THE VERNACULAR VEDA

Studies in Comparative Religion
Frederick M. Denny, General Editor

THE VERNACULAR VEDA

Revelation, Recitation, and Ritual

Vasudha Narayanan

The University of South Carolina Press

Published in Columbia, South Carolina, by the
University of South Carolina Press

Manufactured in the United States of America

Library of Congress Cataloging-in-Publication Data

Narayanan, Vasudha.
The vernacular Veda : revelation, recitation, and ritual / Vasudha
Narayanan.
p. cm.
Includes the translation of the temple Tiruvāymoḻi songs.
Includes bibliographical references and index.
ISBN 0–87249–965–0
I. Nammāḻvār. Tiruvāymoḻi. English. 1994. II. Title.
PL4758.9.N3155T536 1994
294.5′95—dc20 93–44400

For Desika and Ramanujan
who adore their Lord Ranga

CONTENTS

Contents

ILLUSTRATIONS

Following page 79

Painting of Nammāḻvār in Srirangam Temple.

Festival image (*utsava mūrti*) of Nammāḻvār in the eighth-century temple of Tiruvidavendai, near Mahabalipuram, Tamilnadu.

The sixteenth-century Horse Court, outside the Hall of a Thousand Pillars, Srirangam Temple.

Nammāḻvār dressed for his liberation on the tenth night of the Tiruvāymoḻi recitation at the Srirangam Temple.

Main image of Nammāḻvār at his birth place, Alvar Tirunagari.

Picture of Nammāḻvār decorated and mounted on a chariot. Nammāḻvār Cannati, Bangalore.

GENERAL EDITOR'S PREFACE

One of the most fruitful areas of comparative religion research in recent years has been that of the nature and functions of scripture in various traditions. Sam D. Gill, in an essay that appeared in the first book in this series, *The Holy Book in Comparative Perspective* (1985), made a distinction between the "informative" and "performative" dimensions of language and, by extension, sacred texts. The first is what a scripture says, or its message; the second is how a scripture is ritually recited and otherwise appropriated and celebrated through performance.

Vasudha Narayanan's *The Vernacular Veda: Revelation, Recitation, and Ritual* explores the informative and performative dimensions of the principal scripture of Tamil-speaking Hindus, the long devotional poem of Nammāḻvār known as the *Tiruvāymoḻi*. Of the greatest interest is the way in which this text is viewed alongside the ancient Sanskrit Vedas, Hinduism's principal and most sacred scripture. To call anything else, and especially anything in a language other than Sanskrit, by the name of "Veda" is to make a bold claim about God's intentions of revelation. But Śrīvaiṣṇava Tamil Hindus have canonized the *Tiruvāymoḻi* as scripture and the outcome has been of incalculable importance for the spiritual, social, and cultural life of the community. Dr. Narayanan is herself from that community and has been able to conduct field and textual research in a manner that brings the home and temple rituals of reciting and meditating through the *Tiruvāymoḻi* to the reader in rich, clear detail.

Although this book emphasizes the performative aspects of Śrīvaiṣṇava use of the *Tiruvāymoḻi,* the author also pays careful attention to its exegesis, for the two aspects must finally be seen in their dynamic complementarity within the Śrīvaiṣṇava Tamil belief and action system, at both the individual-personal and communal levels. *The Vernacular Veda* is a study that has been influenced by the renewed interest in comparative scriptural studies. In its comprehensive attention to one scripture, within one sub-tradition of Hinduism, it offers a level of complex detail and texture that will be of value to both field and textual research on other traditions as this type of scholarship gains a greater following.

Frederick Mathewson Denny

ACKNOWLEDGMENTS

The writing of this book was made possible through the generous help of several people and institutions. My initial research was done with summer stipends from the National Endowment for the Humanities, 1987, and the Division of Sponsored Research, University of Florida, 1988. A translation grant from the National Endowment for the Humanities (1989–91) made the translation of large sections of Tiruvāymoḻi possible, for this and another project. I was able to get information on the recitation of the Tiruvāymoḻi in temples and witness the performances during the Festival of Recitation (1989–90) with the help of a senior fellowship from the American Institute of Indian Studies and the Smithsonian Institution. The final draft of this book was done under a fellowship from the John Simon Guggenheim Foundation.

Frederick Denny encouraged this project from the very beginning, and his writings on Quranic recitation inspired much of the early research. Harold Stahmer (Department of Religion, University of Florida) gave me Ong's *Orality and Literacy* in 1982 and since then has encouraged my interest in the subject. He has shared his vast resources on "aural" literature over the years, drawing my attention to important articles and books, which have increased my awareness of the oral/aural/visual modes of apprehending the sacred. John Carman (Harvard University) has read the drafts of this book and the translation in many recensions and has offered timely and important advice. A. K. Ramanujan, John Carman, Glenn Yocum, and Francis Clooney have improved upon the drafts of my translations and have kindly agreed to let me use this revised version for my book. A full translation of the Tiruvāymoḻi which I am doing in collaboration with these scholars will appear in later volumes.

I would like to thank Dr. Alex Zhao of the University of Florida for helping me with the illustration in chapter 3. I am also grateful to the University of South Carolina Press for its assistance and patience in the production of this manuscript.

My parents, Sri V. R. Rajagopalan and Srimati Hema Rajagopalan, provided invaluable research help throughout the writing of this book. My mother was principally responsible for arranging for the private recording of the entire *Nālāyira Divya Prabandham,* procuring several important *sthala purāṇas* of the places sacred to the Śrīvaiṣṇava community, and being vigilant about new Divya Prabandham cassettes in the market. My father arranged for visits to many Śrīvaiṣṇava temples in India, drawing and redrawing itineraries for trips to remote temples in Tamilnadu and Kerala. He also arranged for transcripts of interviews and worked through the summer heat in 1988 to get me some vital archaeological information. Every fieldworker knows the frustration of having last-minute questions, months after getting back from the field site, and my parents got me answers to dozens of queries dictated frantically over international phone calls.

The generous help of Sri R. Raghunathan, Kotturpuram, Madras, is gratefully acknowledged. He accompanied me on several visits to the Parthasarathy Temple (Madras), to Srirangam, and many sacred places from 1985 to 1991. He also videotaped modern interpretations of the *araiyar cēvai* which were broadcast by local television stations and procured copies of relevant books. Sri S. Govindarajan, advocate, Chidambaram, very generously spent time getting information on locales near Chidambaram. Srimati Soundra and Sri K. S. Veeraraghavan of Neelangarai, Madras, thoughtfully videotaped the Vaikuṇṭha Ekādaśi celebrations and other rituals between 1987 and 1988. Srimati Jaya Rajagopal of Neelangarai, Madras, gave me programs and books of the Tamil Isai Sangam in Madras, where the *āḻvār* hymns are sung during the December music festival.

Sri Nadhamuni Araiyar of Srirangam spent several hours discussing *araiyar cēvai,* despite his heavy schedule in 1990 and 1991. Professor G. "Veenai" Rangarajan (the resident musician of the Srirangam Temple) and his family spent several hours singing and playing the *āḻvār* songs on the *veena* and discussing their responsibilities in the temples. I am also extremely grateful to the gracious hospitality of Professor Devaki Parthasarathi, longtime resident of Srirangam and former trustee of the temple, for making all the arrangements for me in January 1990. Through her I met Smt. Jayammal, Maithili Rengarajan, and Viji Sudarshanam (all of West Adayavalanjan Street, Srirangam); they were my companions during the days and nights of Tiruvāymoḻi recitation in Srirangam, offering me guidance and information. They took turns accompanying me from the "wake-up" rituals, which began at 3:30 A.M. during the cool dawns of Mārkaḻi month, to the end of the *ēkāntam* singing of the *āḻvār* songs, which concluded the day's ceremonies, anytime between 11:00 P.M. to midnight on a good day. Some nights, as on the eve of Vaikuṇṭha Ekādaśi and during the salvation drama of Nammāḻvār, they kept vigil with me at the temple (along with a crowd of 400,000 people). A very special thanks to them for making my trip there a memorable one.

Sri Ashtagotram N. C. Parthsarathy Iyengar, honorary secretary, Veda Adhyapaka Goshti (Veda Reciters' Association), of the Triplicane Temple in Madras has recorded the entire Divya Prabandham for me and spent several hours discussing the schedules of recitation in the temple context. Sri Venkata Varadhan of Triplicane, the Goda Mandali group at Theagarayanagar, Smt. Kothai of Tiruvanmiyur, Srirama Bharati, Smt. Usha Narayanan, Sri Saranatha Bhattar, and Sri Venkatacharlu (Sri Venkateswara Temple, Pittsburgh), Sri Krishnamacharylu (Malibu Temple, California), all interpreters, singers, or dancers of the Divya Prabandham, were generous in their time and patience and provided me with fascinating information. Their involvement with the sacred word made me see and hear it from their perspective.

Ranganayaki Sampathkumaran of Bangalore was initially responsible for informing me about and taking me to the Andal shrine and, later, to the Nammalvar Cannati, in 1983. I am also grateful for the hours of conversation and discussions I have had with her. In 1989 Usha Rajagopalan of Perumbavur, Kerala, took me to some temples that Nammalvar had sung about and kindly interpreted the information on rituals from Malayalam. I am very grateful to both women for their interest in this project.

My husband, Ranga, has encouraged this endeavor from the beginning; his continuing support, enthusiasm, and keen interest has given life to this project. He has spent several hours sharing with me his love and knowledge of Carnatic music, interest in the recitation of the Tamil and Sanskrit Vedas, and stories of Srirangam, making me see and hear the joyous celebrations of the south Indian culture. Desika and Ramanujan reluctantly freed me from many swimming assignments and monopoly and *pallankuli* tournaments, just so I could "hurry up and finish the storybook" and dedicate it to them. I express my profound gratitude to all these people.

Material from two of the chapters in this book has appeared in slightly different form elsewhere. Parts of chapter 7, "Exegesis and Interpretation: Oral and Written Commentary on the Tiruvāymoḻi," appeared in *Texts in Context: Traditional Hermeneutics in South Asia,* edited by Jeffrey R. Timm (Albany: State University of New York Press, 1992). An earlier version of chapter 2, "The Sacred Utterance of the Silent Seer: Speech and Sight in the Revelation of the Tamil Veda," appeared in *Journal of Vaiṣṇava Studies* 2, no. 1 (Winter 1993).

A NOTE ON TRANSLITERATION

The standard systems of transliteration have been used for Sanskrit and Tamil words in this book, with two exceptions. The Sanskrit letter usually rendered as ṁ is transliterated as ṅ and the letter that is written as ṟ in the Tamil Lexicon appears as ṛ.

I have not used diacritics for names of places like Srirangam or Tiruvenkatam, except when they occur in the context of a translation. Traditional names like Nammāḻvār have been transliterated. However, a number of people I interviewed spell their names in a particular way (Nadhamuni Araiyar, Sri Vipranarayana, Venkata Varadhan et al.) and I have simply retained that spelling. Authors' names, when appearing in the Tamil or Sanskrit script, have been transliterated. Some organizations and groups like Tamil Isai Sangam, Andal Cannati, and Goda Mandali do not use any diacritics and I have used the spelling that they have adopted to refer to themselves.

Commonly accepted spelling for the names of musical ragas is retained throughout the book; for example, "Kambodhi" is the recognized spelling used in music brochures, souvenirs, newspaper articles, etc., and spelling it as Kāmpōti did not make sense.

When Tamil or Sanskrit words appear in quotations, I have retained the marks used in the text from which the quotation is taken.

The names of texts considered to be canonical by the Śrīvaiṣṇava community are not italicized.

THE VERNACULAR VEDA

1 INTRODUCTION

The earliest compositions considered as "revealed" within the Hindu tradition are called *śruti* (that which is *heard*), but those who transmitted the sacred words were called *ṛṣīs,* or seers. This dual emphasis on hearing and seeing what is holy characterizes the Hindu tradition; the sacred is experienced through sound and vision. When Hindus go on a pilgrimage or visit a temple they go to have a *darśan. Darśan* is "to *see* with piety, to behold with faith, and to be seen by the deity." But the prayers uttered by the Hindu at home and in temples usually end with a signature verse called *phala śruti* (fruits of hearing), and this verse recounts the benefits of reciting or listening to the holy words.

The imagery of vision and sound also dominate the ritual patterns of the annual Festival of Recitation at the Srirangam Temple in south India. In Srirangam, as the camphor is lit in the "Hall of a Thousand Pillars" and the flame lights up the visible form of Viṣṇu, the brahmin cantors at the other end of the hall begin the recitation of the poem known as the Tiruvāymoḻi, or "Sacred Utterance." Through light and sound, vision and recited words, with eyes and ears, the congregation is put in touch with the heavenly realm, which they believe descends to earth for those ten days that it takes to recite the poem. For the duration of ten days, when the poem is recited and acted, the "gates of heaven," large doors at the northern side of this temple, are flung open, and the pilgrims (over 400,000 in 1989–90) stream through them to see the divine form of the deity and to hear the recitation of the holy words of the Tiruvāymoḻi.

This book is concerned with the sacred words of the Śrīvaiṣṇava tradition of south India. It is a study of one Hindu tradition's notion of aural revelation, an exploration of the social and ritual context of a sacred text, and a study of the traditions of recitation, music, and verbal and performative commentaries which have been associated with its transmission. Specifically, it focuses on the Divya Prabandham ("Sacred Collect"), which includes the Tiruvāymoḻi, a poem of 1,102 verses.

The Śrīvaiṣṇava tradition of south India became organized around the time of its fifth, and most important, teacher *(ācārya),* Rāmānuja (ca. 1017–1137 C.E.). The word *Śrīvaiṣṇava* occurs in the Tiruvenkatam (Tirupati) Temple inscriptions as early as 966 C.E., and it is probable that a community bearing the name existed even from the ninth century.

The Śrīvaiṣṇava community emphasizes exclusive devotion to the Lord Viṣṇu and his consort Śrī. Like many of the other Hindu traditions, it accepts the Sanskrit Vedas, the epics Rāmāyaṇa and Mahābhārata, and the Purāṇas as "scripture" but, in addition to these, also claims that the poems of the *āḻvārs* are revealed. The word *āḻvār* is traditionally derived from the Tamil root *āḻ* (deep), and the title *āḻvār* was given to eleven men and one woman who are said to have been immersed deep in the love of Viṣṇu. The twenty-four works of the *āḻvārs* are about four thousand verses long, and they came to be known as the *Nālāyira Divya Prabandham,* or the Sacred Collect of Four Thousand Verses. The Śrīvaiṣṇavas refer to the poems simply as the Divya Prabandham. Specifically, the community considers one of the *āḻvārs,* Śaṭhakōpaṉ (ninth c.), known affectionately as Nammāḻvār, or "Our *āḻvār,*"[1] to be a paradigmatic devotee and his Tiruvāymoḻi as the equivalent of the Sāma Veda.

Canonized as scripture, the Tiruvāymoḻi has been of seminal importance in the piety and liturgy of the Śrīvaiṣṇava community of south India and extraordinarily significant in the history of Hindu literature. It was the first "vernacular"[2] work within the Hindu consciousness to be considered as revealed; it was also the first work in a mother tongue to be introduced as part of domestic and temple liturgy. Unlike the Sanskrit Vedas, which could only be recited by male members of the upper castes, the Tiruvāymoḻi has been recited by men and women of all castes of Śrīvaiṣṇava society. It is historically significant as a key part of the Tamil devotional literature that influenced the religious patterns in medieval northern India. The devotion voiced in the Tiruvāymoḻi was transmitted through the Sanskrit text known as the *Bhāgavata Purāṇa,*[3] the teacher Rāmānanda (c. 1360–1470), as well as through Sanskrit hymns and oral tradition and appeared in different forms in the teachings of Caitanya, Vallabha, Sūrdās, Kabir, and Guru Nānak.

According to Śrīvaiṣṇava tradition, Nammāḻvār was said to be of the landowning Veḷḷāḷa Hindu community, traditionally held to be a low caste by south Indian brahmins but which in reality wields considerable economic power. Nammāḻvār claims in the Tiruvāymoḻi that the Lord speaks through him (Tiruvāymoḻi 7.9),[4] and Śrīvaiṣṇavas quote these verses to proclaim the revealed nature of the work. Very little historical information is available about the poet,[5] but it is assumed that he lived about the ninth century C.E. Around the tenth century C.E. the brahmin scholar Nāthamuni (who was later hailed as the first teacher of the Śrīvaiṣṇava community) was entranced by a set of eleven verses that he heard from wandering musicians and inferred from the eleventh "signature" verse that this set was part of a poem with a thousand stanzas. The verses that so moved Nāthamuni were from the Tiruvāymoḻi. According to Śrīvaiṣṇava tradition, in the course of his search to retrieve the other verses of the Tiruvāymoḻi he was also blessed with the revelation of three other shorter works of Nammāḻvār and about twenty other poems composed by other Tamil poet-saints. The primary and, in fact, the "parent" status of the Tiruvāymoḻi and its author to all other poems and poets remains strong in Śrīvaiṣṇava consciousness. The community hails the Tiruvāymoḻi as Veda, or revealed literature, although it is in a vernacular language, and considers its author as one of the greatest devotees of the Lord, despite the perception that he is of a "low caste."

The Tiruvāymoḻi portrays Nammāḻvār's quest for union with the Lord. It reflects the poet's search for Viṣṇu, frequently portrayed as the Lord enshrined in a particular temple in the local landscape or as one of his many incarnations. In about one fourth of the poems Nammāḻvār talks of his separation and talks from the stance of a lovesick "heroine," a persona seen in earlier (2d–4th c. C.E.) secular Tamil poems of love. In thirty-three verses Nammāḻvār identifies himself as a cowherd girl who pines for Krishna. The rest of the Tiruvāymoḻi contains philosophical statements, didactic verses, wonder at the creations of the Lord, descriptions of sacred places where Viṣṇu is enshrined, recollection of past unions with the Lord, and the importance of serving the other devotees. The poem begins and ends with triumphant statements of union with the Lord.

Selections from the Tiruvāymoḻi (about 143 verses, known as the *Kōyil*, or Temple Tiruvāymoḻi) are recited every day at home and in temples. The whole poem is recited for auspicious, domestic rituals such as investiture with the sacred thread and sixtieth birthday celebrations and also for inauspicious events such as funerals and annual ancestral rituals. There are also regular cycles for reciting the whole work over periods of ten days. Some temples and shrines have about twelve to thirteen annual cycles of recitation, and others may have only two. In addition to these cycles, some verses of the Tiruvāymoḻi are danced and enacted in Śrīvaiṣṇava temples during the Festival of Recitation. Nammāḻvār is the paradigmatic soul searching for the Lord; the Tiruvāymoḻi portrays his and the Śrīvaiṣṇava community's quest for salvation. Recitation is always in front of the deity; there is an experience of the sacred through sound and visualizing the deity in the temple or at home.

The recitation of the Tiruvāymoḻi in the context of ritual is itself a kind of commentary and elaboration of the holy word. In the formative years of the Śrīvaiṣṇava community the "sounding" of the Tiruvāymoḻi through song or recitation continued side by side with the tradition of explicit verbal commentaries on the verses. Importance was given both to the *sound* of the recitation—this, after all, was the Tamil Veda, and the power of the Sanskrit Veda derived principally from its sound—and to the *meaning* of the verses, as was elucidated in the commentarial literature. There has also been a long verbal commentarial tradition on the Tiruvāymoḻi since the late eleventh century C.E. There were oral and written commentaries, and five classical commentaries written between the eleventh and thirteenth centuries C.E. were given authoritative status in interpreting the Tiruvāymoḻi. Although the five commentaries have been considered as authoritative, there is no sense of closure with the commentarial tradition; oral and written commentaries have continued through the centuries and still flourish today. The commentaries on the Tiruvāymoḻi elucidate the meaning of key phrases, show parallels with Sanskrit traditions, and recount diverging interpretations on the meaning of some verses, but their discussions on how earlier Tamil literature informs the poems are extremely brief. The poem has also been summarized in Sanskrit and Tamil verse over the centuries. While the oral (ritual) and written (commentarial) elaborations of the word did not convey messages that were at variance with each other, their emphases, as well as the modes and techniques of realizing their aims, were different. This book will discuss the differing but "complementary" emphases between the oral (recitation/ritual) elaboration of hymns and the elucidation of the verses in the traditional commentarial literature.

A study of the Tiruvāymoḻi, therefore, involves a study of its revealed status, recitation schedules, musical renderings, oral and written commentarial traditions, and dramatic performances in temples. It involves an understanding of the learning process by which the verses are committed to memory, the details of the almanac which dictate the selection of verses to be recited every day, the process by which the commentaries were recorded, and the ritual context of the temples where the Tiruvāymoḻi is performed. This book will address these issues and, in the process, participate in the current academic discussions on the aural nature of scripture, oral and written forms of communication, and the centrality of sacred sound and vision in the Hindu tradition.

Several studies in the history of religions and the Hindu tradition have helped in the formulation of this book. The importance of sound and vision in the religious experience of the Hindu traditions have been the focus of many studies. The early transmission of the Vedas,[6] importance of Vedic recitation, and the early Hindu distrust of writing have been studied by Staal (1961 and 1979). Donna Wulff, in her sensitive study, draws our attention to the identification of *nāda* (sound) with brahman, the Supreme Reality. Gonda's work (1963) on the centrality of *vision* in the Vedas and the revelation of the Supreme Reality through the sound *(śabda brahman)* is an excellent study of Vedic compositions. Coward and Goa's *Mantra: Hearing the Divine in India* (1991) seems to be a welcome addition to the study of sacred sound, but, unfortunately, I did not get the book in time to profit from it for the present study. Eck's now classical work (1981), dealing with medieval Hindu literature, emphasizes the importance of *darśan* (vision) in the perception of the "image," or the Lord enshrined in a temple.

The works of Kelber (1983) and Graham (1987) have been seminal in the study of the aural/oral nature of scripture. In his sustained study Graham studies the oral dimensions of scripture in Christianity, Islam, and Hinduism and points out the central importance of the aural experience of the religious texts in these traditions. Coburn (1984) has clarified the various categories of the Hindu Word and has given us a typology of holy verbal utterance in Hindu life. He sketches what Hindus have done with the holy word, through the centuries, and arranges them into five areas: they have frozen it, as in the Vedas; told salvific stories; composed commentaries; written holy texts that imitate texts with stature; and, finally, been receptive to new additions to scripture. He notes that there is considerable overlap between the categories, although some pure types do exist. He also proposes a second typology that is a drastic simplification of the first: the holy words of Hinduism can be seen as two basic types, scripture and story. One may say that the Tiruvāymoḻi can fit into at least four of these categories: it is scripture, the Veda; it contains references to salvific stories; it is the focus of a commentarial tradition; and, while it is not a self-conscious imitation of the Sanskrit Veda, the Śrīvaiṣṇavas considered it to *be* a Veda itself, and one can say it is an addition to the scriptural canon of a tradition.

In the last few years there have been important studies on the category of scripture/"holy book." The anthologies edited by Denny and Taylor (1985) and Levering (1989) have compelled us to rethink our notions of scripture. Gill's article in Denny and Taylor suggests that sacred texts have an "informative function" and a "performative function." This distinction becomes important in our study of the Tiruvāymoḻi, in which it is held as a showcase of Śrīvaiṣṇava theology, and, at the same time, the recitation has complex functions in liturgy and everyday life. Levering has coaxed more categories out of Gill's two basic ones and, based on fieldwork in Taiwan, proposes four kinds of "receptions" of the holy word: informative, transformative, transactive (as in a mantra affecting someone else), and symbolic. We will have the opportunity to see some of these in action in our discussions of the Tiruvāymoḻi.

The aural and written nature of later medieval texts in Hinduism have been studied in Brown's splendid article (1986), in which he gives the details on the transformation of scripture from holy sound to the written word and also offers a critique of Ong's work. Brown's article draws our attention to the deep bias against writing in early India and how, starting from this position, the various traditions within Hindu culture reoriented themselves toward the written word and eventually thought of the writing and presenting of manuscripts as merit-worthy acts. He considers the stages involved in committing a part of the oral tradition to a written form and also offers an interesting theology behind the Hindu book cult, showing how the sacred word becomes the verbal image of God in some medieval texts. Thus, by the Middle Ages, he concludes,

> the visible, verbal image, in the form of a book, is none other than an incarnation of God, parallel to the idea that an iconic image of God is also an incarnation *(arcāvatāra)* of the divine. The book, a manifestation of God's grace and love for his devotees, is infused with his real presence. Seeing the book is tantamount to seeing God. . . . We see here in the "Bhāgavata Mahātmya" the complete transformation of the holy word from sound to image, from mantra to *mūrti.*[7]

Brown's discussions bring together notions of sacred sound, vision, and writing, seen in the medieval Sanskrit texts of the Hindu tradition. Vision is used in a twofold way: to perceive the Supreme Truth, as in *darśan,* and to visually see the writing of the holy word. Both the visible form of the Lord and the visible word are holy. Our discussions in the chapter on the commentarial tradition will note the importance of writing the holy word.

The recitative traditions of the Tiruvāymoḻi or the Divya Prabandham have not been studied, and very little attention has been paid by Western scholars to this very important aspect of Śrīvaiṣṇava culture. There have been studies of music and recitation in other areas of the Hindu tradition. Tamil Śaiva recitation and musical traditions have been discussed by Peterson (1989), and ethnomusical and highly technical accounts of Veda recitation have been written by Staal (1961) and Howard (1986). Hawley (1984) has discussed the role of music in medieval north Indian devotional poetry. My discussion of the issues and approach to the material on recitation has been fostered more by studies in Islamic culture than by any single work on the topic in Hinduism. The works of Denny (1980 and 1989), Nelson (1985), and Martin (1982) have been particularly stimulating and have helped focus many of the discussions in this book.

The Tiruvāymoḻi was also choreographed and acted out and may well be one of the earliest surviving enactments of scripture within the Hindu contexts. Performances of oral epics have been and continue to be popular in urban and rural areas, but the performance of the Tiruvāymoḻi is different from them in many respects. Rooted in a strong brahmanical context, it is formal, based on a family tradition of performance, with strict adherence to the text. Hiltebeitel (1988), Beck (1982), and Blackburn (1981) have studied south Indian performances, but there is considerable freedom and improvisation in the narration and enactment of these oral folk epics. Blackburn has discussed an oral performative tradition of the "bow song" found only in the Kanyakumari district of Tamilnadu and has identified "fictive" and "realistic" expressions of birth, death, and sexual conflict and how the performance system involves alternating patterns of fictive-realistic-fictive sequences. None of these performances (which roughly fall under the category of *terukūttu,* or street dancing) are similar to the *araiyar* performance of the Tiruvāymoḻi in temples. They are not viewed as the Veda, in which the recitation of the exact words and pronunciation is all important, the performance is not in a temple worship context, and the gods and myths alluded to (except in the case of Hiltebeitel's study) do not have pan-Indian recognition.

Extensive studies have been done in north Indian Vaiṣṇava performances: Hein (1972) and Hawley (1981) have studied the Krishna plays of Mathura and the Braj-land extensively; Haberman's *Acting as a Way to Salvation* (1988) focuses on the plays of the Gaudiya Vaiṣṇavas. Schechner and Hess (1977) and Kapur (1985) have written on the Ramlila; John D. Smith (1990) has discussed Rajasthani versions of the Mahābhārata performances in the larger context of orality and literacy; and Sax has written about the Pāṇḍav Līlā of Uttarkhand. Lutgendorf's work (1991) on the narration of the Rāmcaritmānas highlights the importance of *kathā,* or "story," in the Hindu tradition. All these studies describe the dynamics of the performances and their social contexts in great detail, but, while there are some similarities, none seem to approach the content, techniques, and spirit of the Tiruvāymoḻi performances discussed in chapter 8.

The materials for the ritual context of the poem were collected over several years, from many visits to Śrīvaiṣṇava shrines, temples, and classical music concert halls; from interviews with those who recite and sing in temples; and through reading and hearing Śrīvaiṣṇava compositions. The primary text for the study, of course, is the Divya Prabandham, of which the Tiruvāymoḻi is considered to be the fourth thousand. The many recitation manuals, called *nityānusandhānam* (daily contemplation and recitation) and the Temple Tiruvāymoḻi selections are frequently printed separately and sold outside temples. These publications print the verses and the order in which and the number of times they are to be recited. The hagiographic literature of the community which began around the twelfth century C.E. gives us a clear understanding of the community's perception of the importance of the Tiruvāymoḻi and of Nammāḻvār. It also makes us conscious of the paradoxes inherent within the discussions: Nammāḻvār is simultaneously human and divine; the Tiruvāymoḻi is authored by him, by God, and, in a sense, is authorless. I have also used the verbal commentarial literature on the Tiruvāymoḻi to show the process of exegesis and, occasionally, the difference in style between verbal and ritual comment on the verses.

Information on recitation and performances was collected from visits to the temples and extensive conversations with reciters, priests, and other personnel. In all I traveled to 60 of the 108 places that the Śrīvaiṣṇavas hold as sacred, to observe, question, and participate in the ritual celebrations. I observed some of the worship ceremonies several times, to get both a cognitive knowledge and a "feel" for the ceremonies. People in the temple town of Srirangam were extraordinary in their hospitality and help, introducing me to people whom they thought I should meet and taking turns accompanying me to the various rituals in the temple almost around the clock. I am a native speaker of Tamil, fairly fluent in Śrīvaiṣṇava modes of expressions, and my appearance was not very different from the other south Indians at the temple, so I was practically "invisible" in the crowds. This proved invaluable in the process of understanding the phenomena.

Interviews with temple servants, reciters, and *araiyars* (those who recite and perform in some temples in south India) were supplemented with extensive information gathered from pamphlets and brochures about temples. Some of these give the *sthala purāṇa* (stories establishing the sacrality of the place) along with details of recitation during the various festivals. Larger temples such as those at Srirangam and Alvar Tirunagari (Nammāḻvār's birthplace) print pamphlets giving the details of the major rituals, including when and where the recitation of the Divya Prabandham takes place; some of the older pamphlets were also available during visits to these temples.

Because of the nature of the project, I also made extensive use of audio and video sources. I have recorded over a hundred hours of Divya

Prabandham recitation and singing in temples, concert halls, and homes and have also listened to the popular prerecorded cassette tapes that are sold in the shops. I have also extensively recorded the morning Divya Prabandham singing broadcast over All India Radio, Madras, and videotaped the classical dances in the Bharatanatyam style in which Divya Prabandham verses have been choreographed. Some of these dance performances, including creative versions of temple dancing (based on the interpretation done by traditional male performers during the annual Festival of Recitation), have been broadcast on national television in India. These recordings are a testimony to the rise of electronic *bhakti,* or devotion, in the south Indian context.

In the following pages we will see various facets of the Śrīvaiṣṇava community's passionate involvement with the Tiruvāymoḻi. Central to the importance of the text is the understanding of its revealed nature and the exalted nature of Nammāḻvār, and this will be the focus of the second chapter. From the third to the sixth chapters we will consider the traditions of recitation and music, observing the movement from temples and shrines to secular concert halls and the rise of electronic devotion through the proliferation of cassettes and records. The beginning of the verbal commentarial tradition, both oral and written, will be considered in chapter 7, and, finally, in chapter 8 we will enter the "Sacred Arena," or Srirangam, and witness the powerful salvation drama of Nammāḻvār. The appendix contains translations of selected verses from the Tiruvāymoḻi.

THE TRANSLATION OF THE TEMPLE TIRUVĀYMOḺI

The 143 verses of the Temple Tiruvāymoḻi which are considered to be important enough to be recited regularly, if not every day, are translated in the final section of this book. Since the poem was considered to be the "sacred word of the Lord," it was not translated into any other language within India, though it was summarized in Sanskrit and Tamil and has been commented upon extensively since the twelfth century C.E. Several verses attesting to its importance were composed and ritually recited prior to the chanting of the Tiruvāymoḻi. The first translation into an Indian language was in the nineteenth century, when it was rendered in Sanskrit.

Attempts at translating the poem into English by Śrīvaiṣṇava scholars have not been successfully accomplished because they have been criticized for not incorporating the commentarial interpretation into the translation; in fact, it was not until 1983 that a complete translation in English was published in two volumes.[8] It is possible that, because the Śrīvaiṣṇava community has shielded the Tiruvāymoḻi from translations because of its sanctity and because the commentarial traditions covered the text, this major religious document was never rendered into English by some of the earlier Indologists. It has, therefore, been less known in the Western world than both Sanskrit works and other Tamil works such as the Śaiva poem *Tiruvācakam*.

The poems were meant to be recited, sung, and heard, more often than not in a liturgical milieu, and reading them in translation, without the trappings of contextual familiarity, will be an experience that is vastly different from the Śrīvaiṣṇava community's enjoyment of the sacred word. The Śrīvaiṣṇava's experience of the Tiruvāymoḻi is predominantly aural and visual because she or he was always in close proximity to the deity when reciting or hearing it. The experience is also closely connected with the sounds, sights, and fragrances associated with liturgy. Bells, waving lamps, and fragrant flowers and incense frequently form the context of hearing the sacred word, with its rhymes and rhythms. My aim is to present to a modern audience a translation that is close to the spirit of the poem and evocative of the milieu in which the poem lives. The meters, alliteration, and rhymes will not be reproduced in the translation, nor will the linking style of *antāti* (end-beginning), whereby the last words of one verse become the opening words of the next one, be employed.

My earliest recollections of hearing the Divya Prabandham is when I was about five years old. My grandmother would bathe early in the morning, go to the front of the family shrine, clap her hands to wake up the Lord, and start reciting the opening words of the first song of the Divya Prabandham:

> pallāṇṭu pallāṇṭu pallāyirattāṇṭu
> palakōṭi nūṟāyiram mallāṇṭa tiṉ tōḷ maṇi vaṇṇā
> uṉ cēvaṭi cevvi tirukkāpu

> Many years, Many years,
> for many thousands of years

Many hundreds of millions,
for hundreds of thousand years
O Gem-colored one! Lord with strong shoulders
    who vanquished the wrestlers
May your fair feet be ever blessed!

I did not know the meaning of all the words, but the first words of the verse, *pallāṇṭu pallāṇṭu,* seemed to rhyme with the Tamil word *kalkaṇṭu,* or "rock sugar." Perhaps that early association was not all that far off; over the centuries, starting with the *ā̲lvārs,* people have considered their words to be sweet as sugar and honey. As a child, I also heard several verses of the Tiruppāvai being recited and sung by the women around the house, heard the stories of Āṇṭāḷ and Nammā̲lvār, and saw the shrines of the *ā̲lvārs* in the temples. While growing up, these words, stories, and sights faded into the background, while I became interested in other subjects. Even with my deepening interest in the Divya Prabandham in later years I looked only to the books: the text of the Tiruvāymo̲li and the commentaries, which were all written by men. In 1983, while translating the first commentary on the Tiruvāymo̲li, I went to a temple in Bangalore and seemed to *hear* for the first time the almost imperceptible transition between the Sanskrit and Tamil Vedas. I also heard the entire Tiruvāymo̲li recited during a domestic ritual and soon after that met the people of the Nammā̲lvār Shrine in Bangalore. This congregation celebrated the birthday of Nammā̲lvār by reciting the Tiruvāymo̲li and venerating him with rituals; on the last day the saint was taken in a procession through the streets in a large chariot. It was during that spring that I began to pay close attention to the recitation of the Tiruvāymo̲li and other works of the *ā̲lvārs;* it was then that I began to hear them anew. For several years after 1983 I revisited Śrīvaiṣṇava temples all over south India, taking detailed notes on what was recited and when and where they were recited. Details were not always forthcoming immediately, and sometimes it was only after extended conversations that patterns emerged. Occasionally, I forgot to ask or note something, and my parents, through their network of relatives and acquaintances, would get me the relevant information.

It is my hope that the interpretation of the Tiruvāymo̲li in this book will convey the texture of Śrīvaiṣṇava religious discourse in terms of its oral and written communication and its apprehension of the sacred through sight and sound. Through this study of the Tiruvāymoḻi we might understand one Hindu tradition's enchantment with the power and the beauty of the chant and something about this community's celebration of bringing the joy of heaven to earth.

2

THE SACRED UTTERANCE OF THE SILENT SEER

Speech and Sight in the Revelation of the Tamil Veda

Who is this [child]
who does not open his mouth
who does not open his eyes?
Is there a son
who does not drink his mother's milk?
—Vaṭivaḻakiya Nampi Tācar, Āḻvārkaḷ Vaipavam

So sang Vaṭivaḻakiya Nampi Tācar (15th–16th c. C.E.) in his biography of the poet Nammāḻvār. The irony of his words are grasped by the audience listening to the biographical poem; this child, Nammāḻvār, "who does not open his mouth," is to proclaim the Sacred Utterance; this child, "who does not open his eyes," is the seer (*ṛṣī*) who will see the eternal truth and reveal it.

The Śrīvaiṣṇava community calls the Tiruvāymoḻi a Veda and Nammāḻvār a *muni* ("silent one") and *ṛṣī*. The words *silent one* and *seer* have traditionally been used within the Hindu tradition to refer to those individuals who are said to have intuited the eternal Sanskrit Vedas and transmitted them to human beings. This chapter will explore the Śrīvaiṣṇava understanding of *revelation* by focusing on the paradox of the saint who remained silent until he started uttering eternal truths, the poet who was apparently granted blessed visions, which he communicated through words that have been considered sacred. Was the author of the poem God, or Nammāḻvār? Was Nammāḻvār divine or human? What is it that the community thinks he "saw," and how did he "say" it? In trying to respond to these questions, we shall initially discuss the Śrīvaiṣṇava notion of Veda and then address the issues concerning the authorship of the poem and Nammāḻvār's divinity.

While the Śrīvaiṣṇava community considers the Tiruvāymoli̱ to have had a transhuman *(apauruṣeya)* origin, it is also known that the poem embodies several literary devices from earlier Tamil poetry and allusions to mythology found in Sanskrit and Tamil works. The Tiruvāymoli̱ and the other works of the *āl̠vārs* were also similar to the poems composed by the devotees of Śiva around the same time. Any serious discussion about revelation of the Tiruvāymoli̱ should take into account the literary and religious climate around the ninth century C.E., when the poem was composed, and also attend to the notion of the Veda prevalent in the twelfth to fifteenth centuries C.E., when the poem was considered to be a new "incarnation" of Sanskrit revelation.

A sophisticated body of Tamil literature existed in south India two thousand years ago. The earliest literature, usually referred to as "Caṅkam" (Academy) poems were said to have been composed at the time of three great Tamil academies.[1] These classical poems were secular and focused on the "outer" *(puṟam)* and "inner" *(akam)* worlds. The poems that dealt with the outer sphere were those concerned with kings, nobles, and warfare; these poems of chivalry, honor, and generosity were composed by bards who praised the valor of kings. The inner poems focused on love and romance: secret meetings between lovers, forbidden love, the anguish of separation, and the overwhelming joy of union. Nammāl̠vār's hymns include several verses in which he speaks in the voice of one of the characters—a young girl in love, for example, or the mother or friend of the young girl—found in the classical Caṅkam poems. The Tiruvāymoli̱, therefore, incorporates many of the earlier literary conventions, but the passion is not addressed to a king or human lover but, rather, is directed to Viṣṇu, the supreme protector and beloved of the human soul.

ŚRĪVAIṢṆAVA PERCEPTIONS OF THE SANSKRIT AND TAMIL VEDAS

The Tiruvāymoli̱, unlike the Sanskrit Vedas, is a work that can be understood in a definite historical and literary context. While the earliest commentators have largely ignored the Tamil literary context in their analyses, twentieth-century scholars have attended to the connections between classical Tamil poetry and the Tiruvāymoli̱.[2] Unlike the Sanskrit canon, there is a known historical author for the Tamil poem, a person who signs himself as Māṛaṉ Caṭakōpaṉ in the last verse of every subunit of the poem. Māṛaṉ Caṭakōpaṉ came to be known as Nammāḻvār (our Āḻvār) by the Śrīvaiṣṇava community.

Maturakavi Āḻvār, the disciple of Nammāḻvār, sang that his master had rendered the Vedas in Tamil, and Śrīvaiṣṇava theologians, starting in the twelfth century, elaborated on this idea in the commentarial literature. Calling it Veda was the most important way in which the Tiruvāymoḻi was spoken of as revealed literature, for the Sanskrit Veda was considered to be synonymous with revelation.

The Śrīvaiṣṇava community does not usually call the Tiruvāymoḻi *śruti*,[3] the term that is used for the Sanskrit Vedas. The words used most often to refer to the Tiruvāymoḻi are *Veda* and *maṛai*.[4] Several philosophers from the Hindu tradition, especially from the Nyāya (Logic) and Mīmāmsaka schools, had already discussed the term *Veda* in some detail, and the Vedānta teachers, including Rāmānuja, the most important Śrīvaiṣṇava teacher, had clearly discussed the transhuman nature of the Sanskrit Vedas in commentaries on the *Vedānta Sūtras*. All schools of thought agreed on the transcendental aspect of the Vedas and their authoritative nature but differed on what was meant by the transhuman nature of their composition. The followers of the Nyāya school believed that God was their author, and, since God was perfect, the Vedas were infallible. The Mīmāmsakas, on the other hand, starting from at least the second century B.C.E.,[5] said that the Vedas were eternal and authorless. The Vedic seers saw the mantras and transmitted them; they did not compose or author them. The seers were

> aided in their sight or vision both by the transparence of their being and by the power of *vāc* to . . . articulate their visions. What is significant is that the ṛṣī-vision entailed the Mīmāmsa claim that aspects of the eternal truth revealed themselves *to the seers in the form of sound representations*.[6]

The Mīmāmsakas do not assume the role of God or any other being in the authorship of the Vedas. The word that gains currency in exegetical literature here and in later Vedānta is *apauruṣeya*—literally, "superhuman, not of the authorship of man, of divine origin."[7] The transhuman origin of the Vedas is also upheld by the later Vedānta thinkers.

It is against this background that we consider the Śrīvaiṣṇava position as articulated by Rāmānuja.[8] He agreed with the Mīmāmsaka school of philosophy that the Vedas are authorless and eternal, but, unlike them, he insisted that the Vedas teach us about the Supreme Being, Viṣṇu, in the form of Nārāyaṇa:

> This is what is meant by the impersonal character and eternality of the Vedas. . . . A body of words is said to possess impersonal character and eternality if their order of utterance conforms to a pre-established order and proceeds from a remembrance of that order. . . . This order is maintained by the tradition of recitation. The groups of words, so preserved in a fixed order, constitute the Vedas divided into *Ṛk, Yajus, Sāman, Atharvan*. . . . Now through all [the] divisions, branches and forms, the Vedas in their totality teach us the nature of Nārāyaṇa, the supreme Brahman, the mode of worshipping him and purposes whose fulfillment is brought about by him as a result of such worship. Even as the supreme Person is eternal, the system of words embodying the knowledge concerning him, his worship and fruits accruing therefrom, is eternal.[9]

Because the Vedas were not touched by human hands, they were faultless. They were the supreme source of knowledge, according to Rāmānuja, and thus we could know that Viṣṇu was the Supreme Being. It is important to note that for Rāmānuja the Vedas were transhuman and, therefore, the perfect and supreme source of knowledge; by their authority we know that Viṣṇu is supreme. Rāmānuja did *not* say that Viṣṇu is the author and, therefore, the Vedas are perfect.[10] The Vedas constitute "eternal knowledge as embodied in an eternal form, [and their form and content] are co-terminus with the Supreme Reality that they reveal."[11]

The Śrīvaiṣṇava tradition affirms that, because the Vedas make known the supreme person, the Lord is called "Vedāngaḥ," or "He, whose limbs are the Vedas." Rāmānuja's disciple, Parāśara Bhaṭṭar, commenting on the *Viṣṇu Sahasranāma,* explains the divine name Vedāngaḥ thus: "*Vedāngah* means that the Vedas, with all their innumberable branches, are his limbs *(aṅga),* body; because they manifest his inner portion."[12] Clooney rightly points out that this soul-body analogy is standard in Rāmānuja's school and that to "say that the Veda is God's body is therefore to stress its dependence on, essential inherence in and its inseparability from him": "just as our bodies make us perceptible to other people, the Veda is God's way of being known."[13]

The similarities and distinction that the Śrīvaiṣṇava community perceived between the Sanskrit and Tamil Vedas can be understood by perusing the literature of the twelfth and thirteenth centuries. We may start with the name Tiruvāymoḻi, a name that was probably granted to the work several years after its composition and about the time that its status as Veda came to be affirmed. The word *Tiruvāymoḻi* does not occur in the poem itself, or even in the hymn of Maturakavi Āḻvār, in which it is compared to the Veda; as far as I can ascertain, it first occurs in literature only in the late eleventh century, when Piḷḷāṉ wrote his commentary on the poem. *Tiru* is the Tamil word used to denote the Sanskrit *śrī:* "that which is auspicious, that which is sacred." The word *vāy* means "mouth," and *moḻi* means "words" or "language." *Tiruvāymoḻi,* therefore, is "sacred word [of] mouth" or "words [of] sacred mouth." The first translation emphasizes the sacrality of the words, and the second focuses on the revealed nature of the words. Perhaps the closest we can come to translating the word into English is *sacred speech* or *sacred utterance.*

The word *vāy,* or "mouth," highlights the *spoken,* or uttered, aspect of the hymn. In earlier (4th–5th c.) Tamil classical literature, the word *vāymoḻi* was used to indicate either the Sanskrit Veda or words spoken by any holy man. Thus, the words spoken by a Jain monk in the fifth-century Tamil poem *Cilappatikāram* (The Epic of the Anklet) are called *vāymoḻi.*[14] By using the Tamil words for "sacred speech," the Śrīvaiṣṇava community also distinguished itself from the Śaiva movement, in which the Sanskrit word *vāc* was used in the names of hymns to indicate their spoken nature. Zelliot points out that the word *vacana* (a word meaning "sayings, or having said")[15] is found in the Tamil Śaiva poet's work *Tiruvācakam; vacana* also refers to the hymns of the Śaiva saints who composed in the Kannada language between the tenth and twelfth centuries C.E. Zelliot also points out that Śaiva *bhakti* uses the word for "having said" *(vak)* for its poetry in Kashmir and the hymns of the female saint Lāl Ded (14th c.) are called Lalleśvari *Vākyani.*[16]

Clearly, giving the name Tiruvāymoḻi, when the Tamil word *vāymoḻi* evoked associations with the Sanskrit Vedas, was deliberate. If the compositions of Nammāḻvār were equivalent to the Sanskrit Vedas, the parallelism in structure and content had to be pointed out as explicitly as possible. In its formative years, between the eleventh and fourteenth centuries C.E., the Śrīvaiṣṇava community focused on the many perceived similarities between the Tamil and Sanskrit Vedas. No similarity was considered to be too trivial to be overlooked. Nammāḻvār's four compositions were considered to be like the four Vedas, and the Tiruvāymoḻi, which is the most important work, was seen as the "Sāma Veda."[17] Like the Sāma Veda, which was supposed to have been divided into a thousand *śakhas,* or "branches," the Tiruvāymoḻi had about a thousand verses, and both works were musical.

Specifically, the Śrīvaiṣṇava tradition today considers the Tiruvāymoḻi to be similar to the Sanskrit Veda in two important ways but different in one aspect. Both the Tamil and Sanskrit Vedas are the *eternal* word, and, second, they contain the same message; the Tiruvāymoḻi, however, is perceived to be more lucid and accessible than the Sanskrit Veda. These views were clearly articulated by the teachers between the twelfth and sixteenth centuries C.E. and eventually prevailed in the entire community. In presenting the similarities between the Tamil and Sanskrit Vedas as perceived by the Śrīvaiṣṇava community, I have chosen those authors and works that most compellingly and elaborately articulate a certain view for the first time within the tradition. My sources are primarily the first commentary on the Tiruvāymoḻi, written around the twelfth century C.E. by Piḷḷāṉ; Aḻakiya Maṇavāḷa Nāyaṉār's *Ācārya Hṛdayam* (The Heart of the Teacher), a work composed around the thirteenth century C.E. and commented upon by Maṇavāḷa Māmuṉi in the fifteenth century; and Vaṭivaḻakiya Nampi Tācar's fifteenth-century biography of Nammāḻvār, *Āḻvārkaḷ Vaipavam* (The Glory of the Āḻvārs).

THE ETERNAL AND PREEXISTENT NATURE OF THE VEDAS

An intense and fascinating discussion of the Tiruvāymoḻi as the Tamil Veda occurs in Aḻakiya Maṇavāḷa Nāyaṉār's *The Heart of the Teacher* (thirteenth century). Aḻakiya Maṇavāḷa Nāyaṉār says that there are many kinds of Vedas; the commentator adds that, because there are different kinds of people who recite and differences in the worlds, there are many kinds of Vedas, and the Tiruvāymoḻi is one of them.[18] Vedas are classified as Tamil or Sanskrit, just as the Sanskrit Vedas are classified as Rig, Sāma, Yajur, and Atharva. Like Sanskrit, Tamil is beginningless, he says, and, just as the Sanskrit Vedas have ancillaries, all other Tamil works in the Divya Prabandham (The Sacred Collect of Four

Thousand Verses) form ancillaries to the works of Nammālvār.[19] The author of *The Heart of the Teacher* and its commentator list a detailed comparison between both the Sanskrit and Tamil Vedas: they are important books (Tamil: *nūl*), commandments of the Lord, without fault, sweet to hear by the ear *(śruti cevikkiniya),* [transmitted] through recitation, contain no falsehood, are preexistent, and without beginning or end.[20] We may briefly note that the Vedas are spoken of as *books,* which is rather unusual because the Vedas have usually been perceived as eternal sound and authorless words, seldom as a book. About a century later Vaṭivalakiya Nampi Tācar places a lot of importance on the writing of the Tamil Veda; it appears that by the fifteenth century the Śrīvaiṣṇava tradition understood scripture as written as well as spoken.

Of the many claims made by Alakiya Maṇavāḷa Nāyaṉār, perhaps the most unusual is that of the preexistent and eternal nature of the Tamil Veda. As noted, the Mīmāmsaka school of philosophy and later Vedānta thinkers, including Rāmānuja, believed that the Veda had no beginning or end; Alakiya Maṇavāḷa Nāyaṉār applied this notion for the Tamil Veda as well. Just as [the worlds] are created as they existed before (a reference to the cycles of creation and destruction), so too the Tiruvāymoli is created as it existed before. In other words, there is an *eternal* Tiruvāymoli, which the poet has sung now. The commentator explains that, just as the sun and moon are created by Brahmā, the creator god, as they existed in previous ages of time, so too now "this sacred work which is the Tamil Veda was brought about as it has been manifested as before."[21] This application of the eternal preexistent nature of sound and truth to the Tamil Veda is strikingly bold and deliberately lifts the work out of a historical context. It also alters our understanding of Nammālvār as the author of the poem.

PERCEPTIONS OF SIMILARITY IN THE TAMIL AND SANSKRIT VEDAS

Along with the preexistent and manifest forms of the Tiruvāymoli, the *content* was also said to be similar to the Vedas. Śrīvaiṣṇava literature is consistent in what it perceives to be the content of the Vedas: Viṣṇu is the Supreme Being, the other gods are his devotees, and the entire universe forms the body of Viṣṇu. Surrendering to the Lord is another issue that becomes increasingly projected as a message of the Vedas. After quoting from the Vedas and later literature to "prove" these points, the discussions in Śrīvaiṣṇava literature generally end with a statement such as "thus Lokāyata, Māyāvāda, Bhāskara, Yādavaprakāśa and other sectarian viewpoints different from the Vedas are rejected."[22]

While almost all Śrīvaiṣṇava works perceive these issues (i.e., supremacy of Viṣṇu, soul-body analogy, and the importance of surrender) to be the main content of the Vedas, I shall illustrate the points by referring to two works: the commentary on the Tiruvāymoḻi by Piḷḷāṉ and Vaṭivaḻakiya Nampi Tācar's poetic biography of Nammāḻvār. I have chosen these two works as representative of the early formative years of the Śrīvaiṣṇava community and of the late medieval period when doctrinal issues were fully developed and the beginnings of the sectarian dispute were already seen. Piḷḷāṉ, who lived in the late eleventh–early twelfth centuries, stands at that stage of the Śrīvaiṣṇava community during which oral *maṇipravāḷa* commentaries were being transformed into written documents. Thus, the elaboration of the doctrine of a dual Vedānta, or philosophy (Ubhaya Vedānta), based on Sanskrit and Tamil scriptures is clearly seen in his commentary. Vaṭivaḻakiya Nampi Tācar's poetic biography on Nammāḻvār and other *āḻvārs* (*The Glory of the Āḻvārs*) was written possibly in the fifteenth or sixteenth centuries C.E.[23] I have chosen his work as representative of the later Śrīvaiṣṇava tradition because it includes details of Nammāḻvār's life along with Tācar's summary of the content of the poem. His views on the *writing* of the Tamil Veda, and notions of seeing the truth and hearing the holy word, also shows his familiarity with the careful discussions of Aḻakiya Maṇavāḷa Nāyaṉār. His biography is not as well known as the fourteenth-century prose biography of Piṉpaḻakiya Perumāḷ Jīyar, *Guruparamparā prabhāvam, āṛāyirappaṭi* (The Splendor of Succession of Teachers; henceforth, *The Splendor*), which is in *maṇipravāḷa,* or the Sanskrit poem of Garuḍa Vāhana Paṇḍita, *Divya Sūri Caritam* (The Story of the Divine Sages). These earlier biographies give us, in a pious mode, considerable information on the life of the *āḻvārs,* which is elaborated in later biographies such as *Nammāḻvār Tiruttālāṭṭu* (The Lullaby for Nammāḻvār) and *Āḻvār Vaibhavam* (The Glory of the Āḻvārs). Unlike *The Splendor*, the last two include summaries of the Tiruvāymoḻi within the context of the hagiography.

Piḷḷāṉ, the eleventh-century theologian who wrote the first commentary on the Tiruvāymoḻi, was usually very brief in his interpretation. Indeed, his commentary is the shortest among all that have been written, and he was sparing in his use of proof texts. Yet he quoted extensively from the Sanskrit Vedas and other canonical texts at key passages to show his perception of the similarity in content between the Sanskrit and Tamil Vedas. These overwhelming strings of quotations from Sanskrit came in the comment for two Tiruvāymoḻi verses that spoke about doctrines cardinal to the Śrīvaiṣṇava community. The first of these concepts related to the relationship of the Lord and all of creation; the Lord was the inner soul, and the universe was his body (TVM 1.1.7); in commenting on this passage, Piḷḷān̲ lists seventy-three proof texts:

> Becoming all things,
> spread on the certainties of sky, fire,
>
> Wind, water, and earth,
> he is in each of them;
>
> hidden, he pervades
> like life in a body,
>
> yet according to the sacred word
> all flame
> he is the one
>
> who devoured them all,
> this god.

Piḷḷān̲'s commentary, *The Six Thousand:*

> In the earlier three verses it is said by *sāmānādhikaraṇa* [grammatical coordination which assumes the predicate shares the substance of the subject] that the creation and movement of the earth are dependent on the Lord. Now by *sāmānādhikaraṇa* we say that the union between the universe and the Lord is that between the body and soul.
>
> Just as this soul rules this body and pervades it, the Lord also pervades and rules the world, the five elements and all other objects. This is established irrefutably by valid sources of knowledge. He is different from all objects in the two states of cause and effect, as well as the beings who are bound, free and eternally free. His essential nature consists of wisdom, bliss and purity. He is opposed to all filth, possesses unlimited auspicious glorious attri-

> butes; his pastime is the sport of creating, protecting and destroying the worlds; he is the soul of the entire universe; his body is the entire universe, he is without any karma; he has as his body all souls and matter, and is their soul; he is pure and not affected by the happiness, sorrow, change and the imperfections of all other things. This is the Supreme Person. [Here there are seventy-three scriptural quotations.] So say *smṛti* and *itihāsa*. These [statements] are also found in radiant revealed literature *(śruti)* which has not been composed by human beings and which is irrefutable. Thus, Lokāyata, Māyāvāda, Bhāskara, Yādavaprakāśa and other sectarian viewpoints (Tamil: *camayam*) which are different from the Vedas are rejected.

Piḷḷāṉ's style is scholastic, and he is at pains to show the similarity of the Sanskrit and Tamil Vedas by quoting extensively from Sanskrit scripture while commenting on a Tamil verse. The second verse in which Sanskrit Vedas were quoted at length was at a verse in which the supremacy of Viṣṇu was emphatically stated.[24] Sections of the Sanskrit Vedas were carefully chosen to elucidate these concepts, but it must be noted that, at least for the supremacy of Viṣṇu, selective choice and distinctive interpretation were vital to make the points in question.

Vaṭivaḻakiya Nampi Tācar also emphasizes that the Tiruvāymoḻi is the Tamil Veda and that Viṣṇu is supreme, but he does it in a manner different from that of Piḷḷāṉ's. Tācar focuses on the birth and life of Nammāḻvār and highlights his *ṛṣī*-like qualities. The biographer says that the Vedas praised Nammāḻvār as he sat in a "lotus position" as a child and meditated on the supremacy of Viṣṇu's incarnation as a boar.[25] As the seven seas rose to the sky (and chaos reigned), says Tācar, the Lord appeared as a wild boar in order to save the earth and all the lives, thus proving the doctrines of the Śaivas to be false.[26] After three more verses that speak of Viṣṇu's supremacy, Vaṭivaḻakiya Nampi Tācar articulates his polemic: by his gracious deeds (which Nammāḻvār contemplates on) the Lord annihilates the beliefs of the Śaivaites and the Advaitins. The Śaivaites, "who say that Viṣṇu is *not* supreme, and the [nondualist Advaitins] who say 'That thou art' are all to be proved wrong" by the Vedas, which are to be revealed in Tamil.[27]

Tācar says that, even though Nammāḻvār petitioned the Lord to take him to heaven immediately, the Lord answered that he was born to render the Vedas in Tamil and so kept him on earth to give the aural revelation *(śruti)*, which *visually shows* (Tamil: *kāṭṭu*) the blissful heaven to human beings.[28] Nammāḻvār began to recite the Tiruvāymoḻi, the Sāma Veda:

> So that the people of this world
> may conquer the grief of lust and other [vices];
> [So that] they may behold the grace
> of [the Lord] who has a thousand names
> and see the higher goal;
> So that the prosperity of Kurukur,
> the town where the smoke from [Vedic] sacrifices
> floats high and covers the sky,
> may ever increase;
> he rendered the Sāma Veda as the "Sacred Utterance"
> with which [the Lord] could be praised.[29]

Triumphantly, Vaṭivaḻakiya Nampi Tācar says that, "in order to show that the . . . beliefs of the followers of the *Liṅga Purāṇa* were wrong, [Nammāḻvār] proclaimed the meaning of the Vedas and Vedānta."[30] This becomes the occasion for the author to summarize the entire Tiruvāymoḻi and pause at those verses that he considers to give the absolute essence of the Vedas. Like Piḷḷāṉ, Tācar pays close attention to Tiruvāymoḻi 4.10, in which Nammāḻvār praises the temple in his own hometown and in ringing tones celebrates the supremacy of Viṣṇu. It was here that Piḷḷāṉ had showered Sanskrit quotations to show how the agenda of the Tiruvāymoḻi and the Sanskrit Vedas was the same—the declaration of Viṣṇu as the only Lord. Tācar now repeats the sentiments, with a new twist:

> And he declared that the Primordial Viṣṇu
> who wears the cool basil garland
> is the Supreme Being.
> Even as he proclaimed this [message],
> the Jainas, Śaivas and others cried,
> "O *āḻvār*, we have not *heard* the Vedas *utter* this;
> this must be your imagination."
> But [Nammāḻvār], who wears the garland
> of fragrant *vakuḷa* flowers replied:
> "I have only said the meaning of the Vedas
> which have no imperfection."
> . . . .

And the others cried, "O *āḻvār*,
we have not heard this proclaimed
by those who recite the Vedas
from the beginning to the end;
nor have *you* learnt[31] them.
But if you apprehend [these truths]
by the [favor] of the *divine glance*,
tell us that this is the only meaning."[32]

In these verses the philosophical opponents of Nammāḻvār are made to say that *he* could not have learnt the Vedas because he was of the lowest caste, which did not have the authority to study scripture. If, however, he had apprehended the truths by the favor of the Lord's divine glance, he is asked to declare them and clarify the issue.

The message of the Sanskrit Vedas is given one more time in the poem, and the verses (6.10) in which Nammāḻvār surrenders himself to the Lord at Vēṅkaṭam—a set of verses that are considered to be crucial in later Śrīvaiṣṇava soteriological discussions—are seen to portray the essence of the Vedas:

[This] is the [set of] ten [verses] where he takes [refuge]
with [the Lord] who ate the worlds.
[The *āḻvār*] who graciously gave the precious Vedas
  to the people of this earth,
  in a manner that they may understand its meaning,
mentally[33] proceeded to the wondrous Lord
  [who abides] in Venkatam, the golden hill.
Through the mediation[34] of the sacred lady
  who [abides] on the breast of Viṣṇu
[the *āḻvār*] took refuge with him.[35]

Tācar states here a doctrine that is central to the Śrīvaiṣṇava community: that surrendering oneself to Viṣṇu, through the mediation of his consort, Śrī, leads to salvation. What is interesting is that this message is now considered to be part of the Sanskrit Vedas as well.

The emphasis of the theologians in pointing out the perceived common themes between the Sanskrit and Tamil Vedas was clearly on the supremacy of Viṣṇu. Clearly, this was of utmost concern to the Śrīvaiṣṇava community, which prided itself on having a "dual Vedānta," the philosophy based on the "twin" scriptures, Sanskrit and Tamil. The Sanskrit Vedas were being quoted by philosophers of diverse movements and interpreted to support their claims, and earlier, in the thirteenth century, Aḻakiya Maṇavāḷa Nāyaṉār had said that the various kinds of philosophers, the Advaitins, Dvaitins, and Dvaitādvaitins, had all [mis]interpreted the Vedas. The Vedas were not just common heritage for all Hindu traditions; one's philosophy always had to be shown to be the correct and only acceptable interpretation of the Vedas. On the sectarian side the Śaivaites were competing with the Vaiṣṇavites in the south for royal patronage and new converts; on the philosophical side the Advaitins, the Bhedābhedins, and later the Dvaitins and Dvaitādvaitins were clamoring to interpret the Vedas in their distinctive ways. We notice that by this time the perceived dangers of the Buddhists and Jains were on the wane; these people had *rejected* the Vedas and, therefore, were not under immediate criticism by the Śrīvaiṣṇavas. Politically, these movements were not flourishing at this time and were not as threatening as the Śaivaites, who were appealing to the devotional sentiments of the people and pouring out sweet Tamil verses, as the *āḻvārs* had. The Śaivaites saw the Vedas as proclaiming Śiva as the supreme God; their temples were as accessible as the Vaiṣṇavaite ones, their Tamil songs as attractive. Hence, the Śrīvaiṣṇava theologians quoted proof texts more often against the Śaivaites than anyone else and never lost an opportunity to show the Vedic portrayal of Viṣṇu's supremacy.

Despite the perceived similarities in structure and content between the Sanskrit and Tamil Vedas, there were also important distinctions that the community recognized. The most important difference concerns the notion of accessibility; whereas the Sanskrit Vedas were only open to study by brahmin men, the Veda in Tamil could be heard and recited by almost everyone,[36] which meant, in south Indian society, people of all castes and both sexes. Further, unlike the Sanskrit Vedas, the words of the Tiruvāymoḻi would have been easily understood by people hearing them, and even now, after several centuries, the words are not very difficult to comprehend for those who know Tamil.

ACCESSIBILITY OF THE TAMIL VEDA

The importance of accessibility was emphasized by Aḻakiya Maṇavāḷa Nāyaṉār. The Sanskrit revelation is like an ocean, he says, and cannot be utilized easily; the Tiruvāymoḻi is like drinking water in a jug from which a thirsty person can easily get a drink.[37] While the Śrīvaiṣṇava community generally accepts the equality of the Sanskrit and Tamil Vedas, A<u>l</u>akiya Maṇavāḷa Nāya<u>n</u>ār argues that the Tamil Veda is superior. His analogies, expanded by the commentator Maṇavāḷa Māmu<u>n</u>i, are fascinating. Rivers such as the Kaveri and the Tamaraparani, he says, originate in hills and fall to the plains, but near the source the waters are said to be cloudy and mixed with sand. It is much later, downstream, that they become clear and drinkable. Similarly, the Sanskrit Vedas, the source of all knowledge, may be confusing, and, because of their cloudy waters, people who look at them perceive different things. So, concludes the commentator, there are diverse philosophies such as Advaita, Dvaita, and Dvaitādvaita, and all of them purport to be the correct interpretation of the Vedas. Just as the early muddy waters of a river clear as they go on, the later Vedas, manifested through Nammā<u>l</u>vār, are clear and pellucid; there is no argument about their meaning.[38]

A second analogy follows immediately: the sea water is not drinkable, but the water that pours down as rain when the clouds absorb moisture from the sea is clear and sweet. Similarly, the Tamil poets gather the essence, the moisture from the salty ocean of the Sanskrit Vedas, and pour it down as accessible rain.[39]

This accessibility of meaning, however, has to be qualified by at least two points: first, the perception that the poem contained many hidden truths; and, second, the Tamil words were not understood when new converts were made in Telugu and Kannada–speaking areas. Śrīvaiṣṇava teachers have always felt that there were deeper and deeper layers of meaning embedded in the Tiruvāymo<u>l</u>i—truths that would lead one to salvation. The Śrīvaiṣṇava teachers tried to elucidate the Tiruvāymo<u>l</u>i in several commentaries and showed how this sacred poem contained many salvific truths.

While people in the Tamil-speaking areas understood the meaning, this was clearly not the case both with new converts in the Kannada and Telugu–speaking areas (in the modern states of Karnataka and Andhra Pradesh) as well as for later generations of Śrīvaiṣṇavas who settled in these areas. These people learned the Tiruvāymo<u>l</u>i by oral transmission but were not clear about the meaning. Later generations began to copy the words in other scripts, and, in fact, even today Śrīvaiṣṇava residents of these areas, whose ancestors spoke Tamil, read from the Tiruvāymo<u>l</u>i written in the Kannada-Telugu script.

It is important to note that there was no attempt made to translate the Tiruvāymoḻi into any other language until the nineteenth century. This meant that, for those people who did not know Tamil, even the superficial meaning of the Tiruvāymoḻi was as inaccessible as the Sanskrit Vedas. The Tiruvāymoḻi itself was considered to be a new incarnation of the Vedas and, in other contexts, the word of God spoken through Nammāḻvār, and so it was a unique document that could not have an equal. So, while there were no translations—not even for the Śrīvaiṣṇavas in other areas—there were extensive commentaries. The commentarial tradition started in the late eleventh century and still continues to grow. There were also summaries of the poem which would offer the general meaning in a nutshell. Such summaries were composed in Sanskrit and Tamil and included the Sanskrit work of Vedānta Deśika, "Dramiḍopaniṣad Tātparya Ratnāvaḷi" (The Gem Necklace of the Tamil Upaniṣad [13th c.]) as well as Maṇavāḷa Māmuṉi's Tamil poem "Tiruvāymoḻi Nūṟṟantāti" (The Tiruvāymoḻi in a Hundred Verses [late 14th or early 15th c. C.E.]).[40] Both these works tried to summarize the perceived meaning of every unit of ten verses in the Tiruvāymoḻi into one verse. As we saw earlier, in his biography of Nammāḻvār, Vaṭivaḻakiya Nampi Tācar also summarized the meaning of each set of ten Tiruvāymoḻi verses, but, unlike other boiled-down versions, he sometimes took several verses to give the meaning of a particular set. These new summaries emphasized the philosophy of the young Śrīvaiṣṇava community and tended to make the sorrow and pain of Nammāḻvār more removed from the listener. The synopses were elegant, polished literary works that highlighted the similarity in content between the Tamil and the Sanskrit Vedas, but in that process they also made the intensely human Nammāḻvār of the poem more distant, more impersonal.[41]

THE AUTHORS: GOD, NAMMĀḺVĀR, OR NEITHER?

The Tiruvāymoḻi is different from the Sanskrit Veda in one obvious and striking manner. It portrays the longing of one particular human being, Nammāḻvār, for union with the Lord. It is an intensely personal and passionate description of the poet's love, his agony at being separated from the Lord, his crying out to *see* and serve the Lord, and, finally, a triumphant union with him. It is therefore very different in texture and spirit from any of the Sanskrit Vedas—in fact, any Sanskrit work up to that point.[42] In the Tiruvāymoḻi itself, however, Nammāḻvār makes a startling claim that the Lord used him as an instrument and sang the entire Tiruvāymoḻi:

> What can I say of the Lord
> who lifted me up for all time,
> and made me himself, every day?
> My radiant one, the First One,
> my Lord, speaks of himself,
> through me, in sweet Tamil.
>
> What can I say of him
> who unites with my sweet life today?
> He makes my words, the sweet words I say,
> seem as if they were mine,
> [but] the Wondrous One praises himself
> through his own words.
> The Primary One of the three [divine] forms
> says my words ahead of me.
>
> Entering my tongue first,
> he made clear to me that,
> yes, he was the primeval one.
> Would I forget any day,
> the father who, through my mouth,
> spoke about himself
> to the foremost, pure devotees
> in fine sweet verse?
>
> (7.9.1 to 7.9.3)

In this entire set of verses, and in some later ones (TVM 10.7.2), Nammāḻvār claims that the Lord spoke through him. There is no reference to his suffering and his longing; the Lord has united with him and speaks through him. The commentators understand this to mean that the Lord has spoken the *entire* Tiruvāymoḻi through Nammāḻvār, not just the verses in which the poet speaks through the ecstatic words of union. Obviously, this is very different in one sense from the notion of the Sanskrit Veda, which is "authorless," but in another sense Nammāḻvār approaches the Vedic seer closest in these verses when he claims that the Lord "makes my words, the sweet words I say seem as if they were mine. . . . the Primary One . . . says my words ahead of me."

Nammāḻvār is almost *seeing* the words that the Lord says ahead of him. Consider the following verses, which mingle senses of vision and speech:

> When I *saw* his wealth,
> sweet poems, worthy and good,
> came about as I *said* them. . . .
>
> Caṭakōpaṉ from cool Kurukūr
> who *saw* that without Tirumāl
> there is no existence, anywhere,
> *spoke* these thousand verses. . . .
>
> (TVM 7.9.5 and 7.9.11)

Nammāḻvār, like the Vedic seer, visually apprehends what he considers to be the ultimate truth—the infinite attributes and possessions of the Lord—and the words are then spoken aloud, without any effort, almost as if they already existed, and, as we saw earlier, Aḻakiya Maṇavāḷa Nāyaṉār affirms that the Tamil Veda is a newer version of an earlier preexistent model. Many Śrīvaiṣṇava authors declare that Nammāḻvār was given divine eyes *(divya cakṣu)* to apprehend the truth and then enunciated it.[43]

Rāmānuja had stated that the Vedas spoke about Viṣṇu-Nārāyaṇa. It is clear that the content of the Tiruvāymoḻi also focused on Viṣṇu, but, unlike the Sanskrit Vedas, the Tamil Veda is also at times considered to be spoken *by* Viṣṇu. In spite of the perception of divine authorship, note the last verse quoted above: in the traditional "signature" verse—for example, the last verse of every subset of poems in which the author identifies himself—Nammāḻvār (who refers to himself by his proper name Caṭakōpaṉ) says that *he* spoke the poem. Both Nammāḻvār and the Lord share the billing for the poem; while Nammāḻvār says that the Lord entered his tongue and spoke through him, he also clearly asserts his own authorship. The Śrīvaiṣṇava tradition refers to Nammāḻvār as he "who rendered the Vedas in Tamil." The ambiguity of the authorship is maintained by Piḷḷāṉ, the first commentator on the Tiruvāymoḻi. In his introduction to 7.9, in which the poet talks about the Lord speaking through him, Piḷḷāṉ says: "[Nammāḻvār] experiences the Lord's auspicious attributes such as omnipotence, gracious condescension and motherly love. Through the excessive love that was born of this experience, in which [the Lord] took the [*āḻvār*] and graciously sang the Tiruvāymoḻi, [the *āḻvār*] now speaks." While Piḷḷāṉ says that the Lord sang through the poet, he also preserves the exultation that Nammāḻvār felt at the joy of union and says that he spoke because of that exhilarating experience.

Aḻakiya Maṇavāḷa Nāyaṉār, in *The Heart of the Teacher,* has a specific discussion on the notion of authorship and, in fact, brings up the question of signature verses in which the poet identifies himself as Caṭakōpaṉ. The poet usually ends his poems with the line "these verses, *said by* Kurukur Caṭakōpaṉ. . . ." Aḻakiya Maṇavāḷa Nāyaṉār discusses the words *said by* and declares that Nammāḻvār's authorship of the poem is like saying that Brahmā, the creator god, composed the Vedas. According to the commentator, the Sanskrit *smṛti* literature says that Brahmā composed them; what they mean is that, "since the Vedas which have no origin, spring from Brahmā's words *(vāk),* Brahmā is considered to be their composer." The Tamil Vedas, he adds firmly, are not composed by any human being and are eternal.[44]

Immediately following this discussion, Aḻakiya Maṇavāḷa Nāyaṉār says that Nammāḻvār is like the seers who *saw* the Vedas and who visualized the mantras. Nammāḻvār, like these wise men in the past, is a seer *(ṛṣī),* a silent one *(muni),* and a poet *(kavi).* These are words used traditionally for the composers of the Vedas.[45] The commentator explains the words by quoting from an (unidentified) source: "Since he *sees,* he is called a *ṛṣī,* since he possesses the disposition of thinking silently *(manana),* he is called *muni* ('the quiet one'); a *kavi* (a poet) is one who has *insight* into the books *(nūl).*"[46] These discussions highlight the divine vision of a person who perceived the eternal truth and transmitted it; his human nature is made distant. Śrīvaiṣṇava theologians present the Tiruvāymoḻi as the communication of a seer; this is the sacred utterance of a seer who, in biographies, was silent until he was ready to render the Vedas in Tamil.

NAMMĀḺVĀR: HUMAN BEING OR INCARNATION OF GOD?

The ambiguity that is pronounced in Śrīvaiṣṇava discussions on the authorship of the Tiruvāymoḻi is even more apparent in their preoccupation with the question: "Is Nammāḻvār a human being, or is he an incarnation of God?"

Nammāḻvār tells us very little about himself. The name Nammāḻvār was used by the community much later; he refers to himself usually as Māṟaṉ, Kāṟi Māṟaṉ (which leads to the supposition that his father's name was Kāṟi), or Caṭakōpaṉ. He says he is from Kurukūr and praises the town in extravagant terms. He also sings about the deities in thirty-two other places, many of them in neighboring districts, and gives an accurate, though usually nonspecific, description of the places. It was in later biographies that we get more details, including the perception that he was a Veḷḷāḷa, a powerful landowning community but one that was considered from the brahminical standpoint as the "fourth class" of society—for example, a *śūdra*—and thus not eligible to study the Vedas.

The hagiographies describing his life were written *after* the acceptance of the Tiruvāymoḻi as the Veda, the beginning of a commentarial tradition on the poem, and its inclusion in home and temple liturgies. It is probable that, like all other Śrīvaiṣṇava literature, these hagiographies are based on earlier oral traditions, but it is still puzzling how little we know of Nammāḻvār's life. While the biographies give more and more details, the basic construction of his early life remains the same, with minor variations. The following discussion is derived from three works of comparatively later date: *The Splendor of Succession of Teachers* (late 13th c.), *The Sacred Lullaby for Nammāḻvār* (written possibly in the 14th c.),[47] and *The Glory of the Āḻvārs,* composed by Vaṭivaḻakiya Nampi Tācar.[48]

Vaṭivaḻakiya Nampi Tācar's account is filled with the cosmic configurations of time; he gives details of the aeon and life span of the creator god Brahmā to announce when the birth of Nammāḻvār occurred, for his incarnation into this earth is supposed to hold cosmic significance.[49]

The biographies speak of seven generations of holy men who were ancestors of Nammāḻvār, and some even name them. Poṟkāriyār, for instance, the grandfather of Nammāḻvār, arranged the marriage of his son Kāṟi to a fine woman called Uṭayanaṅkai. The young couple were very happy for a while, but Uṭayanaṅkai grew despondent when she did not get a child. The couple went to Tirukkurunkuti, a village a few miles away, and were engaged in intense penance *(tapas).*

At this point Vaṭivaḻakiya Nampi Tācar turns his attention to heaven; Viṣṇu thinks that he should incarnate on earth one more time. He decides that he "will come to earth to show all human beings the way to [everlasting] life, cut through their confusion and show them how to attain [him]."[50] Viṣṇu is usually attended by the eagle Garuḍa and the serpent Ananta (Śeṣa), so he orders them to descend to earth before him and herald his arrival. Ananta is born as a tamarind tree under which the poet Nammāḻvār will sit; then come the instructions to Garuḍa the eagle, who in Sanskrit mythology is the symbol of the Vedas:

> The Vedic [brahmins] who recite the Vedas
> that reveal me as I am
> do not understand what they chant
> and are caught in delusion. . . .
> I do not see any soul acting well
> or a person who knows what he should do
> to reach heaven.
> . . . .
> O Incomparable Ananta,
> I shall render the Vedas in Tamil
> and to see the earth filled with devotees,
> I shall incarnate myself to earth.
> and you shall go ahead, to give me shade.
> O Garuḍa, you shall [write down] my poems
> and *make them into manuscripts.*

Garuḍa is said to incarnate as the brahmin Maturakavi Āḻvār, who became the disciple of Nammāḻvār (this account is not given in earlier biographies).

By the time of Vaṭivaḻakiya Nampi Tācar, we also see an increased preoccupation with the writing of the Tiruvāymoḻi, one that is not at all present in earlier biographies. We must put this in context. In the early days of the Śrīvaiṣṇava community the Tiruvāymoḻi and a commentarial tradition were part of an oral culture, but after the twelfth century there was an intense effort in recording commentaries in leaf, manuscripts *(paṭṭōlai)*. The author of *The Glory of the Āḻvārs* imagines this writing of the Tiruvāymoḻi to have happened at the same time as the original proclamation. It is possible that the author insisted on immediate recording in order to clearly assert that there was no interpolation or change made between the original utterance and eventual recording. It is important to note that, by the fifteenth-century author's perception, the Tamil Veda was immediately written; it was perceived as a *book* and not just as the eternal word transmitted by oral tradition. This notion is reinforced by earlier discussions of A̲lakiya Maṇavāḷa Nāyan̲ār and Maṇavāḷa Māmun̲i, who called the Veda *nūl,* or "book."

The Lord decides to be born as the son of Kāṛi and Uṭayanaṅkai and tells them in a dream (in *The Splendor's* account it is through the voice of the temple priest) that he himself will be born as their son. He tells them that, according to their fate decreed by the creator god Brahmā, they are to remain childless but that, moved by their intensive penance, he has decided to take a "pure body" and be born as their child. The poet reflects that the Lord decided to appear as his own servant on earth, and so, "in the month of Āvaṇi (August–September), as the Vedas celebrated the event, the lord of Wisdom (Viṣṇu) enters Uṭayanaṅkai's womb."[51]

The Lord is born as Kāṛi and Uṭayanaṅkai's son in the month of Vaikāci (15 May–14 June), and the entire town rejoices. But for Uṭayanaṅkai the joy soon turns to bewilderment, for the child refuses to open his eyes or his mouth, either to cry or to drink milk from the mother's breast.

From this point in Vaṭivaḻakiya Nampi Tācar's poem the divinity of the child is not visible. There is an abrupt transition from the perception of God's incarnation as a child to the distress felt by the infant Nammāḻvār. The newborn baby wonders whom he can talk to; there seems to be no one who can receive what he has to say. All the verses from this point in the narrative speak of Nammāḻvār as a human being, one who is enlightened and unique but not God. Both Nampi Tācar's biography and *The Sacred Lullaby for Nammāḻvār* spend several verses focusing on the mother's distress and pathetic words; it is a clear place to show one's poetic talents. And with all the pleading and cajoling the child still does not open his mouth, still does not eat, but his body does not seem any worse for it.

Eventually, the child is taken to the temple; here something startling happens. The child, who was motionless, starts to crawl; *The Sacred Lullaby for Nammāḻvār* contains several verses describing the grandeur and majesty of the child's gait, moving slowly around the Lord, circumambulating him. The child then finds the tamarind tree—the incarnation of Ananta—and crawls under it. There, to everyone's amazement, with his fingers turned around in a teaching symbol he sinks into a meditative trance. He sits in a lotus position, a yogic stance, and seems oblivious to the world.[52]

Meanwhile, Maturakavi Āḻvār, who has undertaken a pilgrimage in northern India, sees a brilliant light in the south. He follows it, and it eventually leads him to Tirukkurukur, where he approaches Nammāḻvār. Knowing intuitively that the Vedas are going to be revealed, he approaches Nammāḻvār with the *manuscript pages* and *stylus* in hand![53]

According to *The Splendor,* Viṣṇu, in all his glory, appeared in front of the poet, who was in deep meditation, and Nammāḻvār sang four poems, which were born from his intense enjoyment derived from visualizing the Lord and his devotees. The four works, says this biography, are the four Vedas, and the Tiruvāymoḻi is the last and most important of these poems.[54]

The other biographies deal with this vision in more detail. One verse from *The Glory of the Āḻvārs* is particularly noteworthy: Viṣṇu, it says, appeared in front of "Tamil Māṟaṉ" (Nammāḻvār), and he heard the rustling of Garuḍa's wings and opened his eyes.[55] While the biographer does not analyze this image, the import of this scene would be clear to a Śrīvaiṣṇava: *Garuḍa represents the Vedas* in the Hindu tradition. Nammāḻvār hears the sounds of Garuḍa, the embodiment of the Vedas, and opens his eyes, thus visually perceiving the supreme truth. Notice the juxtaposition of hearing Garuḍa, the embodiment of the Vedas, and seeing the truth. The biographer continues:

> Opening his gracious lotus-like eyes,
> [the *āḻvār*] scanned the firmament and there he saw
>   with hordes of devotees surrounding him
>   with the glorious incomparable goddess on his breast
>   with the Vedas singing his praises,
> Nārāyaṇa holding aloft his whirling wheel and white conch,
> sitting astride on the fortunate Garuḍa.[56]

The *āḻvār,* trembling, bowed low and begged the Lord to take him to heaven, but the Lord, firm in his resolve, asked him to render the Vedas in Tamil. He ordered Nammāḻvār to recite and to set to music the "aural revelation which shows us heaven; heaven which is filled with wisdom and bliss."[57] Having said this, Viṣṇu-Nārāyaṇa departed for heaven, and Maturakavi Āḻvār got his palm leaves to write down the words of Nammāḻvār. Nammāḻvār then gave the essence of the Rig Veda in his poem

"Tiruviruttam," continued with the essence of the Yajur Veda in his "Tiruvāciriyam," then sang the Atharva Veda in "Periya Tiruvantāti." Finally, came the essence of the Sāma Veda in his Tiruvāymoḻi.[58] Vaṭivaḻakiya Nampi Tācar then proceeded to summarize the Tiruvāymoḻi in about a hundred and forty verses and concluded his biography of Nammāḻvār with a lengthy account of his ascent to heaven.

BIOGRAPHICAL LITERATURE: THE SECOND REVELATION TO NĀTHAMUNI

The second revelation is described in a chapter in *The Splendor.* The songs of the *āḻvārs,* we are told, became "lost" to human beings and so had to be revealed for a second time: by the poet Nammāḻvār, to the first teacher, Nāthamuni, around the tenth century. *The Splendor* narrates his efforts in recovering the lost poems. Nāthamuni heard ten verses from the Tiruvāymoḻi, went in search of the other verses to Nammāḻvār's birthplace, and meditated intensely on the poem written by Maturakavi Āḻvār.

> With restraint he meditated repeatedly on the poem "Kaṇṇinuṇ Ciruttāmpu" twelve thousand times. The *āḻvār,* pleased with Nāthamuni . . . asked him . . . "Why do you meditate so intensely on me?" Nāthamuni submitted, "I want you to take pity on me and [teach] me the Tiruvāymoḻi and other sacred works." The *āḻvār,* pleased, graciously gave Nāthamuni eyes of divine knowledge. . . . Just as the Supreme Lord graciously gave [the *āḻvār*] "wisdom and love to cut all sorrow" (Tiruvāymoḻi 1.1.1), he gave Nāthamuni the "three secrets," the Tiruvāymoḻi and the other 3000 verses, the truth of all philosophies and the secret of the eight-fold yoga.[59]

The poems of the second revelation are collectively called the *Sacred Collect.* Nāthamuni, it is said, instituted the chanting of verses from this anthology (alongside the Sanskrit Vedas, which alone had been traditionally recited) both in home and temple worship.

Several elements in this story are worth noting in connection with our understanding of how this work became the Vedas. Earlier, in looking at Tiruvāymoḻi 7.9, God seems to be the author of the Tiruvāymoḻi, and it may appear that the Tamil poem is *different* from the Sanskrit Vedas, which were *not* composed by God. According to the Mīmāmsaka school of thought and Rāmānuja, they are eternally existing and coterminus with the Lord, though in the Śrīvaiṣṇava tradition they are later understood to be a part of him. The Sanskrit Veda is authorless; the Tiruvāymoḻi has not one but two authors, God and Nammāḻvār, depending on one's perspective. But by the time of Aḻakiya Maṇavāḷa Nāyaṉār this notion of the "authorlessness" of the Veda was extended to the Tiruvāymoḻi also.

There is yet another major difference between the Vedic seers who instituted the eternal words and communicated them and Nammāḻvār. According to the Śrīvaiṣṇava understanding, the seers are passive transmitters; they are the conduits of an impersonal revelation. Nammāḻvār, on the other hand, is the suffering hero (or "lovesick heroine," if one adopts the terminology of classical Tamil poetry) whose experience is as intense and personal as any experience can be. It is the story of one man, one soul, who does not want God to play hide-and-seek with him. The poet frequently seems to be speaking, even as the action is going on, as the drama is unfolding. He is the actor who does not know the end of the script. This intense personality is removed in the biographical tradition: we see a yogic personality impervious to heat and cold, one who sat under a tree singing in obedience to the commands of the various "images"—incarnations of Viṣṇu from local temples who appear in front of him and say "sing about me, sing about me." By accentuating his nonhuman nature—he does not eat, cry, speak, marry—the biographies remove Nammāḻvār from the human realm. It is, therefore, no surprise to learn that in some texts in the Śrīvaiṣṇava tradition he is considered as an incarnation of the Lord and sometimes of a celestial being known as Viśvaksena. Viśvaksena is considered to be Viṣṇu's commander in chief, but, as far as I can see, there is no obvious reason why Nammāḻvār was thought to be the incarnation of this particular divine servant.

But the stories also make this important point: the Tiruvāymoḻi was forgotten and obliterated from human recitation, with the exception of one set of poems, which attracted the attention of Nāthamuni. And so we have a scenario in which there is a *preexistent* set of holy words that are formed in a particular order, just as the Sanskrit Vedas are, and the sage Nāthamuni "hears" these words, like the Vedic seers hear and see the eternal words in Sanskrit. Whereas Nammāḻvār was the active participant of the salvation drama seen in the Tiruvāymoḻi,

Nāthamuni, like the Vedic seers, is the passive transmitter of the divine words of the Tamil Veda.

The Tamil Veda is like the Sanskrit one in content. Both reveal Viṣṇu as the Supreme Being. The Sanskrit Vedas, however, are authorless, but the Tiruvāymoḻi is spoken both by the human being Nammāḻvār and at the same time considered by the poet and the community as the utterance of Viṣṇu. In time it, too, is considered to be authorless. Nammāḻvār, therefore, is not the only analogue to the Vedic seer; it is also Nāthamuni, the first teacher of the community, who is the recipient of the second revelation. Just as the Vedic seers formed the spiritual ancestors for all of the Hindu tradition, Nāthamuni becomes the first full teacher of the Śrīvaiṣṇava community.

The notion of Veda as applied to the Tiruvāymoḻi is complex and multifaceted. It is not just that the Tiruvāymoḻi was considered revealed and made part of the temple liturgy that qualified it as a Veda: the dynamics of the revelation of the Sanskrit and Tamil Vedas were considered similar in great detail. Just as the Vedic seers "saw" the mantras, Nammāḻvār, with his divine eyes, saw and "uttered" the preexistent words. By the fifteenth century these words were said to be immediately recorded in writing, a concept that fits Aḻakiya Maṇavāḷa Nāyaṉār's portrayal of the Vedas as books. Nammāḻvār's life was described in a manner that made him a yogic seer; he simply did not display any discernible "normal" human behavior. Finally, the contents of both Sanskrit and Tamil Vedas were considered to be the same. These contents reflected the political climate of the day (the superiority of Viṣṇu and the showing of Śaivaites to be "wrong") as well as the doctrines important to the fledgling Śrīvaiṣṇava community. By seeing and uttering the divine truths, Nammāḻvār became the *ṛṣī* who intuited and communicated an old Veda for a new age. That new age was to be realized in the "sacred arena" of liturgy and worship of the faithful in "Srirangam." Srirangam became the sacred stage upon which the paradigmatic journey of Nammāḻvār was enacted with the recitation of the Tiruvāymoḻi, and the words of the Tamil Veda became a new revelation to every devotee who participated in the recitation.

3

RECITERS OF THE SACRED TEXT

Contemporary Exemplars of Teaching and Learning

In the last chapter we saw how the Śrīvaiṣṇava community perceives the Tiruvāymoḻi to be equivalent to the Sanskrit Vedas and discussed the ambiguous divine-human status of Nammāḻvār in the biographical literature. According to tradition, the recipient of Nammāḻvār's revelation of the Tiruvāymoḻi was initially Maturakavi, and apparently after several centuries the first Śrīvaiṣṇava teacher, Nāthamuni. In many traditional paintings Nammāḻvār is depicted with Nāthamuni and Maturakavi next to him. Maturakavi is represented as having a manuscript and stylus in hand; biographical literature portrays him as recording the Tiruvāymoḻi as it was being revealed. The manuscript and pen, we may suppose, also symbolize the long line of commentarial and exegetical literature on the Tiruvāymoḻi which the community has produced over the centuries. Nāthamuni, on the other hand, is portrayed with cymbals in his hand, ready to keep rhythm; he represents the recitation of the Tiruvāymoḻi and the tradition of interpreting the poem through music and dance. In this chapter (and also in chap. 6) we shall discuss the importance of recitation and music and their transmission within the Śrīvaiṣṇava community; in later chapters we shall look at the commentarial traditions on the poem, including the literary (chap. 7) and the performative (chap. 8) interpretations.

While the word used frequently in the Śrīvaiṣṇava community for the recitation of Sanskrit Vedas is *adhyayana* (recitation)—and, in fact, the annual Festival of Recitation is called *adhyayana utsava*—Nammāḻvār does not use the word in the Tiruvāymoḻi. The other word used in Śrīvaiṣṇava parlance today to describe recitation is *anusandhānam;* in

Sanskrit it means "investigation, inquiry, close inspection"; in Tamil it came to mean "to contemplate, meditate, to say and to express."[1] The daily cycle of prayers from the Divya Prabandham which are recited every day is called *nityānusandhānam,* or daily meditations. *Anusandhānam,* therefore, has connotations of prayerful meditation. To do the daily *anusandhānam* is not just to recite the words; it also involves a total mental, intellectual, emotional, physical, and spiritual commitment to what is being recited and a complete involvement with the subject matter. This word also does not occur in the works of Nammāḻvār or the other *āḻvārs.*

The most frequently used word today to recite the Tiruvāymoḻi is *cēvai,* meaning "service" (from the Sanskrit *sevā*). The ritual of reciting the Divya Prabandham, including the hours of recitation in a temple or during a funeral, is called *sevā kālam,* or "time of service." According to the Śrīvaiṣṇavas, recitation is service to the Lord, and it is this attitude that one should take when articulating the words. Although this word is commonly used by the Śrīvaiṣṇava community today, the poet does not use it in the meaning of recitation. What then does the Tiruvāymoḻi say about itself? Did Nammāḻvār perceive his verses as being silently meditated upon, sung, or recited? How were the traditions of music and recitation transmitted? What is the content of the verses recited in daily liturgies? Historically, how long, and in what context, has the Tiruvāymoḻi been recited in brahmanical temples and in scheduled caste ("outcaste") shrines? While recitation and singing the Tiruvāymoḻi were supposed to be religious events, they have to be studied in a social and political context, in which tensions between the different castes and different families connected with ritual recitation led to bitter fighting and occasionally to legal battles. While it would be outside the scope of this book to answer all these questions in overwhelming detail, we shall try to get a historical and contemporary understanding of the phenomena of Tiruvāymoḻi recitation at home and in temple by studying the text, considering inscriptional data, and by meeting the people who teach, learn, and recite the poem.

THE TIRUVĀYMOḺI'S PERCEPTION OF ITSELF

The Tiruvāymoḻi is composed in an old Tamil style called "end-beginning" *(antāti),* in which the last words of one verse also become the first words of the subsequent verse. The verses are thus linked together, and the last words of the last verse also form the first words of the first verse, and the entire poem is thus woven together like a garland. Nammā̱lvār himself talks about his "garlands of words" and "garlands of song":

> Praising the lord,
> is there any need [unfulfilled]
> in seven generations
> for one who can say
> *garlands of words* [for the Lord]?
>
> With soft words
> I praised the Lord
> with *garlands of song* . . .
>
> I obtained the fortune
> of singing with my tongue,
> *garlands of song,*
> praising the Lord . . .
>
> (from 4.5.1, 4.5.2, and 4.5.4)

This format of linked verses could thus deter interpolation, though, of course, it would still be possible. The linking or weaving of the verses makes the poem resemble a wreath or a garland, and this imagery is seen in the Tiruvāymoḻi itself. Sometimes Nammā̱lvār calls his poem a garland (1.2.11), sometimes a garland of words (7.2.11, 8.1.11, 8.3.11, 9.3.11, 10.4.11), a "Tamil-garland" (2.7.13, 5.6.11, 6.2.11, 8.9.11, 10.6.11),[2] and sometimes as a wreath of song (3.2.11, 4.8.11).

It is obvious from the poem itself that the author envisaged it as being set to music and dance:[3]

> . . . those who can *sing (pāṭu)*
> these ten verses
> from the thousand set in *antāti*
> with melody and rhythm
> are devotees of Kēcava<u>n</u>.
>
> (2.6.11)

> . . . those who can *sing* and *dance*
> these ten verses
> from the thousand Tamil [songs]
> will ascend to heaven.
>
> (4.7.11)

Although he delights in saying that his words are to be sung, he sometimes uses the Tamil word *ōtutal,*[4] which specifically refers to the recitation of the Sanskrit Vedas:

> These verses on Mātavan̲
> are spoken by Caṭakōpan̲
> without malice or pride.
> Those who can recite [*otu*]
> these ten verses
> from the thousand songs
> which have no blemish
> will not have more births.
>
> (1.6.11)

The word *ōtutal* occurs only twice in the Tiruvāymoḻi, in 1.6.11 and 9.1.11. The Śaiva tradition, however, uses this word frequently to describe the recitation of its hymns, and its singers are called *ōtuvārs.* The Śrīvaiṣṇavas, who have an entire subculture concerning the "correct" and "proper form" in usage of words, have consciously refrained from employing the word *ōtutal* in referring to the recitation of the Tiruvāymoḻi, quite possibly to distinguish themselves from the Śaivas.[5] The poet suggests that the verses are to be articulated correctly, and audibly: the Tamil word *oli,* which means "sound, roar, articulate sound; loud or audible recitation of a mantra," is sometimes used by Nammāḻvār. Frequently, he just asks people to say or utter his verses;[6] listen to (*kēṭṭu* [10.6.11]), learn (*kaṟṟu* [1.10.11, 4.4.11, 5.5.11, 10.4.11]), and consider *(ōrtal)* them carefully (1.8.11). While these specific verbs are used frequently, Nammāḻvār uses a generic word, *vallār,* several times in connection with his songs. The word *vallār* comes from *van̲mai,* which simply means "having the strength for, or being capable of." Although Nammāḻvār has used the words *sing, recitation,* and *dance,* he uses the word *vallār* by itself frequently, possibly to indicate that, if one can, one should sing, recite, dance, utter, listen to, learn, or carefully consider the Tiruvāymoḻi and that all these activities will bear fruit. While all these ways of being involved with the poem are recommended, in the initial stages of instituting the poem in domestic and temple worship, singing the verses seems to have been popular.

ARAIYARS AND ADHYĀPAKAS

The Divya Prabandham has been recited by the *araiyars* and *adhyāpakas* in the Śrīvaiṣṇava temples.[7] The *araiyars* are said to be the descendants and disciples of the first people who sang and danced the Divya Prabandham in the temples. These were Kīḻaiakattāḻvār and Mēlaiakkatāḻvār, the nephews of Nāthamuni. Although the *araiyars* have the formal right to render "loving service" to the Lord by reciting the Tiruvāymoḻi and other works from the Divya Prabandham in some of the temples, in others a group *(goshti)* of men, known as "reciters" *(adhyāpakas)*, do it. *Adhyāpakas* are always male and can be chosen from the congregation at large, if they have the necessary qualifications, but to be an *araiyar* one has to be born into an *araiyar* family and then be trained in the art. Today the *araiyar* tradition, with song and dance, lives only in the Śrīvaiṣṇava temples of Srirangam, Alvar Tirunagari, and Srivilliputtur. In Melkote, Karnataka, the *araiyars* sing but do not dance. The tradition has died out in the other sacred places, but there is inscriptional evidence to tell us that it flourished in other centers, such as Kanchipuram, in the past. In an inscription dated 1242 in Kanchipuram we hear that twenty-two *viṇṇappam ceyvārs* (another name for *araiyars*) lived and performed there.[8]

While both the *araiyars* and the *adhyāpakas* recite the sacred verses, only the *araiyars* beat the rhythm with their cymbals. Further, the modes of recitation are quite different between the *araiyars* and the *adhyāpakas;* the *adhyāpakas* break the sentences at regular intervals, emphasizing the sound patterns, but this sometimes leads to the breaking up of sentences and even words at awkward places. The *araiyars,* on the other hand, carefully break the sentences by looking at the meaning of the verse. Placing emphasis on the meter and the meaning is important to the *araiyars;* since the entire Divya Prabandham is like Veda, they believe that the words have potent power like a mantra and that breaking them up in wrong places when concentrating on the meter may lead to disastrous consequences. Their belief is based on the notion that the mantras of the Vedas have power when uttered; thus, if one mispronounces a word or utters a sentence in such a way that it alters the meaning of the verse, then what was uttered in ignorance will actually be caused to happen. There is a famous Vedic story to illustrate this point: Tvaṣṭṛ, a mythological character, blesses his son to be the destroyer of Indra. He accidentally mispronounces the words *Indra śatruḥ* (Indra destroyer), however, and the sentence takes new meaning: Indra is to become the destroyer of the son![9]

Sri Nadhamuni Araiyar, the chief cantor in the Srirangam Temple today, quoted a few verses from the Divya Prabandham, for which if recited according to the *adhyāpaka* style, the meaning of the lines will become garbled; more important, the wrong meaning will become like a prophecy, and calamities will occur.[10] This is an extended illustration of what Levering calls "transactive reception," in which "the recitation of even those texts not specifically meant for the purpose of taking action also causes things to happen."[11] As examples, Sri Nadhamuni Araiyar quoted verses from the Tiruvāymoḻi of Nammāḻvār and the Periya Tirumoḻi of Tirumaṅkai. The first example is from Tiruvāymoḻi 7.4.7, in which the verse ends with the line: "O the way in which my father set Laṅkā ablaze and destroyed it." The Tamil words are followed by a word-by-word translation in the Tamil order and then translated:

> *appaṉ nīru paṭa ilaṅkai ceṟṟa nērē*
> father-ablaze-set-Laṅkā-destroy-way
> The way in which my father set Laṅkā ablaze and destroyed it!

Ideally, when reciting the line, the pause should come after the first word, *appaṉ* (father), in the Tamil verse. To get the right rhythm, however, the *adhyāpakas* pause after the third word, *paṭa,* and say the first three words, *appaṉ nīru paṭa,* together; this by itself translates as "my father was touched by fire" or "my father was set ablaze." Thus, with wrong intonation, and by splitting up the sentence in a wrong way to get uniformity in recitation, the line may mean "my father was set ablaze." Sri Nadhamuni Araiyar said that, because of this mispronunciation, there was actually fire in the inner shrine of the Srirangam Temple, and the chamber in which the Lord is enshrined was enveloped in flames. Likewise, he added, in the Periya Tirumoḻi, composed by Tirumaṅkai Āḻvār, the words in the verses dedicated to the Lord at Tillai Citrakūṭam (the modern city of Chidambaram) are split up in the wrong way. In these verses (3.2.1–10) the word *Tillai* in the name Tillai Citrakūṭam was split up by the *adhyāpakas* as *tī illai. Tī* was then attached to the word preceding the name, and *illai,* which means "no," was uttered separately. Thus, instead of a line meaning "Tillai Citrakūṭam, where the flag flies," the line, as enunciated by the *adhyāpakas* came to mean "Citrakūṭam, where the flag *does not* fly."[12] In later verses there are lines that come to mean, as the *adhyāpakas* recite it, "Citrakūṭam, *which is not* surrounded by golden, gem-covered walls" and "the four Vedas are *not sung* in Citrakūṭam" (Periya Tirumoḻi 3.2.3 and 3.2.6).

It is important to note that the Viṣṇu temple at Tillai Citrakūṭam is part of the famous and larger Śiva temple complex in the same place, and common walls surround them. Sri Nadhamuni Araiyar said that the splitting of the lines by paying attention to the meter and not the meaning was like a prophecy, leading to the discontinuation of several festivals in this temple. Thus, the *brahmotsavam,* the main festival in any shrine, which is marked by the hoisting of the temple's flag, was not conducted for a while in Tillai Citrakūṭam because the *adhyāpakas* had recited, "Citrakūṭam, where the flag *does not* fly." The temple had lost its own territory surrounded by towering walls and had become enclosed in the Śiva temple, making the line "Citrakūṭam, *which is not* surrounded by golden, gem-covered walls" come to pass. The Festival of Recitation was also discontinued there, and the four Vedas were not sung there for a while. The words of the Divya Prabandham, therefore, have mantralike power, causing action to happen even if it is not the intention of the reciter. Careful enunciation and proper recitation, said Sri Nadhamuni Araiyar, are extremely important.

Notwithstanding the mantric power of the uttered words, even the meaning of the words seem powerful enough to move people. The power of the sacred words of the Divya Prabandham has been reiterated in biographic literature. Once during the Festival of Recitation the teacher Yāmuna (10th c. C.E.) was listening to Tiruvaraṅka Perumal Araiyar sing and dance Tiruvāymoḻi 10.2.1, a verse in which the poet urges everyone to go to Tiru Ananta Puram (modern Trivandrum). The *araiyar* apparently sang some of the lines over and over again, looking at Yāmuna's face. Moved, Yāmuna rose immediately and undertook the pilgrimage, forgetting all else.[13] A generation later Rāmānuja, while listening to a verse in praise of the Lord at Tirupati (3.3.1 [see app.]) was inspired to send someone to permanently abide in Tirupati and serve the Lord. The verses thus seem to jog one's memory and remind one of the duties of human beings.

Both the *araiyars* and the *adhyāpakas* undergo years of learning and practice before they recite in the temples. They learn the Divya Prabandham from their parents, teachers, or in seminary-style schools, which educate them in Tamil and Sanskrit literature.

THE SERVANTS OF THE LORD: LEARNING AND RECITING THE DIVYA PRABANDHAM

The Tiruvāymoḻi has been taught and learned from teacher to disciple for generations, and the lines of transmission are still visible. When the theologians said that the Tiruvāymoḻi was better than the Sanskrit Veda because it was more accessible, they meant that women and lower-caste people had the authority to recite it. Men and women of all ages and castes participate in the transmission, teaching, and learning the Tiruvāymoḻi in special schools established for the purpose, at homes, and in small informal classes held in community centers or temples. People learn to recite or sing the Tiruvāymoḻi for different reasons, and the purpose for which they learn it determines the formality and structure of the classes. For instance, a group of women meeting twice a week in a suburban home in Madras to learn and sing verses from the Divya Prabandham will concentrate on the musical modes and sing by looking at their books, but a class of young brahmin boys training perhaps to be *adhyāpakas* or eventually to recite in temples may be told to repeat a verse about a dozen times, over and over again, to memorize it, and recite it with the correct rhythm and intonation. In this section we shall meet a few people serving in Śrīvaiṣṇava temples in India and the United States and hear how they learned to recite the Divya Prabandham.

1. Sri Saranatha Bhattar, Sri Venkateswara Temple,[14] *Pittsburgh.* Sri Saranatha Bhattar is a Śrīvaiṣṇava Vatakalai priest and has mastered the recitation of the entire Divya Prabandham.[15] He studied up to the eighth "standard" (grade) at a secular school and after that was taken to the Madurantakam *pāṭhaśāla* (a seminary-style school), where he studied in the Sanskrit college for seven years. He came from an orthodox Śrīvaiṣṇava family and was initiated into the Śrīvaiṣṇava community formally with the sacrament of *samāśrayaṇam* (taking refuge with the Lord) administered by Sriman Garudapuram Chinnaswami. After having studied the various subfields in Sanskrit, including logic, drama, and poetry, he almost finished the work needed to attain the Siromani title. He searched for a job in secular fields but eventually came to work at the temple in Sri Mushnam, near Chidambaram. This was his mother's hometown. Later he joined the entourage of Srimad Andavan, an extremely learned pontiff, who heads the Munitrayam branch of the Vaṭakalai Śrīvaiṣṇavas and who has a large following. He learned the entire Divya Prabandham here, over a four-year period.

Sri Saranathan emphasized that he learned the Divya Prabandham, especially the Tiruvāymoḻi, *after* he had been invested with the sacred thread. Since the Tiruvāymoḻi was the Tamil Veda, the boys had to undergo the Upanayana ceremony in order to be qualified to study it. This is an interesting twist in the interpretation of the notion of Veda. The Sanskrit Veda was only to be studied by "twice-born" males, after they underwent the initiation-rebirth ceremony of the Upanayana, but the Tiruvāymoḻi, the Tamil Veda, was considered to be accessible to all Śrīvaiṣṇavas. But, by calling the Tiruvāymoḻi a Veda, in popular imagination it is immediately considered to be like the Sanskrit one, and the qualifications required for the study of the Sanskrit Veda are now transferred to the study of the Tamil Veda.

The learning process to memorize the Divya Prabandham was arduous; for fourteen to fifteen days (one *pakṣa,* or "fortnight," roughly corresponding to one half-cycle of the moon), they would learn fifty verses—the same fifty verses—over and over again, repeating each one over *(uru)* ten times. During the next *pakṣa* they would learn fifty new verses and do *tiru* (repetition) for the old fifty, repeating each verse three times. Attention was paid to meter and rhythm; careful recitation was all important. There would be no classes on feast days and ritual days. During these recitation classes the sound was emphasized; this was not the time for meaning and exegesis. In the evenings the pontiff would have a *kālākṣepam* (literally, "whiling away time" but referring, in fact, to exegesis and storytelling, when scriptural passages are explained at length). In these the commentaries on the Tiruvāymoḻi, known as "sacred matters" *(bhagavad viṣayam),* were the subject matter of discourses. Sometimes the Andavan would lecture on Vedānta Deśika's (1268–1368) works, and so Saranatha Bhattar got a good grounding, not just in the art of recitation but also in the meaning of the verses. The two necessarily do not go hand in hand, but he felt fortunate in getting this instruction along with many others.

The special feature of the discourses was that the pontiff would frequently bring in scriptural quotations from outside the books and introduce them in his lectures to illustrate a point; no book learning could bring this wealth of knowledge to illuminate a verse, he said. It is evident that he mastered the art of giving religious discourses, using the proper Śrīvaiṣṇava technical words and phrases unique to the community; when he recorded his recitation of the entire Tiruvāymoḻi for me in 1988 he prefaced it with a formal narrative of the life of Nammāḻvār, embellished with scriptural quotations from Sanskrit and Tamil texts. Sri Saranatha Bhattar underwent further initiation to be a temple priest and now feels comfortable reciting both Sanskrit prayers and Tamil hymns at temple and home rituals. He recites selections from the Divya Prabandham regularly at the Pittsburgh temple and looks forward to several years of serving the Lord and the community.

2. Students of the Tirupati Pāṭhaśāla. Sri Samudrala Krishnamacharylu and Sri Venkatacharlu are brothers and priests; Sri Krishnamacharylu is at the Hindu Temple Society of Southern California, where he serves at the Venkateswara Temple, and Sri Venkatacharlu is at the Venkateswara Temple in Pittsburgh.[16] Both studied at the Tirupati Pāṭhaśāla, or "school," located near one of the most famous temples in India. According to Sri Venkatacharlu, the regimen was rigorous for the four hundred young male students at this residential school. Most of the students were brahmins, and the twenty-two teachers certainly were Śrīvaiṣṇava brahmins. The daily schedule is interesting, as it forms the rigorous orthoprax context against which we understand the process of learning the Divya Prabandham. The day began very early, and before they had any coffee they were to have had a cold bath by six in the morning. In the cold weather of the hills a student was not enthusiastic about having a chilly shower, and he would occasionally try to sprinkle water on himself and pretend that he had taken a bath. But, if the teacher was suspicious, he would feel the "sacred thread" on the student's shoulder to see if it was damp, to ensure that indeed the boy had bathed. The ritual bath is more than just a cleansing act for the Hindu; without it the person is ritually impure and cannot partake in any religious activity. They said the morning prayers, including the *suprabhātam* (literally, "good morning," a prayer recited daily to wake up the Lord in the Tirupati and some other temples). After the *sandhyā vandanam* (prayers said at dawn, midday, and dusk) at 7:30 A.M. they had breakfast at 8:00 A.M., and classes began at 8:30 A.M.[17] There were many subjects: logic, Mīmāmsa, recitation of Sanskrit Vedas, Tamil hymns, and so on. After the midday *sandhyā vandanam* lunch was served between noon and 1:00 P.M., and this was followed by one hour of extra tuition, followed by more classes until 4:30. Immediately after that there was a half-hour study of the Bhagavad Gītā. The evening *sandhyā vandanam* had to be performed between 5:30 and 6:00 P.M., followed by the recitation of the thousand names of Viṣṇu *(Viṣṇu Sahasranāma)*. Dinner was between 7:00 and 8:00 P.M., and special classes and tuition were held between 8:00 and 10:00 P.M. This rigorous schedule was followed every day; the only holidays were the eighth day after the new moon and full moon *(ashṭami)*, new moon and full moon days.

Venkatacharlu joined this school after his fifth standard and was there until he finished the final year of schooling. His classes included the study of Pañcarātra, Divya Prabandham, Yajur Veda, prayers *(stotras)*, and other subjects. Examinations involved both oral recitation and practical competency to do the *ārādhana*, or daily worship rituals. Although most students took six or seven years to learn the Divya Prabandham, he learned it in just four; his brother Krishnamacharylu learned the poems in about three and a half years. Venkatacharlu learned the *iyaṛpā* section first ("that which is to be recited"; the third thousand in the corpus of the Divya Prabandham), and this was followed by the Tiruvāymoḻi, the First Thousand, and finally the Periya Tirumoḻi of Tirumaṅkai Āḻvār.

This is not necessarily the order in which other students learn the Divya Prabandham; most of them start with the First Thousand and finish with the Tiruvāymoḻi. While the instruction was completely oral, and the student repeated the verses after his teacher, he also had a copy of the Divya Prabandham not in Tamil but in Telugu script. The teacher would make him learn about a hundred verses every fortnight; he had to repeat each new verse ten times (a process called *uru*). He had to use the digits in his fingers in his right palm to keep count; each time he repeated a verse he would move his thumbs to one part of his fingers. The mid section of the student's middle finger was supposed to denote Mount Meru, the *axis mundi,* in a symbolic way. When he kept count by moving his thumb up and down his fingers, he moved in a clockwise manner (see fig. 1), and, thus, each time he recited a verse ten times it was as though he circled Mount Meru once.

In the following fortnight the students learned a hundred new songs and then had to repeat (an action called *tiru*) the old hundred verses to ensure that they remembered it. At the end of the learning

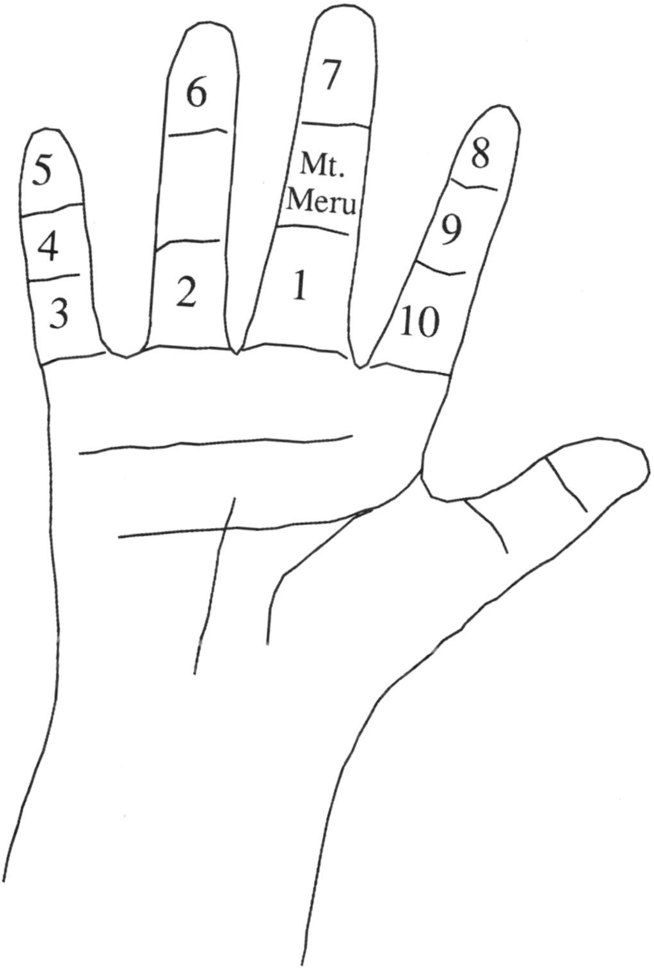

Figure 1. Keeping count of repetitions of verses.

period they were quizzed, and the teachers looked for clarity of expression, intonation, modulation, splitting of the words and lines at regular intervals, and sense of timing and rhythm. In addition, they would sometimes quiz a student by giving him a certain word or name of a place and ask him to recite the verses in which that term occurred—almost like the "search" mechanism in modern computers. The student would race through his mind mentally to find all the passages in which that word occurred; this was to test the accuracy of the memorization process. While most of the students were brahmins, Sri Krishnamacharylu remembered that, of the seven students in his class, there were two *bhāgavatas* (literally "devotees," used frequently in modern Śrīvaiṣṇava parlance to denote nonbrahmin devotees) from the city of Coimbatore and one *bhāgavata* in Sri Venkatacharlu's class.

Both brothers passed the Sanskrit Siromani examination. Sri Krishnamacharylu came to the United States in 1983. While there was no time to do the full recitation of key sections from the Divya Prabandham at the Malibu temple,[18] he does say some verses during the concluding ceremonies of the ritual recitation, which is known as *cāṟṟumuṟai*. *Cāṟṟumuṟai* literally means "to bring to a close" and refers to the concluding verses, some of which are benedictory in nature. Sri Krishnamacharylu recites Tiruvāymoḻi 6.10 (see app.) every day; these verses refer to the hills of Tiruvenkatam, or Tirupati, from where he hails. Further, it is the Lord of Tiruvenkatam (Venkateswara) who is enshrined both in the temple at Malibu and in Pittsburgh, so these eleven verses are deemed to be particularly appropriate.

3. *The Veda Adhyāpaka Goshti of Sri Parthasarathi Temple, Triplicane*. Sri Ashtagothram N. C. Parthsarathy Iyengar has been the honorary secretary of the Veda Adhyāpaka Goshti (Veda Reciters' Association) at the Parthasarathi Temple in Triplicane and is in charge of the daily Divya Prabandham recital in the temple. The temple is old (it is mentioned by the earliest *āḻvārs*, who perhaps lived in the eighth century); it is large and influential, being a sacred place *(divya deśa)* located at the center of Madras city, a large metropolitan area.[19] The Veda Reciters' Association has nineteen carefully chosen male members, a relatively small group compared to that of the 1920s, when there were sixty members. Of the nineteen members five people are retirees, having worked in secular jobs all their lives, and two are full-time priests. The others work full-time outside the temple. Sri Parthsarathy Iyengar worked in the accountant-general's office until his retirement, but his work as the honorary secretary in the temple's recitation group took up a great deal of his time. He stresses that he and the other *adhyāpakas* in the temple do honorary service, volunteering several hours a day, and this is to be regarded purely as "loving service, without expecting anything in return" *(ananyaprayojana kaiṁkarya)*. In some months, such as

Mārkaḻi (15 Dec.–13 Jan.), the service begins at 3:00 A.M., when the Tiruppāvai of Āṇṭāḷ is recited, and concludes about ten or eleven at night, when the Tiruvāymoḻi verses for the day are finished. For this voluntary service they are given about one pint of food (a rice and lentil dish called *pongal*) and about a quarter of a *vaṭai*, a fried snack. This is considered to be *prasādam*, or food blessed by the Lord.

In a legal case in 1923, when some of the trustees (who apparently were not brahmin), alleged that the *prasādam* constituted payment and, therefore, the *adhyāpakas* could be dismissed, the judge ruled (in 1925) that the *prasādam* was hardly enough payment or inducement for the reciters to spend so many hours in the temple and dismissed the case. The legal case, according to some of the local informants, had its roots in tensions between brahmins and nonbrahmins and issues of monetary control; the reciters' association became a focal point of such tensions. The finer points involving the 1925 judgment are still quoted by the group with pride, because it affirms their religious and legal status as an autonomous group rendering "loving service" to the Lord.

The litigation of the 1920s is not just history for the Veda Reciters' Association; it has relevance to present-day politics and the group's desire to establish the temple under a category recognized by the local government as "scheme temples." These temples have apparently existed from the time of the East India Company, and, according to Sri Parthsarathy Iyengar, twenty-three such scheme temples are recognized today. These temples are outside the purview of government control, and the executive officer is also the management officer of the temple; there is no "outsider" appointed by the government to look over the shoulders of the local management.

Sri Parthsarathy Iyengar, the present secretary, was born on 7 September 1928 in Olalur, near Madras. His great grandfather, Nallan Chakravarti Ramanujachari, was from Tiruvehendipuram, and he had decided to come to the Triplicane Temple and renovate the shrine of Rāmānuja there. Sri Parthsarathy Iyengar studied at the Hindu High School in Triplicane. At the same time he joined the Veda Vedanta Vardhini Pathasala, a small group dedicated to the teaching and learning of the Sanskrit and Tamil Vedas. The classes for Sanskrit Vedas and the Divya Prabandham were held simultaneously, and he elected to study the Divya Prabandham. It is important to note that, while his father and uncles did not know the Divya Prabandham, his mother had learned it completely. He studied the Divya Prabandham under Sri Agaram Kandoor Narasimhachariar and Sri Agaram Kandur Rangaswamy Iyengar between 1946 and 1956 and won several prizes for recitation. But Sri Parthsarathy Iyengar's real interest was sports; he was an avid cricketeer. He initially formed a team called the Triplicane Friends' Union Cricket Club and won the minor league games sponsored by the Madras Cricket Association. He joined the accountant general's office and even there was involved for two years in the A.G.S. Recreation Club's cricket team, spending all his spare time in practicing and taking part in the league competitions. In 1955, when he was about twenty-seven years old, he acceded to the requests of Sri T. A. Varadachariar Swami and Sri N. Srinivasachariar Swami, two older people serving the Lord at the Triplicane Temple, and gave up his involvement with cricket. He joined the Veda Reciters' Association at the temple to render *kaiṁkarya* (loving service) to the Lord. In 1959 he became the secretary of the Udayavar Kaimkarya Sabha (Association to Render Service to Rāmānuja), an association in which his father and uncles had served previously.

The Veda Reciters' Association is proud to trace its continuous existence back more than 760 years and, in commemoration of this, Sri Parthsarathy Iyengar brought out a special volume celebrating the recitation of the Divya Prabandham in the various Vaiṣṇava sacred places. The volume honors the names of many devoted reciters and recounts the details of their service. Sri Parthsarathy Iyengar worked hard to raise funds for the volume, which contains details on recitation of the Divya Prabandham in the various temples of south India. The raising of funds for that volume took several years; the original publisher produced it on credit, after he asked Sri Parthsarathy Iyengar to visit the Sankaracharya of Kanchi and seek his permission.[20] The monies were paid up in 1989. It is not just for occasional ventures such as the publication of a commemorative volume that the Veda Reciters' Association feels the lack of money; it also lacks funds for the proper conducting of the Festival of Recitation and inviting competent reciters of the Sanskrit Vedas.

The Veda Reciters' Association regrets that, although their members are well versed in the Divya Prabandham, the temple lacks people who are competent to recite the Sanskrit Vedas. It is important to note that at present the word *Veda* in the title Veda Reciters' Association refers strictly to the recitation of the Tamil Veda. Sri Parthsarathy Iyengar has heard the lore about the previous volunteers in that group. He said that in 1923 there were thirty brahmins who recited the Sanskrit Veda with great majesty; by 1935 that number had shrunk to three old men. The trustees of the temple (with whom the Veda Reciters' Association has had its share of legal battles) were asked to invite Sanskrit Vedic reciters from other places for the annual Festival of Recitation, when the Sanskrit and Tamil Vedas are both to be recited, and just for travel expenses and local hospitality they were able to attract a handful of scholar-reciters. Even now the temple is dependent on Sanskrit reciters coming in from other towns, but the money granted by the trustees for the celebration of the Festival of Recitation is apparently extremely low. They grant a total of about Rs. 300 (approx. U.S. $12) for the *entire* festival, and the cost of importing the Sanskrit reciters is at least Rs. 475 a person, and eight reciters are needed for the festival. So, despite its prestige, its ancient history, and the vitality of its volunteers, funds are tight, and the group has had to do a considerable amount of fund raising.[21]

As mentioned earlier, Sri Parthsarathy Iyengar is also the secretary and the principal organizer of the Sri Udayavar Kaimkarya Sabha, which is responsible for celebrating various festivals in Rāmānuja's shrine at the Triplicane Temple. The daily schedule of recitation that he is responsible for is exacting and has to be arranged according to the lunar calendar and the important feast days of the month. A detailed description of this schedule will be given in the next chapter on "Recital of Divya Prabandham at Homes and Temples."

While Nammāḻvār and other poets saw their verses as being sung and recited, they are almost entirely recited in the major temples today. The *adhyāpakas* do the recitation on a regular schedule in all the Śrīvaiṣṇava temples, and it is for special occasions such as the Festival of Recitation that the *araiyars,* when available, perform. Those who recite in the temples are either full-time priests working at the temple, such as Sri Saranathan, Venkatacharlu, or Sri Krishnamacharylu, or they hold secular jobs, such as Sri Parthsarathy Iyengar, and do the recitation by volunteering their time. When the recitation has to take place at a time when they are at work or if they have to leave town for a business trip, they make arrangements with others in the Veda Reciters' Association to fill in for them. Some of them are trained in special schools, for which the Divya Prabandham classes are part of a larger curriculum in which Sanskrit texts, both sacred and secular, grammar, and modes of worship are learned. Others, like Sri Parthsarathy Iyengar and many of the *adhyāpakas* who work with him at the Triplicane Temple, learn from instructors in small classes held in the evenings or weekends.

It is very important to note from the case of Sri Parthsarathy Iyengar that, while his father and uncles did not know the entire Divya Prabandham, his mother did, and, in fact, even now she informally teaches the Divya Prabandham to many young students. This fits in with the history of the Śrīvaiṣṇava recitation; inscriptional evidence from some of the temples, such as Kanchipuram, indicates that there were women who recited regularly. An inscription from the thirteenth century in the Kanchipuram Temple registers a special endowment by the Telugu chieftain, Ganda Gopala, for the maintenance of women reciters *(perumāḷ muṉ pāṭum peṇṭukaḷ nimitatu)* in the temple.[22] As late as 1535, women seem to have been reciting at this temple, because an inscription from that date provides for a share in the "blessed food" *(parasādam)* for them.[23] Women continue to recite the Divya Prabandham but only at home shrines and not as part of a choir at temples. As we will see in chapter 6, in the last five years there has been a renewed surge of interest in learning the Divya Prabandham among women; many of them are also setting it to music and singing in public/secular forums, not just temples or shrines.

From the case of the Veda Reciters' Association and on the basis of many other interviews, it seems evident that an enormous amount of time has to be volunteered by the *adhyāpakas,* without any remuneration. This means giving up almost all other forms of recreational activity and quite a bit of family time. Sri Parthsarathy Iyengar was passionately involved with playing cricket, and two senior teachers persuaded him to give up that sport and spend the time reciting and rendering service to the Lord.

The history of the Veda Reciters' Association has also been fraught with many struggles and legal battles. We have noted that in the 1920s the trustees tried to dismiss members of the association, holding that the food *(prasādam)* they received constituted payment, until the high court ruled otherwise. The basis for this feud was traced to caste issues, with tensions between some brahmin-reciters and nonbrahmin trustees. These tensions occasionally surface, especially with the granting of money for the celebration of festivals. Thus, the reciters' association has had to do a considerable amount of private fund raising in order to celebrate festivals in the individual shrines. Even though their service is honorary, the proper conduct of the rituals may involve expenses in connection with the importing (from neighboring towns) of reciters well versed in the Sanskrit Vedas, expenditures for flowers, playing of the *nādaswaram* and other musical instruments associated with temple festivals, decorations for the shrine, gas lights for processions, sandalwood paste, mailing, publications, and preparation of food.[24] While some of the Śrīvaiṣṇava temples, including the Triplicane Temple, receive enormous amounts of money from devotees, these are frequently managed by other officials, some of whom are government appointed, and the allotment for individual festivals is abysmally low. The reciters' association thus contends with the politics of caste, of secular appointees, and of temple servants.

Some of the current social issues in the temples today involve the recruiting of Vaṭakalai and Teṅkalai reciters. The Vaṭakalais and Teṅkalais are the two major subsects within the Śrīvaiṣṇava tradition, and in the last two centuries there have been several legal battles over the control of temples.[25] The Vaṭakalais and Teṅkalais both revere Rāmānuja as their premier teacher and accept the validity of both the Sanskrit scripture and the Tamil Divya Prabandham, but they differ in the lineages of teachers they follow. Since the recitation of the Divya Prabandham is always preceded and concluded by laudatory verses paying respect to one's lineage of teachers, the Vaṭakalais and Teṅkalais have different verses to begin and conclude the rituals. Thus, if a temple is primarily Teṅkalai, the *adhyāpakas* there are also Teṅkalai and do not generally recruit from the other subsect. The Vaṭakalais begin their recitation by honoring the lineage of teachers, including Vedānta Deśika, who lived between 1268 and 1368. The Teṅkalais revere Maṇavāḷa Māmuṉi (b. 1365) in their invocatory prayer.

Some of the priests, such as Sri Venkatacharlu and Sri Krishnamacharylu, and the *adhyāpakas* who are trained in states other than Tamilnadu may not be very familiar with the Tamil script and learn the Divya Prabandham with the help of a book written in Telugu or Kannada characters. While the learning process is primarily oral, because books are easily available, they are used as prompts. It is extremely important to note that the learning process sometimes takes place with printed material and, then, with the Tamil verses written in the script of a different language such as Telugu. In the formative centuries of the Śrīvaiṣṇava tradition the Divya Prabandham was considered to have extra merit because it was composed in Tamil, supposedly a language that everyone could understand, unlike Sanskrit. But in time, as Śrīvaiṣṇavas settled down in non-Tamil-speaking areas of the south, Tamil became the unknown language, the metalanguage of scripture. While the priests trained at the Tirupati Pathasala certainly speak Tamil and can understand it, they are far more familiar with the Telugu language. Others do not even speak the Tamil language and learn the Divya Prabandham like they learn Sanskrit, focusing on the sound rather than the meaning.

As we saw in the above cases, with the exception of Sri Saranathan, who had the opportunity to learn the meaning of the Tiruvāymoḻi and the other works in the Divya Prabandham, all the others learn only the correct and proper recitation of the poem without the benefit of the commentary. One obvious reason for omitting this is the lack of time: the learning of the commentarial material would lengthen the course of study by several years. So, a clear distinction is made between the traditions of exegesis and recitation, and learning recitation does not necessarily indicate knowledge of the meaning of the verses.

The process of learning itself involves constant repetition; the student commits the verses to his or her memory and literally learns it by heart. After learning each set of ten or eleven verses a mnemonic strategy is learned, whereby he or she is able to repeat the first word of all the verses. These opening words remind him or her about the verses in each set of poems. Constant repetition and learning by rote at an early age fix the words in the students' minds; as one *adhyāpaka* said, the words are ingrained in them after a while.

The people who so learn to recite the Tamil Veda also learn the correct order of recitation and the sequence of verses to be recited on special occasions. As we will see in the next chapter, there are specific patterns of recitations for domestic and temple liturgies and for the birthdays of the saints and teachers.

4

RECITAL OF THE DIVYA PRABANDHAM AT HOMES AND TEMPLES

Unlike Sanskrit scripture, for which the recitation for "auspicious" and "inauspicious" occasions is clearly delineated, the Divya Prabandham is recited at both kinds of rituals. Recitations take place at home for the celebration of sixtieth birthdays, pregnancy rituals such as the *puṁsavana cīmantam* (which takes place in the eighth month of pregnancy), and investiture of the sacred thread for a young boy. The Divya Prabandham, especially the Tiruvāymoḻi, is also recited for those rituals traditionally considered to be inauspicious by the Hindu society, as in the rites following a funeral. In brahmin communities (the days vary according to the caste) the ritual recitation of the verses takes place on the twelfth and thirteenth day after death, and the occasion is called *sevā kālam,* or "time of service." Recitation in these contexts is seen as service to the Lord. What is interesting to note is that the word *service* (*sevā*) is used in this context specifically for an aural activity, but in Śrīvaiṣṇava temples to see the Lord *(darśan)* is also called *sevā*. The Lord's regal manifestation and his splendid decorations in temples contribute to his "granting a good *sevā*" to the devotee. Thus, after a good *darśan* a devotee may say: "I had an excellent *sevā* of the Lord," and in this context use the word *sevā* as an equivalent of *darśan*. Thus, in Śrīvaiṣṇava parlance, *sevā,* or service, is used both to serve the Lord through oral/aural recitation and for having a good *darśan,* or vision of the Lord. Both are different forms of revelation, and the proper attitude in both is that of humility and service.

In hagiographic literature we see that verses from the Tiruvāymoḻi were recited near a person who was perceived to be on his deathbed; *The Splendor* narrates that when Yāmuna (Āḷavantār) was dying the last twenty verses of the Tiruvāymoḻi were recited for him.[1] In the last twenty-two verses (10.9 and 10.10; see app.) Nammāḻvār speaks of devotees ascending to heaven and finally of his being the recipient of the Lord's grace. These verses are still recited during the enactment of Nammāḻvār's salvation in the temple rituals of the annual Festival of Recitation (and we shall discuss them in chap. 8).

While the recitation of all four thousand verses of the Divya Prabandham is encouraged, many people shorten the proceedings and arrange only for the recitation of the Tiruvāymoḻi. At temples and homes, when there is no time for the recitation of the entire Tiruvāymoḻi, the extracts, known as *Kōyil Tiruvāymoḻi* (Temple Tiruvāymoḻi), are recited. During the daily liturgy a representative sample of verses from the poem, voicing the major concerns of the Śrīvaiṣṇava community, are recited. These verse are called the Temple Tiruvāymoḻi and are specially honored at the Srirangam Temple. Because of the importance of these Temple Tiruvāymoḻi verses, and because they seem to form a special kind of scripture within scripture, I have translated them in full in the appendix.

CONTENT OF THE TEMPLE TIRUVĀYMOḺI

The entire Tiruvāymoḻi is 1,012 verses long and takes from six to eight hours just to recite in its entirety, and, so, the representative verses of the Temple Tiruvāymoḻi songs are supposed to be recited every day. While, ideally, all the Temple Tiruvāymoḻi verses are to be recited every day in temples and at homes, each Śrīvaiṣṇava temple makes its own selection for daily recital, and there is a certain amount of flexibility involved in this choice. But when considered as a whole the Temple Tiruvāymoḻi list of verses reflects some of the issues that have preoccupied the Śrīvaiṣṇava community for centuries. The translations in the appendix will show that there are some sets that speak about the superiority of Viṣṇu (1.1 and 4.10); the relationship between the Lord and the universe compared to that between the soul and the body (1.1); didactic verses urging people to be detached from the world and attached to the Lord (1.2); the importance of some holy places (2.10, 3.3, 5.8, 6.10, 7.2, 9.10); the importance of serving the servants of the Lord (8.10); the centrality of submitting oneself to the Lord and surrendering oneself to him (6.10); the *āḻvār* expressing his love in the guise of a lovesick girl (7.2); and a description of the final ascent to heaven

(10.9–10). It is important to note that verses in honor of the Lord enshrined in popular pilgrimage and worship centers such as Srirangam, Tirumaliruncolai (modern Alagar Koyil), Tiruvenkatam (Tirupati), and Tirukannapuram are all included in this corpus. As we saw in the incident about Yāmuna, who was inspired to visit Tiru Ananta Puram (Trivandrum) after listening to a Tiruvāymoḻi verse, pilgrimage is held in high esteem by the Śrīvaiṣṇava tradition. Travelogues on how to get to the sacred places *(divya deśa)* sung about by the *āḻvārs* are extremely popular, and every edition of the Divya Prabandham has an appendix listing the sacred places sung about by the *āḻvārs,* the local name that Viṣṇu is known by there, the individual myths that speak about the sacrality of that land, and so on. Thus, out of the approximately twelve sets of verses in the Temple Tiruvāymoḻi,[2] seven sets reaffirm the sacred nature of the land where Viṣṇu has chosen to manifest himself to human beings.[3]

One set of verses from the Tiruvāymoḻi that is *not* part of the Temple Tiruvāymoḻi but which, nevertheless, is recited in almost every temple that I visited is 7.4. The various magnificent deeds and cosmic acts of Viṣṇu are celebrated in this set of verses, and the poems are recited regularly. In talking to Sri Venkata Varadhan of Triplicane, Madras, I learned that he had been told that these verses were "protective" in nature and assured the reciter of triumph and victory. Therefore, he said, he had been taught that, in effect, these verses are like the Sanskrit prayer called "The Heart of the Sun" *(Āditya Hṛdayam),* which is found in the epic the Rāmāyaṇa. This Sanskrit prayer is supposed to ensure success if recited regularly. The Tamil verses do, in fact, talk of the Lord's triumphant activities, but including them in the daily recitation seems to be more a matter of oral tradition; books containing the Temple Tiruvāymoḻi do not include that set of verses.

DIVYA PRABANDHAM RECITAL AT TEMPLES

MONTHLY CYCLES

The Veda Reciters' Association of the Triplicane Temple is responsible for conducting the birthday celebrations of the *āḻvārs,* the Śrīvaiṣṇava *ācāryas* every year, and the anniversary of their "birth stars" every month, with the proper recitation of the appropriate verses.[4] The birth star refers to the asterism, or constellation, near which the moon was present at the time of one's birth. There are twenty-seven such asterisms, and these repeat themselves in cycles. Thus, almost every south Indian Hindu would know under which star or asterism he or she was born, and the regional calendars always say where the moon is that particular day. Birthdays are celebrated in the Hindu calendar with reference to these stars; thus, even though one is born, say, on 15 April of a particular year, when the moon was near the star Rēvati (which is in the Pisces constellation), the following year, his or her birthday will be reckoned to be not on 15 April, but, instead, on the day when the moon is closest to that constellation that month. Yearly almanacs and calendars educate the people on every last astrological/astronomical detail. Thus, Rāmānuja's birth star is Tiruvātarai (Sanskrit: *ārdra*), and every month when Tiruvātarai comes around there is a celebration with the entire recitation.

The Veda reciters are responsible for the celebration of the birth stars of every *āḻvār* and every important teacher every month. This involves reciting the appropriate poems and verses; usually, it involves the recitation of a poem composed by or in honor of the *āḻvār* or teacher whose birth star is being celebrated. Thus, in any given lunar cycle of twenty-eight days (the Hindu calendar is based on a lunar time frame but is adjusted to the solar calendar every few years) there are twenty-seven stars, and within this time major sections of the Divya Prabandham are recited. It must be noted that the birth stars assigned to the various *āḻvārs* are only mentioned in hagiographies after the thirteenth century, possibly a full four or five hundred years after they lived, and their authenticity is historically debatable. The pattern of recitation, based on the importance of these stars, allows for the showcasing of representative segments from the Divya Prabandham at least once a month, and this may well be the rationale behind this schedule.

The schedule of recitation and celebration of the birth stars followed at the Triplicane Temple is typical of those adopted in many of the 106 Viṣṇu temples that have been sung about by the *āḻvārs*.[5] Out of the twenty-seven stars in the Hindu calendar there are only six that are not considered to be the birth stars of an *āḻvār* or a teacher, and on these days the songs in the canon called the "daily contemplation and recitation" (*nityānusandhānam*) are chanted. The cycle repeats itself approximately every twenty-seven to twenty-eight days.

Star	Āḻvār or Teacher	Poem from the Divya Prabandham
1. Aśvini	—	*nityānusandhānam*
2. Bharaṇi	—	*nityānusandhānam*
3. Kārthikai	Tirumaṅkai Āḻvār	Tirukkuruntāṇṭakam Tiruneṭuntāṇṭakam
4. Rohini	Tiruppāṇ Āḻvār	Amalanātipirāṉ
5. Mirugaśīrṣam	Tirukkachi Nampi[6]	Rāmānuja Nūṟṟantāti
6. Tiruvātarai	Rāmānuja	Rāmānuja Nūṟṟantāti
7. Punarvasu	Kulacēkara Āḻvār, Empār and Mutaliyāṇṭāṉ	Perumāḷ Tirumoḻi[7]
8. Pūsam	—	*nityānusandhānam*
9. Āyilyam	—	*nityānusandhānam*
10. Makam	Tirumaḻicai Āḻvār	Nānmukaṉ Tiruvantāti
11. Pūram	Āṇṭāḷ	Nācciyār Tirumoḻi
12. Uttiram	The Goddess Laksmi	Ciriya Tirumaṭal
13. Hastam	Kūrattāḻvāṉ	Rāmānuja Nūṟṟantāti[8]
14. Citirai	Maturakavi Āḻvār	Kanninun Ciruttāmpu
15. Svāti	Periyāḻvār	Periyāḻvār Tirumoḻi
16. Vicākam	Nammāḻvār	Tiruviruttam
17. Anucam	Nāthamuni	Rāmānuja Nūṟṟantāti
18. Kēṭṭai	Toṇṭaraṭipoṭi Āḻvār	Tirumālai
19. Mūlam	Maṇavāḷa Māmuṉi	Upadeśaratnamālai[9]
20. Pūrāṭam	Viśvaksena[10]	Rāmānuja Nūṟṟantāti
21. Uttirāṭam	Yāmuna (Āḷavantar)	Rāmānuja Nūṟṟantāti
22. Tiruvōṇam	Poykai Āḻvār, Piḷḷai Lōkācarya, Vedānta Deśika	Mutal Tiruvantāti
23. Avittam	Pūtatt Āḻvār	Iraṇṭām Tiruvantāti
24. Catayam	Pey Āḻvār	Mūṉṟām Tiruvantāti
25. Pūraṭṭāti	—	*nityānusandhānam*
26. Utiraṭṭāti	—	*nityānusandhānam*
27. Rēvati	Raṅganātha, Viṣṇu's manifestation at Srirangam.	Tirumālai[11]

Thus, the schedule for twenty-seven days is fixed, and, depending on the birth star, the portion recited each day is different. It is significant that, on the days that are held to be the birthdays of Rāmānuja's teachers or disciples, it is a work in praise of Rāmānuja and not their own composition which is recited. This apparently minor detail reveals an important belief of the Śrīvaiṣṇava community—that it is because of one's connection with Rāmānuja that one is assured of salvation. Even Rāmānuja's teachers are supposed to get salvation because of their connection with their disciple; symbolically, they are spoken of as being connected through "Rāmānuja's head" *(tiru muṭi sambandham)*. This means that Rāmānuja sat at the feet of his teachers and learned from them; metaphorically, he placed their feet on his head. Similarly, his disciples, even though removed by several generations, learn at his feet and are connected with him through his feet *(tiru aṭi sambandham)*. It is because of their linkage with him that both the disciples and teachers get their importance and, ultimately, their salvation. And, so, on their birthdays it is Rāmānuja who is honored with recitation.

On those six days in which there is no celebration of a birth anniversary, extracts from the Divya Prabandham, known as the *nityānusandhānam* (daily contemplation and recitation) are recited in temples and at homes.

The "daily contemplation" consists of representative verses from the *ālvār* poems which are to be recited daily by Śrīvaiṣṇavas. These verses, along with those of the *Kōyil Tiruvāymoḻi* (Temple Tiruvāymoḻi) are deemed to be almost a scripture within a scripture and repeat themes and sentiments that are considered to be extremely important to the devotee. It is not clear when this compilation was organized, though, according to tradition, the first teacher, Nāthamuni, is credited with instituting the daily procedure at home and temple liturgies. The total recitation can take almost two hours, and in temples it is usually split up into the morning and evening services. The verses used for daily contemplation are as follows:

Poem	*Author*	*Time Recited at Temples*
1. Tirupallāṇṭu (benedictory verses)	Periyāḻvār	Morning
2. Tirupaḷḷiyeḻucci (songs urging the Lord to wake up)	Toṇṭaraṭipoṭi Āḻvār	Morning
3. Tiruppāvai (Āṇṭāḷ's desire to wake up her friends and serve the Lord)	Āṇṭāḷ	Morning

Poem	*Author*	*Time Recited at Temples*
4. Pūcūṭṭal (calling the young Krishna to come and be adorned with flowers) Periyāl̲vār Tirumol̲i 2.7.1–10	Periyāl̲vār	Evening
5. Kāppiṭal (asking Krishna to come and wear protective amulets) Periyāl̲vār Tirumol̲i 2.8.1–10	Periyāl̲vār	Evening
6. Periyāl̲vār Tirumol̲i 5.4.1–10 (general praise)	Periyāl̲vār	Evening
7. Amalanātipiran̲ (poem describing the Lord at Srirangam)	Tiruppāṇāl̲vār	Evening

While, ideally, the recitation of these verses is to be followed by the recitation of the Temple Tiruvāymol̲i verses, in practice only three sets of poems from the Tiruvāymol̲i are recited in the Triplicane Temple. These are Tiruvāymol̲i 6.10, in which the *āl̲vār* seeks refuge at the feet of the Lord at Tiruvenkatam; 7.2, in which the *āl̲vār*, in the guise of a young girl, expresses her love for the Lord at Srirangam (both sets are translated in the app.); and 7.4, which speaks of the Lord's triumphant deeds.

ANNUAL RECITATIONS

While representative sections of the Divya Prabandham are recited in the daily and monthly cycles, there are annual festivals in the temples when the entire Divya Prabandham or, at least, the entire Tiruvāymol̲i is recited. These festivals are usually the Brahmotsavam (the main temple festival, which takes place at different times in different temples); the Festival of Purification *(pavitrotsavam);* the Festival of Recitation (15 Dec.–13 Jan.); and Nammāl̲vār's birthday (15 May–14 June). In addition to these, the full recitation also takes place during the time of Rāmānuja's birthday in April or May. During the Festival of Recitation all other recitation is suspended, and a special schedule is followed for that month. (This festival will be discussed in detail in chap. 8.)

It is important to note that, while all other works from the Divya Prabandham may be recited in the streets by the *adhyāpakas* while the

Lord is being taken in a procession, the Tiruvāymoli̲ alone is recited within the precincts of the temple when everyone is seated. This is because the Tiruvāymoli̲ is considered truly to be a Veda, and one has to have a proper attitude in listening to it.

Most of the recitation patterns discussed above are followed in brahmanical Viṣṇu temples in south India and are seen in an abbreviated form in the Vaiṣṇava temples in the United States, especially at Pittsburgh and Malibu. Many of the temples in south India have a long history and inflexible schedules of recitation and rituals. These traditions are passed through the generations to those who serve the Lord in the temples. It is interesting to note that even in small shrines, administered by "scheduled caste" devotees, a certain rigidity and inflexibility has developed in patterns of daily worship. We shall now turn our attention to recitation in the Nammāl̲vār Shrine, a shrine set up by a community whose ancestors were considered to be outcastes.

5

RECITATION IN NAMMĀḺVĀR'S CONGREGATION

The Exclusive Devotion of the Excluded Servants

THE SERVANTS OF THE SERVANTS OF GOD

This section explores the significance of Nammāḻvār and his poem, the Tiruvāymoḻi, to a scheduled caste Śrīvaiṣṇava community in Gowthamapuram, Bangalore.[1] These Śrīvaiṣṇavas are members of Śrī Nammāḻvār Sabhā, a congregation that was formed in 1881 under the leadership of Sri Parasurama Dasar, and live around a shrine called Śrī Nammāḻvār Cannati (Sanskrit: *sannidhi*).[2]

The material for this section is drawn from observation and participation in the rituals of the Sabha in 1983 and 1985 and from discussions with two of its leaders.[3] Sri Vipranarayana, whose ancestors founded the shrine, and Sri Govinda Ramanuja Dasar, their advisor and ritual supervisor from Ganesapuram, Madras, graciously spent several hours recalling the history of their shrine and sharing details of their recitation rituals and textual authorities. Sri Gopalakrishna Ekangi Swami, a "nonbrahmin" *saṁnyāsi* from Srirangam,[4] was present during some of these conversations. I have also made use of some textual material to help us better understand this congregation's relationship to Nammāḻvār and to the larger Śrīvaiṣṇava community. The texts include a small book written by Sri Govinda Ramanuja Dasar (the advisor of the Gowthamapuram community) in which he exegetes a key section in the *Śrībhāṣya* discussing the authority of the *śūdras* to study the Vedas.[5]

RECOLLECTIONS, RECITATION, AND RITUALS

Sri Vipranarayana of the Nammāḻvār Shrine directs, supervises, and conducts the main recitation in a manner conforming to the traditional way in which he believes they were performed. He takes pride in continuing an unbroken chain of ritual and recitation since the inception of the *cannati* in 1881, when the land was obtained from the British and the shrine was built by the devotees in the evenings and nights. Parasurama Dasar, who built the shrine, was a bartender at the Indian Army mess hall close by; in fact, even now many of the devotees who worship at the shrine and who live within a one-mile radius in Gowthamapuram work at the army workshop. Sri Vipranarayana, the grandson of Sri Parasurama Dasar, worked at the army mechanical workshop until 1985; he now has a little shop outside his house.

It is possible, though not known for sure, that these scheduled caste Śrīvaiṣṇavas, who speak Tamil and who know some Sanskrit, originally came from Mysore and are descendants of a community converted to Śrīvaiṣṇavism by the *ācārya* Rāmānuja in the eleventh century C.E. According to biographical tradition, some outcastes helped the teacher, and, in recognition of their devotion, he gave them the name *tirukulattār* (sacred clan). Apparently, he also granted them privileges to visit the temple on certain days at Melkote and Srirangam. These privileges are still exercised by members of the *tirukulattār* community.[6]

Sri Vipranarayana believes that the traditional recitation was carried on by his ancestors even before the building of the shrine in the nineteenth century. Parasurama Dasar, who was a disciple of a person called Tiruvaymoli Acarya of Mysore, established contact with a number of Śrīvaiṣṇava scheduled caste communities and organized their recitation rituals by encouraging the formation of congregations that could recite the Divya Prabandham.[7]

The first shrine to be built was in honor of Tiruppāṇ Āḻvār (known today as the Pāṇ Perumāḷ Cannati, located near the Ulsoor lake of Bangalore Cantonment), and Sri Nammalvar Cannati was built not long after that. Twelve such shrines were built at the time; as far as I could learn, however, only the Nammāḻvār Cannati and the Andal Cannati (est. 1888)[8] celebrated the rituals and recitations with some fanfare. In addition to those dedicated to Nammāḻvār and Āṇṭāḷ, there are shrines dedicated to the *āḻvārs* Tirumaṅkai, Kulacēkara (located in Ashoknagar), and Toṇṭaraṭipoṭi; some dedicated to the teachers *(ācāryas)* Maṇavāḷa Māmuṉi and Rāmānuja (known as Uṭaiyavar Cannati, located at Murphytown and at Nehrunagar). Other shrines located at Austin Town and Nilachandra are dedicated to manifestations of Viṣṇu.

Of the twelve shrines eight are dedicated to *āḻvārs* or *ācāryas* and only four to the Lord Viṣṇu.[9]

Sri Vipranarayana said several times that for twenty-four generations prior to Sri Parasurama Dasar, his family had been Śrīvaiṣṇavas.[10] The worship of Nammāḻvār by his ancestors is important to his identity; in the terms that Moffatt uses in his study of "untouchable" communities in south India one may say that, for Sri Vipranarayana, Nammāḻvār is the chosen god *(iṣṭa devam)*, the household god *("viiTTu devam")*, and the "lineage god" *(kula devam)*, the divine being shared by the worshipper with the kin of his immediate family and of his patrilineage.[11]

The Nammāḻvār Shrine is a modest building set in a lower-middle-class neighborhood. There are no towers or imposing structures, but the Śrīvaiṣṇava emblems of conch and discus are conspicuous on the walls. There is a large hall with several calendar pictures of Viṣṇu and an "altar" that looks similar to many Śrīvaiṣṇava home shrines. There are several adjoining rooms that serve as the living quarters for Sri Vipranarayana's joint family. His brothers as well as his own family live there. Near the entrance is a foundation stone giving particulars of the date when the building was constructed.

Although the altar looks like a home shrine, this serves as a place of public worship used by the local community as well as devotees from other neighborhoods. There is no inner shrine or separate room set apart for the deity or an image of Nammāḻvār. The focus is on a large picture of Nammāḻvār, which almost looks three-dimensional because of the lighting.[12] A collection was under way in 1985 to get an image of Nammāḻvār. In front of the picture are several small images of the *āḻvārs* and a normal-sized *śaṭhāri*, a small silver crown on which the feet of the Lord are carved. "Śaṭhāri" is another name of Nammāḻvār, and it is significant that the Lord's feet are called by the name of the saint. Unlike most home shrines, but like a temple, the *cannati* has a *śaṭhāri*. When there is no worship in progress, the picture of Nammāḻvār is cordoned off with a satin drape inscribed with a conch and discus, the sacred Śrīvaiṣṇava symbols. The primary focus of worship is Nammāḻvār, and this in itself is unique, for in Śrīvaiṣṇava temples it is the Lord and his consorts whose shrines are central, and the chambers of Nammāḻvār and Āṇṭāḷ are by the side. In a few small Śrīvaiṣṇava temples there is no separate shrine for Nammāḻvār; he is represented by the

Lord's feet on the *śaṭhāri,* and his inseparability from the Lord's feet is emphasized.

The principal rituals of the community may be divided into the life cycle rituals and the rituals that honor Nammāḻvār. The life cycle sacraments include *vaḷakāppu* (celebrating and protecting a pregnant woman and giving her protective amulets), childbirth, coming of age for girls, the giving of the sacred thread for men, wedding, the *pañca-saṁskāra* (the five initiatory "sacraments" of surrender), and death rituals. In all these events selections from the Divya Prabandham, especially the Tiruvāymoḻi of Nammāḻvār, are recited. Here I shall focus only on the daily, monthly, and annual rituals of recitation which celebrate Nammāḻvār and will also note the distinctive features of the liturgy at Śrī Nammāḻvār Shrine.

DAILY AND MONTHLY RECITATION AT THE NAMMĀḺVĀR SHRINE

Sri Vipranarayana does the daily recitation, and members of the family sometimes join in. The selections for the daily recitation are similar to the *nityānusandhānam* (daily contemplation) verses, except for the order in which they are recited. Sri Vipranarayana first recites the poem that Maturakavi Āḻvār composed in honor of Nammāḻvār and then continues in the order that is observed by other Śrīvaiṣṇavas. In other Śrīvaiṣṇava households and in the temples the first work to be recited from the *āḻvār* anthology is a poem by the saint Periyāḻvār. Maturakavi Āḻvār was the first disciple of Nammāḻvār; unlike all other *āḻvārs,* his only work in the Divya Prabandham is not in praise of Viṣṇu but, rather, is exclusively in praise of his master, Nammāḻvār. In reciting Maturakavi's poem first the congregation reaffirms the primacy of Nammāḻvār and its unmediated connection with him; its members reiterate that they are the servants of the servant of the Lord.

It is in the monthly and annual festivities that the real difference between this congregation and the other temples is seen. Members of the Nammāḻvār Shrine recite the entire Tiruvāymoḻi *every* month, starting ten days before the monthly anniversary of Nammāḻvār's birthday and culminating on the day when the moon is near the star *viśākha,* the asterism under which Nammāḻvār was born.[13] There is no equivalent to this cycle of recitation in other places of worship. Frequently, only Sri

Vipranarayana and one or two others recite for nine days, and on the tenth day all members of his family and some other neighbors join in. This is in addition to the daily cycle of recitation. Members of the family are taught the correct way to recite the works of the *āḻvārs;* many of them have memorized large sections, but usually the congregation participates in the recitation with a copy of the Divya Prabandham in hand.

ANNUAL RECITATION

In that wonderful month of Vaikāci
When the star Viśākha was ascending,
the handsome lord of Kurukūr
the precious lord, the true one,
who rendered the Vedas in Tamil
was born. I speak
of the grandeur of that day
so the people of this earth
may know.

(Maṇavāḷa Māmuṉi, "Upadeśaratnamālai," v. 14)

The annual recitation of the entire corpus of the Divya Prabandham *(adhyayana utsava),* which is usually undertaken in Mārkaḻi (15 Dec.–13 Jan.) in other Śrīvaiṣṇava temples, is conducted in the Tamil month of Vaikāci (15 May–14 June) in the Nammāḻvār Shrine to coincide with Nammāḻvār's birthday. Celebrations begin ten days before the actual birthday and sometimes last for a few days after as well. Highlights include the recitation of the works of the other *āḻvārs* in the morning and Nammāḻvār's Tiruvāymoḻi in the evenings. This is also a time of religious instruction and entertainment: there are evening lectures, several religious discourses, storytelling, explanation of Nammāḻvār's poems and elucidation of Śrīvaiṣṇava philosophy, *nādaswaram* concerts, and folk dancing. The recitation of the four thousand verses of the Divya Prabandham ends with two similar rituals called *cāṟṟumuṟai* (literally: "the manner of placing or laying" flowers or honors on the saint/deity/teacher). Benedictory verses are recited, and food and water, blessed by the Lord, are distributed.

At the Nammāḻvār Shrine the annual recitation of the entire Divya Prabandham prior to Nammāḻvār's birthday culminated in a morning *cāṟṟumuṟai* for successfully completing the recitation of the first three thousand verses and one in the evening to signify a triumphant completion of the Tiruvāymoḻi. The recitation is strenuous; for nine days prior to the *cāṟṟumuṟais* the congregation, which ranges from ten to one hundred people at any given time, puts in about five or six hours of recitation each day.

The recitation is accompanied every day with the offering of fruit and milk to Nammāḻvār and the waving of lights, camphor, and incense. After the recitation the *śaṭhāri* (crown) is laid on the devotees' heads. Nammāḻvār had pleaded for the Lord's feet to be on his head and in the Tiruvāymoḻi states that his wish was granted.[14] It is in recognition of Nammāḻvār's desire being fulfilled that the community calls the Lord's feet by his name: *Śaṭhakopa, or Śaṭhāri.* After the śaṭhāri the congregation is given sacred water and some fruit as a mark of divine favor. Occasionally, some *dosai* (a thin rice and lentil pancake) is distributed in a manner similar to that done in other Śrīvaiṣṇava temples.

The celebrations climax when the decorated picture of Nammāḻvār is taken with all regal honors from the shrine to a chariot and then in a procession through the streets. The chariot procession usually takes place on a Sunday evening following Nammāḻvār's birthday. This attracts the largest crowds, and anywhere between three to four hundred people attend the gala. If the devotional highlight is the successful completion of the recitation, the outreach and social highlight of the ceremonies is certainly the sacred chariot *(tiru tēr)* festival, held deliberately on a Sunday evening when everyone can participate in the festivities. The only concession made to "auspicious time" is in the avoiding of the inauspicious period (the *Rāhu kālam*), which falls between 4:30 and 6:00 P.M. on Sundays. The chariot, rented from a local Śiva temple at a considerable cost then "purified" and camouflaged to conceal its place of origin, is decorated with flowers and electric lights, and the flower-laden (picture of) Nammāḻvār is escorted to the chariot after *Rāhu kālam.* Sri Vipranarayana waves a camphor light in front of Nammāḻvār, chants verses from the Tiruvāymoḻi, and, with the blessings and approval of two *ācāryas* of the family (the advisor from Ganesapuram, Madras, and the *ekāṅgi* monk from Srirangam), escorts Nammāḻvār to the chariot. Nammāḻvār is seen as a person who graciously permits these celebrations, and, in the language of the congregation, he "graciously ascends" *(eḻuntu aruḷi)* the chariot. This use of the present continuous tense and the strong feeling of Nammāḻvār's actual presence and participation is noteworthy and comes through very forcibly in words and gestures.

In emphasizing that this is the sacred text, some Brahmin Śrīvaiṣṇavas believe that young boys should undergo the ritual of the Upanayana, or being invested with the sacred thread, in order to have the authority to study the Tiruvāymoḻi.[15] In Śrīvaiṣṇava hagiographical literature the various devotees were categorized, and one prominent classification is between the *cāttina mutali* and the *cāttāta mutali. Cāttina* is "to lay or confer" and referred to those devotees to whom the sacred thread had been conferred—for example, the brahmins. The *cāttāta mutali*s were those devotees on whom the sacred thread had not been conferred.[16] In the Gowthamapuram congregation several members, including Sri Vipranarayana's brother, wore the sacred thread; this in itself was unusual because, according to the traditional Hindu scriptures, only the upper three classes could wear the sacred thread. In south India, by popular practice, only the brahmins wear the sacred thread.

The explanation for this custom was given by Sri Govinda Ramanuja Dasar, their spiritual advisor, who was visiting from Ganesapuram, Madras. He first quoted from the *Tolkāppiyam*, the (4th-c.?) Tamil grammatical treatise. A Brahmin was known by a thread (Tamil: *nūl*), a water carrier *(karakam)*, three staffs *(mukkōl)*, and subdued senses, or detachment.[17] Nammāḻvār, he said, had emphasized the importance of detachment and submission to the Lord:

> Leave it all
> and having left it,
> leave your life with the Lord
> who owns heaven.
>
> Less than a lightning flash
> are bodies inhabited by lives.
> Just think on this
> for a moment.
>
> Pull out by the roots
> these things called
> "you" and "yours."
> Reach God.
> There's nothing more complete.
>
> (Tiruvāymoḻi 1.2.1–3)

Sri Govinda Ramanuja Dasar emphasized several times that the Tiruvāymoḻi was Veda and that this congregation was being prepared to study the most sacred of all revelation. The Tiruvāymoḻi dealt with knowledge of Viṣṇu, the supreme Brahman *(brahma vidyā)*, and, since one could not study the word of God without the right preparation, they were given the (sacred) thread. Wearing of the thread seemed optional; Sri Vipranarayana said that the ceremony had been conducted for him in 1945, when he was thirteen, but said he did not wear the thread now. His younger brother, however, had it on throughout the rituals.

With the authority to wear the sacred thread came the authority to study the most essential segments of the Sanskrit Vedas pertinent to daily ritual: the chanting of the *Puruṣa sukta* and some sections of the Taittirīya Upaniṣad. The significance of this recitation has to be noted; in all classical Sanskrit texts only male members of the higher castes had the authority to recite from the Vedas. In the daily ritual at the *cannati* Sri Vipranarayana chanted the Puruṣa, Śrī, and Nīḷā *suktams* as well as the Taittirīya Upaniṣad (*saṁno mitra saṁ varuṇah,* etc.), along with verses from the Tiruvāymoḻi. Sri Vipranarayana also pointed out that one of the meanings of the Tamil word *vāymoḻi* was, in fact, "Veda." The point made repeatedly by Sri Govinda Ramanuja Dasar as well as Sri Vipranarayana was the *superiority* of the Tamil Veda, the Tiruvāymoḻi—and, if they had the authority to recite *that,* surely the authority to chant the Sanskrit Veda could be assumed.

They described the Tiruvāymoḻi as containing knowledge of Viṣṇu, the supreme Brahman, and, therefore this knowledge *(vidyā)* was like *brahma vidyā*. It was in this connection that they showed a pamphlet called *Apaśūdrādhikaraṇam,* written by Sri Govinda Ramanuja Dasar. The name of the pamphlet is the same as a section in the *Śrībhāṣya* of Rāmānuja, in which he takes up the question of the authority of *śūdras* to receive *brahma vidyā*. While Rāmānuja states clearly in the *Śrībhāṣya* that *śūdras* cannot study the Veda, he does admit the possibility of their being wise (like Vidura in the *Mahābhārata*) because of the lingering effects of previous good deeds. He also clarifies some incidents from the Chandogya Upaniṣad, from which it may be superficially assumed that the people enlightened by *brahma vidyā* are *śūdras*. In discussing these incidents,[18] Rāmānuja points out the origin of the word *śūdra,* which derives from the root *suk,* "to grieve."[19] With some interesting exegesis Sri Govinda Ramanuja Dasar shows how an instructor of *brahma vidyā* in the story of Janaśruti, one Raikva, is actually a person without *āśrama* (an identifiable station in life recognized by the Sanskrit law manuals) and is, therefore, a *śūdra.* Thus, in the self-image of the community we find the conviction that the teacher Rāmānuja had believed them to have the authority to have knowledge of Brahman, or what we would call salvific knowledge. Members of the Śrī Nammāḻvār Sabhā believe that this salvific knowledge is obtained by the recitation of the Tamil Veda, which was graciously vouchsafed to them by their teacher, the poet Nammāḻvār, through whom the Lord sang. Nammāḻvār had sung the sacred words and had believed that there was none equal to him here and in heaven in having the fortune of singing the praise of the Lord (Tiruvāymoḻi 4.5.1–11).

The members of Śrī Nammāḻvār Sabhā learn to recite the verses, hear several discourses (many of them having a strong strain of anti-*advaitin* arguments), and know all the fundamentals of the Śrīvaiṣṇava theology. There is, however, no study of the commentarial literature on the Tiruvāymoḻi. As noted, starting with Piḷḷāṉ, a cousin of Rāmānuja, there had been five "classical" commentaries as well as several recent ones, and they are considered to be indispensable in understanding the Tiruvāymoḻi. The congregation did not study the commentaries; instead, there is a sense of *direct discipleship* with Nammāḻvār. In the group's recitation of Maturakavi Āḻvār's poem at the beginning of their daily liturgy this is reiterated; they are direct disciples of Nammāḻvār, just as Maturakavi Āḻvār and the first teacher Nāthamuni were. We may recall that, according to the Śrīvaiṣṇava tradition, the works of the *āḻvārs* had been lost, and by Nāthamuni's meditations on Maturakavi Āḻvār's short poem Nammāḻvār had graciously revealed not only his own compositions but also the works of the other *āḻvārs* directly to Nāthamuni and, hence, was solely responsible for the "descent" of the works to this earth. Thus, it was the grace of Nammāḻvār which was responsible for the presence of the other works of the *āḻvārs* in this world. While Rāmānuja and several other *ācāryas* are held to be important by the Gowthamapuram community, its members say that they are disciples and servants *(dāsar)* of Nammāḻvār.

Why is Nammāḻvār so honored, and why are his works recited with such fervor and devotion? Central to the answer is the apprehension of Nammāḻvār as medium of *revelation* and the notion of Nammāḻvār as *redeemer.*

REDEMPTION

When members of the Nammāḻvār Cannati say that they are disciples of Nammāḻvār it is understood that their teacher is also a savior. The Tiruvāymoḻi does not communicate just *any* knowledge; it is a Veda, and it imparts salvific knowledge. Nammāḻvār is the savior-redeemer of the community, and it is important to note that the community takes this as a "given." Redemption is not just assured, but it is, in a sense, already accomplished. We go back to the rituals, the Tiruvāymoḻi recitation, and recollections of family history to understand this concept.

The importance of spiritual and biological ancestry was very important for Sri Vipranarayana. The recitation was important in itself, but he was also very conscious of carrying on an unbroken tradition that had lasted several centuries. This spiritual heritage and biological ancestry coincided; he was not just a servant of Nammāḻvār but also came from a long line of Śrīvaiṣṇavas who were presumably devoted to the *āḻvār*. He quoted verses from the Divya Prabandham to embellish his points. In the first few lines of the following verse Tirumaṅkai Āḻvār says with pride that he hails from a long line of Viṣṇu devotees:

My father, his father and further seven times more,
were old servants of yours;
    You have entered my heart
    And I shall not let you go.
My dear life! My king!
My Lord who without pause
    grants me grace!
O perfect Lord of Naṟaiyūr!

(Periya Tirumoḻi 7.2.6)

Similarly, says Sri Vipranarayana, he comes from a family in which twenty-four generations were Śrīvaiṣṇavas and servants of Viṣṇu and the *āḻvārs*. This in itself is reason for prosperity and good fortune, as Nammāḻvār himself proclaimed:

Keśava's followers
    for seven generations before
    and seven generations to come
have the great fortune and prosper along with us,
through [the grace] of the Lord, my dark gem, my adored one,
the Lord of the celestials, my god, my Nārāyaṇan.

(Tiruvāymoḻi 2.7.1)

Anyone even remotely connected with a devotee of Viṣṇu would have good fortune because of the Lord's grace. This prosperity was seen on this earth itself, not necessarily in the afterlife, and it is in this context that we can understand both the rituals that venerate Nammāḻvār and the recitations of his poems.

The recitation of the Tiruvāymoḻi was obviously understood to be beneficial by generations of Śrīvaiṣṇavas. The *phala śruti,* or the "fruits of listening" to the verses or reciting them, are significant. Nammāḻvār has a signature verse at the end of every ten verses (there is a total of one hundred in the entire Tiruvāymoḻi), and they promise benefits of bliss on this life and the next if one recites the verses. On one level the congregation understood this recitation as an exercise in piety and that there would be happiness for all *if* the members chanted the verses. But on another level—and this was indicated in several conversations with the members—they viewed the recitation and the rituals not as a *means* to a life with Viṣṇu but, instead, as a *goal* in itself, reflecting the state of salvation which was already accomplished. To sing the praises of the Lord—here through the words of the Lord himself—was the supreme state and the goal that Śrīvaiṣṇava devotees longed for. Again Nammāḻvār was quoted: this time it was verses from a set in which the poet ecstatically sees the world filled with devotees singing the praise of praise:

> Rejoice! Rejoice! Rejoice!
> The persisting curse of life is gone.
> The agony of hell is destroyed
> Death has no place here.
> [The force] of *kali* is destroyed.
> Look for yourself!
> The followers of the sea-colored Lord
> swell over this earth, singing with melody,
> dancing and whirling [with joy].
>
> We see them.
> The whirling age of *kali* ends;
> the divine ones also enter
> the golden age dawns
> and floods of great joy sweep over the land.
> The followers of
>   him who is dark as a cloud, my Lord,

The one colored like the sea,
Fill this earth, singing with melody.
they are all over the land.
(Tiruvāymoḻi 5.2.1 and 5.2.3)

Singing of the divine name and service rendered to the Lord and one's teacher was the activity of a person who had attained the goal, said Sri Vipranarayana. Through the recitation of the Tiruvāymoḻi one glorified and served the deity and the devotee.

It is very significant that in the invitation for the *brahmotsavam,* the birthday celebrations for Nammāḻvār, the congregation calls the recitation a *sevā kālam:* "time of service." This recitation was clearly seen as a service of love *(kaiṁkarya)* rendered to Nammāḻvār, the supreme king, who ruled over their family, clan, and area. Nammāḻvār is clearly spoken of as a sovereign-teacher. The invitation to his birthday celebrations speaks of his rule in the present continuous tense, and the members of the congregation consider themselves to be the servants and slaves of this king:

> With the upcoming Vaikāci Viśaka in the year Rutrōtkāri, there will be celebrations as listed below, celebrated as is the tradition, for ten days preceding the [birthday] in honor of Śrīmad Nammāḻvār who has graciously *(eḻuntaruḷi)* taken Gowthamapuram Bangalore as his Temple *(kōyil:* "residence of a king") and who [sits in state] to grant vision/service *(cēvai < sevā cāttikkum).* We pray that you may participate in the celebrations and complete your loving service *(kaiṁkarya)* to him.
>
> Yours,
> The Servants *(aṭiyār)* of Srimad Nammāḻvār Cannati

Notice the phrase "to grant service"; the word *sevā* is used here in terms of vision. We have already noted how the word *sevā* (service) is understood as participating in aural and visual revelation in the brahmanical contexts and can now see the usage of the word in a scheduled caste shrine.

The notion of Nammāḻvār being a sovereign-teacher is reinforced in ritual: Nammāḻvār rides a chariot on the last day of the festival; he is adorned with garlands and has a royal white umbrella (in fact, there were two of them) and a person fanning him. But Nammāḻvār, the king and the teacher, is also a servant and a slave; in his Tiruvāymoḻi he states that he will be a servant-slave (Tamil: *aṭiyār*) of any *servant* of the Lord, regardless of his or her birth or qualification:

Even if they are lower
than the four castes
that uphold all clans
even outcastes to even outcastes
    without a trace of virtue

if they are the servants
    of the servants
who have mingled in service
with the Lord
    with the wheel in his right hand
    his body dark as blue sapphire
they are our masters.

(Tiruvāymoḻi 3.7.9)

The world that his feet once covered,
he swallowed;
then slept with a full stomach
on a tiny banyan leaf
as a child beyond any comparison

to him, our Lord,

we are the servants of the servants
of the servants of the servants
of the servants of the servants
of his servants' servants.

(Tiruvāymoḻi 3.7.10)

The best way that he could describe himself and the members of the Nammāḻvār Sabhā, said Sri Vipranarayana, was that they were the servants of the servant of God.

For the members of the congregation Nammāḻvār's teaching is salvific, and the recitation of his verses guarantees salvation, no matter what the qualification of the devotee. On a different level the recitation is already indicative of the salvation achieved. Nammāḻvār ultimately is a savior, and the members of the congregation believe that it is because of their relationship to him that they were saved. The congregation's recitation, honoring Nammāḻvār, may be understood as their celebration of the poet and of his procuring salvation for his devotees. Salvation is *contagious,* and a relationship to one who is saved, whether it is biological or spiritual, guarantees the highest state. Sri Vipranarayana quoted an incident from the biography *The Splendor:* when Rāmānuja was asked about the certainty of salvation he replied that there was an unbroken *chain* of devotees going from those bound on earth to the Lord. The links began with Śrī, the consort of Viṣṇu, and then the first human link was "Our Śaṭhakopa"—Nammāḻvār. If Nammāḻvār obtained salvation, and surely he did (said Rāmānuja) because the poet himself had declared in the last verse of the Tiruvāymoḻi that he had obtained heaven, then *all* the teachers who were connected with him obtained salvation. When the gardener watered an areca tree all the plantain trees close by got the water as well. And so, concluded Rāmānuja, just as he—by his connection with his teachers, culminating in Nammāḻvār—was sure of salvation, everyone else connected with him should be assured of it because of their relationship with him. For Sri Vipranarayana there was a biological chain of Śrīvaiṣṇava devotees, on one hand, and a direct link to Nammāḻvār as well. Because the congregation was linked with Nammāḻvār, they were also saved.

While the tradition of recitation is all important in all Śrīvaiṣṇava temples and shrines, in recent years there has veritably been a boom in setting the Divya Prabandham to music and singing it in classical ragas. Many Carnatic music singers are rendering the lyrics in musical forms, and exponents of the Bharata Natyam style of dancing are choreographing the songs of the Divya Prabandham. We shall now turn our attention to the phenomenon of music and its connection with the Divya Prabandham.

Painting of Nammāḻvār in Srirangam temple.

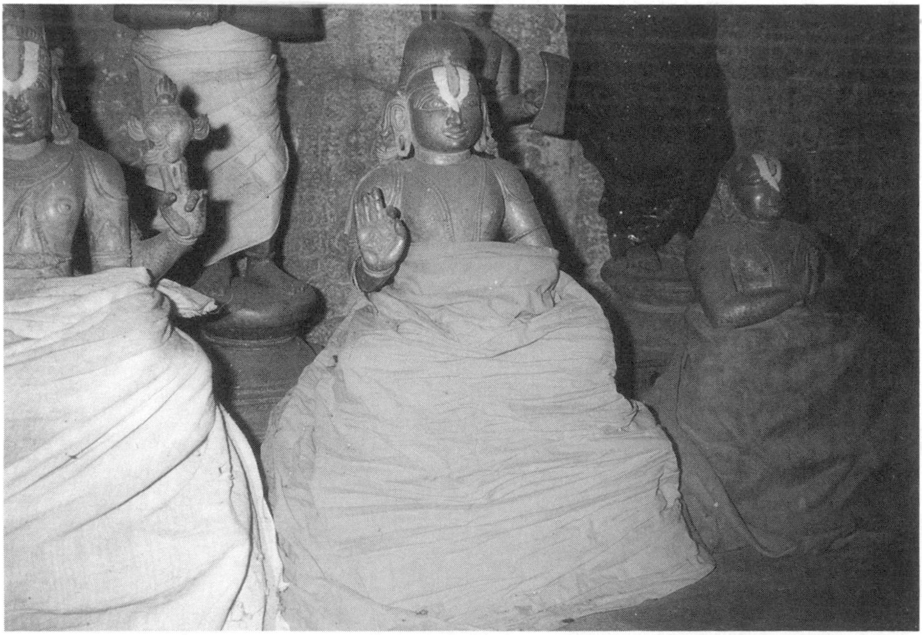
Festival image (*utsava mūrti*) of Nammāḻvār in the eighth-century temple of Tiruvidavendai, near Mahabalipuram, Tamilnadu.

The sixteenth-century Horse Court, outside the Hall of a Thousand Pillars, Srirangam Temple.

Nammāl̲vār dressed for his liberation on the tenth night of the Tiruvāymol̲i recitation at the Srirangam Temple.

Main image of Nammāḻvār at his birth place, Alvar Tirunagari.

Nammāḻvār decorated and mounted on a chariot.
Nammāḻvār Cannati, Bangalore.

6 THE TRADITIONS OF MUSIC

In traditional biographical literature the first teacher, Nāthamuni, is said to have been very knowledgeable in music. He is portrayed as being a referee in a music competition between two courtesans; one of them was adept at *human* music and the other in *divine* music. A local king had apparently ruled in favor of the human music, and the other dancer, piqued, had taken her case to the people. Nāthamuni, who was entranced by the intricacies of her rhythm and singing techniques, explained the superiority of her music to the king and brought her recognition. He is said to have set the entire Divya Prabandham to this form of divine music, choreographed the songs, and taught it to his two nephews.[1]

Nammāḻvār had clearly envisaged the Tiruvāymoḻi as being sung and danced in praise of the Lord:

> O you who want to break
> the hold of deeds
> and stop them from coming close,
> worship the feet of the Lord,
> singing and dancing these ten
> of the thousand Tamil songs
> sung by Caṭakōpan̲ who hails from Kurukūr
> a city with lofty mansions.
>
> (9.10.11)

This art of singing and dancing the verses of the Divya Prabandham, apparently instituted by Nāthamuni, has continued through the male descendents and disciples of the two nephews in what came to be known as the *araiyar* tradition. (We will discuss this tradition in chap. 8 in the context of temple rituals of recitation.) While the major portion of the Divya Prabandham was set to music, some works came under the category of *iyal,* or "that which is to be recited." These thousand verses are called *iyaṟpā,* and the division between *icai-pā* (that which is to be sung) and *iyal-pā* (that which is to be recited) is said to have been created by Nāthamuni.

The modes of singing which existed in those days are no longer in existence; except for the *araiyar* tradition, which claims continuity, there is no other form of singing which is said to reach back over the centuries. The enactment of particular verses of Nammāḻvār, or myths that are alluded to in the Tiruvāymoḻi during the annual Festival of Recitation in December–January, is called *araiyar cēvai,* that is, "service [*cēvai;* Sanskrit: *sevā*] by the araiyar." The *araiyar* tradition is closer to recitation than to classical south Indian music today. The *araiyars* use cymbals to beat time—and the recitation has traditionally been called "singing." For the better part of the last seven hundred years the Divya Prabandham has been recited rather than sung in the brahmanical temple context. It is, however, quite probable that the *āḻvār* hymns have been rendered in song by the nonbrahmanical castes for several centuries.

The power of music is reiterated several times in Śrīvaiṣṇava works. According to biographical literature, even the Lord Viṣṇu is said to be entranced by music; in some instances he is reported as being so under the influence of the beauty of music that he accedes to the requests of the devotee. This point is made in one important incident retold several times in Śrīvaiṣṇava lore. The Śrīvaiṣṇava community in Srirangam is said to have wanted the young Rāmānuja to become its leader. Rāmānuja at that time was serving Viṣṇu enshrined at Kanchipuram, some two hundred miles away. An *araiyar,* well versed in music, is said to have been dispatched to Kanchipuram to seek the permission of the Lord Viṣṇu there to release Rāmānuja from his service and send him to Srirangam. The *araiyar* sang and danced the verses from the Divya Prabandham in front of the Lord Varadā (the local name by which Viṣṇu is known in Kanchipuram), and the Lord, delighted, promised the *araiyar* anything he wanted. The *araiyar* requested that Rāmānuja, the favorite devotee and servant of the Lord, be sent with him, to serve the manifestation of Viṣṇu at the town of Srirangam. Reluctantly, the Kanchipuram god is said to have acceded to the request and sent Rāmānuja away.[2]

The importance of music at least up to the fourteenth century in the Srirangam Temple is recorded in the chronicles of the Srirangam Temple.[3] In this book, which contains several interpolations, there are many stories about the musicians of the temple. In the part mythic, part historic, accounts the *araiyar* is portrayed as one skilled in the performing arts and music. It relates that once Tiruvarangaperumal Araiyar (11th c.) so pleased the Lord by singing the tunes most appropriate to the season and festival that he was honored with titles by the Lord himself.[4] In one anachronistic story, which is placed *before* the time of Nāthamuni, it is related that the Tulukka (from *turka,* or *Turkish,* which is the Tamil word for Muslim) king of Delhi came to Srirangam, entered the temple through the northern gateway, overcame the local resistance, and went away with the treasures of the temple as well as the processional deity, who is known as the "Handsome Bridegroom." The processional deity is a movable "image," and he presides over all festivals. This processional deity, along with the immovable Lord enshrined in the inner chamber, are thought of as full incarnations of the Lord on earth. He is said to be graciously present on earth, as he is in heaven and, so, taking him away was unbearable to the local congregation. A woman from a neighboring village apparently followed the Lord to Delhi and saw him being initially cast into a warehouse, from where he was rescued by the Muslim king's daughter, the "Sultani." The woman came back to Srirangam and recounted the tale. Subsequently, the temple priests went to Delhi, and there they charmed the emperor and requested that he give back their Lord. The temple musicians then called the Lord with an "intense and divine melody," and the Lord, making the Sultani sleep, came away with the temple servants. Because the Lord was entranced by song and thus brought back, the musicians came to be called "the group belonging to the Lord who knows music."[5] The chronicles of the Srirangam temple also indicate that the Lord here has the special title of "Emperor among musicians" (*Gāyaka sārvabhauman*).[6]

The point made in this story is that the temple servants placed great importance on music and believed that the Lord was the monarch of song. In passing, however, it may be noted that, although the story is said to have taken place before the time of Nāthamuni in this narrative, its veracity is questionable; at best it is clearly anachronistic. The Muslim invasion did not take place until about 1311 (with a second one occurring around 1323), and Nāthamuni lived in the tenth century C.E. It is also a "generic" story seen in many Viṣṇu temples in south India which at one time or another were conquered by a Muslim king. Most of these temples have a shrine for a *bībī nācciyār,* or "Muslim consort" for Viṣṇu, and this is probably as far as the medieval Śrīvaiṣṇavas went in terms of "interreligious dialogue."[7] What this story does make clear, however, is that the temple reforms carried out by Rāmānuja, which included establishing groups of musicians to entertain the Lord, were followed in some measure two centures later.

In the last fifty years or so rendering the Divya Prabandham and the Tiruvāymoḻi in song has become popular. Before we consider the recent boom in singing these verses, a phenomenon that has gone hand in hand with the proliferation of aural culture of radio and cassettes, let us briefly consider why singing the Tiruvāymoḻi may have faded out of the temple context.

Commentarial literature on the Tiruvāymoḻi began around the late eleventh century C.E., when Rāmānuja's cousin Piḷḷāṉ wrote the first commentary on it. The many commentaries talk about the emotional involvement of the teachers and the devotees in the meaning of the Tiruvāymoḻi and the emotional commitment that the *araiyars* had in performing it. It is possible that even at this stage the involvement with meaning and forms of exegesis became so important to the teachers that singing was not given as much importance as in earlier centuries. We may also speculate whether the modes of singing undermined the status of the Divya Prabandham as the Tamil Veda in the minds of some people; in certain forms of classical singing a phrase is sometimes repeated several times, or words are rearranged slightly to get the best possible musical effect. Rearrangement of words, even for aesthetic pleasure, would be unacceptable if the poem is considered to be a Veda; every syllable is supposed to be where it is supposed to be, and the order of the words is supposed to follow a cosmic order that outlives even the destruction of the universe. Thus, when the words are to be said in a definite order a musical rendering that would sacrifice this sequence would not be accepted. It is also possible that certain forms of singing came under the purview of certain women who were called "servants of god" (*emperumāṉ aṭiyār* or *deva dāsi*). These women danced and sang in front of the Lord and in time came to acquire a reputation as courtesans;[8] it is quite possible that the brahmanical temple tradition tried to distance itself from this group of singers.

Perhaps the demise of the singing traditions in temple worship can be attributed in part to the disruption in worship caused by Muslim invasions in the fourteenth century and later in the eighteenth century. We have already noted that, according to the chronicles of the Srirangam Temple, the Lord of the temple was carried off during an invasion. In one poem written in the fourteenth century the temple is described as being in a state of ruin and the towers as being in a dilapidated condition.[9] The Vijayanagara kings restored the deity to the temple in 1371.[10] There was also a second disruption of the worship in the eighteenth century, when the forces of Chandasaheb, aided by French soldiers from Pondicherry, occupied the temple in 1751. Although Chandasaheb was beheaded in 1752, the French continued to occupy the temple until 1758, when they were conquered by the British. Haidar Ali from Mysore attacked in 1781 but did not conquer the temple; however, his son Tippu Sultan occupied it in 1790. When the British army approached his camp he fled Srirangam but apparently left a trail of destruction on his way.[11] These military occupations evidently disrupted the traditional worship in the temple, although it was never abandoned, except for fifty-nine years in the fourteenth century.

According to an interesting story (from family lore) told to me by Sri Nadhamuni Araiyar of the Srirangam Temple,[12] apparently, during one of the attacks, hundreds of *araiyars* living in the East Uttara Street (the traditional home of the *araiyar* families in the sixth enclosure around the temple) were put to death; their cymbals were melted and recast into a large bell. The cymbals that the *araiyars* carried symbolized their musical service to the Lord. This story seems to be a poignant account of the dying of certain forms of musical performances in the temple context. I have not been able to find any written account of the story, but, directly or indirectly, it speaks of the demise of musical service rendered in the Srirangam Temple.

While it must be pointed out that *araiyars* continued to perform in other temples in south India, the Srirangam Temple was the heart of Śrīvaiṣṇava culture. It was simply called *kōyil,* or the Temple; all the *āḻvārs,* with the exception of Maturakavi, sang about the Lord here, the early teachers lived here, and so any change in ritual that took place here would have been felt in ripples in other Śrīvaiṣṇava temples. Many *araiyar* families lived in Srirangam, and occupation and destruction here would have cut at the roots of the art. The *araiyar* tradition was based on family lineage; only a son, a direct male descendent or child formally adopted, could claim to be an *araiyar*. Other disciples and relatives could not become *araiyars* and could not be taught the art of reciting, expressing the emotions, and dancing the verses. Thus, the death of a generation of *araiyars* would mean the destruction of a tradition, a whole form of interpretation and commenting on the Tiruvāymoḻi, and perhaps this was the message embedded in the story recounted by Sri Nadhamuni Araiyar.

While there have been disruptions in the singing traditions of the *araiyars*, there are other families near the temples of Srirangam and Tiruvenkatam (Tirupati) which have the hereditary right to sing to the Lord on certain occasions. These families claim that their rights go back several centuries; certainly, it can be documented that the Annamacharya family in Tirupati have been official performers of classical devotional music at the temple from the fifteenth century. This family sings the Telugu songs composed by Sri Annamacharya (1408–1503), who lived there for most of his life. Sri G. Rangarajan (known even in the telephone directory as Veenai Rangarajan after the vīnā, the musical instrument that he plays) and his sons sing regularly in the Srirangam Temple in the classical Carnatic music style. They sing the songs of the famous composers of Carnatic music (e.g., Purandara Dāsa, Thyāgarāja, Shyama Sastri) as well as the verses of the *āḻvārs* which their ancestors set to traditional ragas two generations ago.

VEENAI RANGARAJAN: RESIDENT VĪNĀ PLAYER AT THE SRIRANGAM TEMPLE

Veenai Rangarajan was born on 13 April 1931. He was trained by his father and uncle and began to perform in the temple when he was nine. It was at this age that he was invested with the sacred thread. When he was eleven he was initiated into the Śrīvaiṣṇava community with the sacrament of *samāśrayanam* (literally, "to take refuge," but referring to the branding of the conch and discus on one's shoulders). It is interesting to note, however, that his family were originally considered to be members of the *smārta* community, the brahmin tradition that is generally associated with the philosopher Śaṅkara and which has some

Śaivaite affiliation. According to his family lore, passed on by oral tradition, this *smārta* family was recruited by Rāmānuja to perform music for the Lord at the Srirangam Temple. There is no textual confirmation of this event. The family is considered to be both *smārta* and Śrīvaiṣṇava; the family name has the suffix of *Iyengar,* which is considered to be Śrīvaiṣṇava, but the women wear their clothes in the traditional manner of *smārta* women. Wedding alliances are done with the *smārta* community, but when new brides enter the family circle they are given a Vaiṣṇavaite name (if they bear a name associated with the Śaiva tradition) and are initiated into the Śrīvaiṣṇava community.

When Sri Rangarajan finished high school he was anxious to continue his higher education. His father, however, who performed at the Srirangam Temple, was afraid that, if he allowed his son to proceed to college, he may become influenced by secular forces and reject his right to serve the Lord. After some time he gave permission to his son to continue his education, saying that he had turned over the burden of safeguarding him to the Lord. Sri Rangarajan went on to do graduate work in physics at a Catholic institution (St. Joseph's College), and began his teaching career in a Muslim college (Jamal Mohammad College). However, he never missed his duties to serve the Lord by playing music to him in the temple. He is now the chairman of the department of physics and the vice principal at the National College in Tirucchirapalli (the major town near Srirangam) and has continued the family tradition of ritually performing the music of the *āḻvārs* and other songs for the Lord.

Veenai Rangarajan was married in 1956 and now has four sons. He, or one of his sons, go to the Srirangam Temple every morning, unless it is a special festival day, and sing the poem Tirupaḷḷi eḻucci (The Rising from the Sacred Bed), composed by Toṇṭar Aṭi Poṭi Āḻvār. They sing to the accompaniment of the vīṇā, which they play in the traditional way, by sitting on the ground and placing the instrument horizontally across their laps. While the family has special duties on some festival days and two or more members are in attendance, it is during the annual Festival of Recitation in the months of December and January that the sons get together, and all male members of the family sing for the Lord on the ten nights of the Tiruvāymoḻi recitation. Veenai Rangarajan's sons, who all hold high level secular jobs as well (some in nearby cities), come to Srirangam to serve the Lord with their music during these nights. On these nights, after the Tiruvāymoḻi recitation and dancing done by the *araiyars,* Sri Rangarajan and his family play the vīnā and sing for a full hour, when the Lord comes back to the shrine and the day's rituals are to be concluded. Dressed in traditional garb with an elaborate turban, they stand with their vīnās hanging vertically in front of them (an extremely unusual and difficult position to hold and play the instrument) and entertain the Lord and his small group of worshippers. These concluding rituals are called *ekānta sevā* or *ekāntam,* "exclusive service," and Veenai Rangarajan has been participating in this ritual since he was thirteen. On the first night these rituals begin sometime around midnight, but it is closer to 9:15 P.M. after the second night. Because of the lateness of the hour, there is only a relatively small crowd of about 150 people for the concluding rituals.

The singing commences when the Lord enters the inner enclosure. He is carried on a palanquin, and Sri Rangarajan and his sons face him. After playing what is now called the five classical ragas for about ten minutes, without singing, they walk a few steps backward, all the time facing the Lord. The palanquin bearers carry the Lord close to the singers, and in this new station they sing songs composed by Purandara Dāsa (15th c.) or Thyāgarāja (18th c.), or melodiously render prayers composed in honor of Srirangam or the Lord of Srirangam for about fifteen minutes. Making a sharp right-angle turn, they proceed a few more yards and, standing near the eight steps that lead to the inner shrine, sing the verses of the *āḻvārs* for about twenty minutes. These songs are set in modern (about two- or three-hundred-year-old) ragas and were rendered in this current form two generations back. Thus, there had been deliberate innovation in the rendering of the songs at that time. Sri Rangarajan thinks this need to render the songs in accessible modes of music is built into the dynamism of the *āḻvār* verses. Most of the songs selected, though not all, are addressed to the Lord at Srirangam. The final song of the evening is one that was composed by a king, Vijaya Ranga Chokka Nayaka (d. 1707), who apparently used to sing to the Lord while his wife, Meenakshi, danced before him. The statues of Vijaya Ranga and his family are displayed in a showcase close to where Veenai Rangarajan and his family sing. This final song is almost like a lullaby, in the soothing raga of Yadukula Kambodhi, and, as they sing the four verses, the palanquin bearers carefully lift the Lord over the eight steps, gently rocking the palanquin like a cradle. The Lord finally enters the inner shrine and retires for the night.

Like the *araiyar* tradition, Sri Rangarajan's service in the temple is hereditary in nature, but there is no textual confirmation on how long this has been in place. A male heir in the family is extremely important to carry on the tradition, and two generations ago there was adoption within the family to continue the tradition. Sri Rangarajan has four sons now and a young grandson as well, and he is at peace that the tradition will continue for the foreseeable future. He looks forward to retirement, when he can concentrate on setting more *āḻvār* songs to ragas and singing them.

The cluster of *āḻvār* songs is framed in the night ritual of *ekānta sevā* by other songs of devotion composed over the centuries. The music is what we might call contemporary classical; that is, it is set in ragas of Carnatic music which the audience recognizes and enjoys. It is important to note that rendering the *āḻvār* verses in modes of music which are in tune with the times is an important feature of the vernacular Veda; the Sanskrit Veda, on the other hand, is to be recited in a fixed, inflexible manner.

Classical music in south India has undergone many changes, and in recent years there has been a tremendous revival in setting the Divya Prabandham to ragas. The present form of classical south Indian music is called Carnatic, and a continuous tradition can be traced at least from the time of Purandara Dāsa, a fifteenth-century saint and musician. Verses from the Divya Prabandham are set to classical modes of Carnatic music by many well-known singers and choreographed by dancers in the Bharata Natyam style. The songs of the Tiruppāvai by the female saint Āṇṭāḷ were set to classical ragas by Ariyakudi Ramanuja Iyengar and made popular by him in the 1950s. A raga involves the exclusive use of a set of notes in a scale for rendering a song. By moving between the notes in a manner that is characteristic of the raga, the performer creates a particular mood. While Ariyakudi was a Śrīvaiṣṇava, many of his disciples were not, and, in introducing the songs within the format of a *secular* concert, he brought it out of the context of home and temple worship, out of the Śrīvaiṣṇava community, and introduced the songs to a larger, but not necessarily more pious, audience. In a sense, although one could argue that the singers rendered the songs with appropriate devotion, the context of the songs had become the concert hall and not the temple or home shrine, and the focus moved from the words to the musical raga.

Ariyakudi Ramanuja Iyengar was not the first person to sing the Divya Prabandham in the Carnatic music style, just one of the first to popularize it. In the latter part of the nineteenth century the ancestors of Veenai Rangarajan had set some of the verses to music and had sung them in the hallways of the Srirangam Temple. But, even though the verses had been set to ragas, they were (and are) sung only within the temple. The movement away from the temple onto the secular stage is an important transition in the history of the sacred text: for the first time since their composition the verses of the Divya Prabandham were rendered in front of a purely human audience; until then the primary audience at temples and at homes had been the Lord.[13] It is also important to note that, because the recitation and singing was done in front of the deity, the human audience both listened to the sacred word and simultaneously had a vision of the Lord. In other words, as the audience participated in the process of bearing witness to the *aural* revelation, it also participated in *seeing* the Lord in the temple or shrine, which in Śrīvaiṣṇava theology is like having a visual revelation. This notion of simultaneous oral/aural and visual revelation is seen in a verse from the Divya Prabandham:

> Those who know well
> recite [*ōti*] the Vedas well
> and *see* the Lord . . .
>
> (Mūnṛām Tiruvantāti 12)

The concept of performing primarily for the deity is still seen during the Festival of Recitation, when the *araiyars* first approach the Lord, seek his permission, face him, and recite the Divya Prabandham to him. In all forms of recitation the Lord is perceived to be the listener and the enjoyer.

The Tamil Music Association (Tamil Isai Sangam) has several sessions devoted to the music of the Śaiva hymns (Tēvāram) and the Vaiṣṇava hymns (Divya Prabandham); however, the sessions focusing on the Tēvāram outnumber the Divya Prabandham on a scale of approximately six to one. Many reasons can be noted for this; the obvious one is that there are far more *ōtuvārs,* or traditional performers of the Śaivaite canon, than reciters of the Vaiṣṇavaite verses. There has also been a continuous tradition of singing the Śaivaite Tēvāram, whereas the Divya Prabandham singing in the Carnatic style is still fairly new. A second speculative reason: the audience for Tēvāram singing has been composed of members of all castes, whereas the Carnatic style of music for the Divya Prabandham is now brahmin dominated. There is also a third reason: many performers of the Divya Prabandham still believe it to be *religious* music and to be performed only for the deity and not in front of a secular audience. Thus, Sri Nadhamuni Araiyar of Srirangam told me in January 1990 that he had been asked to perform for the Tamil Isai Sangam but had refused, since he sang only in front of the Lord in a temple; his singing the Divya Prabandham was loving service to the deity and not secular entertainment.

Rendering the songs in the mode of classical music in secular halls has been a phenomenon popular in the latter part of the twentieth century. In the last five years, however—in fact, since the time that I commenced this study—there has been a boom in the popularity of singing the verses of the *āḻvārs,* showcased in the annual Tamil Isai Sangam musical festival and made accessible by the increasing production of audio cassettes. The audience is now human, not divine; the forum is a music auditorium with excellent acoustics, rather than the temple or a home shrine. But even here we encounter the notion of revelation, as we shall see in the case of Sri Venkata Varadhan.

SRI VENKATA VARADHAN: MUSICIAN AND RECIPIENT OF REVELATION

> The music comes without my mind coming in the way; He speaks, the Lord tells me how to sing the gracious words of the *āḻvārs*. . . . Should I pay attention to him [the Lord] and sing, or should I be bothered with writing down the notation? If I can, I make a rough notation later, but *you* should write it down and organize the songs and the singing mood. I am lost in the personalities of the poets and their emotions. If it is a *sṛngāra* mood [a lover's mood], I feel the pangs of love; if the voice of the *āḻvār* is sorrowful, I am sunk in grief and cry out in agony.[14]

Sri Venkata Varaḍhan was born in 1919 and teaches men and women to sing the Divya Prabandham. I first met him on the secular stage, in December 1989, when he sang a full program of songs from the Divya

Prabandham during the annual music festival held by the Tamil Isai Sangam. He teaches a group of about fifteen to twenty women, mostly homemakers, who meet twice a week on Tuesdays and Friday afternoons for about two hours and learn to sing the Divya Prabandham. Unlike the young men who undergo the training process to recite the Divya Prabandham, these women do not follow any particular order in the learning of the songs; they learn the verses as inspiration strikes their teacher.

Sri Venkata Varadhan has had an interesting life.[15] He was born in an orthodox Śrīvaiṣṇava family near Kanchipuram, and his family had traditional ritual functions in the Viṣṇu temple there. He studied the Divya Prabandham, both under his father and another teacher, and also attended secular school for a while. He gave up his schooling because he became overwhelmingly interested in acting and wanted to be involved in stage productions. He was also interested in mythological movies and loved the songs from these musicals. After some training in Carnatic music in Kanchipuram, he studied under well-known male singers such as "Tiger" Varadachariar and Naina Pillai. Naina Pillai belonged to a family of female singers—women who hailed from a family of temple dancers, or courtesans. Sri Venkata Varadhan lived for a while in Naina Pillai's house, along with several other disciples, learning at odd hours and fully participating in their musical lives. He recollects that even the family dog, Tommy, was so musical that if anyone sang out of tune or struck a wrong note on the instrument, the dog would go to the culprit and start barking. After several years of intensive training in Carnatic music he started setting verses from the Divya Prabandham to music. He notes that now *he* does not set the music; it just comes to him, sometimes in the middle of the night, sometimes when he is traveling in a bus. The feeling is overwhelming; he hears, and feels the raga. He gets up and starts scribbling the best he can; sometimes he cannot decipher his writing at a later time. The ragas are based on folk tunes and melodies; he feels that the raga should indicate the mood of the song and that one should sing with emotion.

There are about fifteen to twenty students in his Divya Prabandham class; they are all married women, all of them brahmins, and many of them are Śrīvaiṣṇavas. Only two were *smārta* brahmin women, and all of them had been trained in classical Carnatic music in some fashion or another. It is important to note that the interest in singing the Divya Prabandham in the Carnatic music style seems to be primarily brahmin based.

Sri Venkata Varadhan has named this class "Goda Mandali" (the circle, or group, of Goda). Goda is the Sanskrit name of Āṇṭāḷ, the only female *āḻvār,* and this group is appropriately named after her. The group was first formed in 1970 and met at Bhagavantam Gupta Street; since 1982 it has been meeting at the home of Srimati Chitra Raghunathan, at Mahalakshmi Street, at Theagarayanagar, Madras. The women meet twice a week, Tuesdays and Fridays, from 1:30 to 3:00 P.M., and learn one verse a day. The learning process goes on for about a half-hour to forty-five minutes, and they practice the older verses for the rest of the time. In the classes I attended the teacher and students worked together in matters of rhythm and beat; because the women are familiar with Carnatic music and all have good voices, they were able to grasp the musical modes quickly. Each line was repeated several times; the teacher sang once, and the students repeated in chorus. Almost all the ragas seemed unusual.[16] When I questioned Sri Venkata Varadhan he replied simply: "That is the way it is. I teach what I hear."

All the students sit in a semicircular fashion on the floor, while the teacher alone sits on a chair, facing them. For these lessons there are no accompanying instruments except the harmonium. They frequently sing for events connected with temples, and, occasionally, they sing for a secular audience. For temple events they choose songs appropriate to that shrine: for a Hanumān temple they choose songs that deal with Rāma devotion from the Divya Prabandham, because Hanumān was the paradigmatic devotee of this incarnation of Viṣṇu. For secular performances, which include singing on the radio, television, and annually singing in the Tamil Isai Sangam, they have more freedom of selection and choose from a variety of ragas. For the secular stage they may be accompanied by a violin, a vīnā, and a percussion instrument, but for temple performances the accompanying instruments are generally not included, so as to concentrate fully on the words of the *āḻvār.* The group (as it is formed now) first started performing for the Tamil Isai Sangam in 1982 and, in its debut, sang only fifteen short pieces. In the 1986 performance this was increased to twenty-one and by 1988 twenty-five different songs were sung. In the 1988 performance, of the twenty-five songs, five were from Nammāḻvār, the greatest representation from any *āḻvār* in the program.

The students of the Goda Mandali highlight the importance of the music and the words. One of them stated: "If the audience wants to hear the Kambodhi raga, they can go to the Music Academy [a famous institution in Madras where the classical Carnatic music festival in December is extremely popular]. But, if they want to *hear* the beauty of the words of the *āḻvārs* and the beauty of music, if they want to *see* the beauty of the meaning, they come to hear us."

Sri Venkata Varadhan is one of many Divya Prabandham singers in the late twentieth century who emphasizes the importance of revelation when he sets the words to music. The music comes in dreams or strikes him as he is in the middle of some activity, and he is consumed by the tune. He has no record of how many songs he had thus set to music; his students estimated the number to be between three hundred and five hundred out of the four thousand verses of the Divya Prabandham; they have kept notations for some of the music.

SRI RAMA BHARATI AND THE DEVAGANA PATHASALA

A more organized group is seen in the Sri Sadagopan Tirunarayana Swami Devagana Pathasala, where, under the blessings of their teacher, Sri Sadagopan, the disciples carry on the activity of setting the Divya Prabandham to music. They describe their heritage and mission thus:

> as custodian of the ancient art of Devagana or temple music, it was the lord here [at Melukote in Mysore] who gave the song Ārāvamutē [Tiruvāymoḻi 5.8] to Sri Nathamuni in the 9th century AD [*sic*], inspiring him to collect the sacred four thousand hymns of the *Alvar* Saints and render them to song and dance. The thread has been taken up by Sangitacharya V. V. Sadagopan, who founded the Tyaga Bharati Mission in 1966 and revived the tradition of singing the Divya Prabandham. Over the years the Mission has published, through the Indian Music Journal, a musical notation for the songs, and propagated the works through performances, public lectures, group classes, and cassette recordings.[17]

This particular group also announces in its brochures that "members who have learnt the Divya Prabandham under Tyaga Bharati are available for performance for all occasions like marriage, Poochuttal [a pregnancy ritual, when the mother-to-be is adorned with flowers], Birthdays etc." The principal performer/singer is Sri Rama Bharati, who does his own version of the *araiyar cēvai* and even wears a hat that is peculiar to the *araiyar* families associated with temples. While the performance is inspired and dramatic, it bears no resemblance to the *araiyar cēvai* in the temples. He is also not *biologically* connected with the *araiyars*, which is generally a necessary element for performing the *araiyar cēvai*. He has, however, repeatedly emphasized his spiritual connection to the *araiyar* tradition, the importance of being moved to sing and dance, and the importance of inspiration while setting the Divya Prabandham to music.[18] Sri Rama Bharati was a doctoral student in microbiology at the University of Chicago, when he felt the calling to devote his life to music. After searching for guidance and the right teacher he became a disciple of Sri V. V. Sadagopan. Sri Sadagopan had learned under Ariyakudi Ramanuja Iyengar, who had popularized the singing of the Tiruppāvai. Sri Sadagopan was a professor of music at Delhi University, but after a mystical experience in 1966 he resigned his job, rejected his former training under Ariyakudi, and felt that he had found the creative source of music. In 1980 Sri Sadagopan departed on a train to Madras; he was seen getting down at Gudur Station and has not been seen since.

Sri Rama Bharati, a close disciple of Sadagopan, has recorded several cassettes of Tiruvāymoḻi singing; like Sri Venkata Varadhan, his songs are melodious and sometimes rousing. His wife, Sowbhagya Lakshmi, and he tour India and give performances; meanwhile, at the shrine in Madras, the "time of service" (Sevā Kālam) is conducted regularly, and the Divya Prabandham is recited and sung.

The students of this mission teach the Divya Prabandham in several places in Madras. I met Mrs. Kothai Venkatapathy in Tiruvanmiyur, Madras; she teaches a group of twelve students every Monday. Kothai Venkatapathy is the granddaughter of Karpangadu Swami, a famous exponent of the Śrīvaiṣṇava scriptures, and she grew up in an atmosphere of regular home recitation and commentarial teaching. She now teaches recitation and singing of the Divya Prabandham and acknowledges the inspiration derived from the Tyaga Bharati Mission and Sri Rama Bharati. She encourages her fledgling students, who are members of a group called *bhaktanjali* (devotional worship), to learn a few hundred songs, give performances of the Divya Prabandham at temples, and donate the proceeds of the concert to a particular temple that needs renovation. Kothai Venkatapathy also emphasizes the role of divine inspiration in singing and recitation: without being in touch with the divine one cannot perform. She calls this "intuition" and describes it in terms of getting the music from a divine source and singing songs appropriate to the time. Thus, before the annual celebration of Āṇṭāl's birthday in 1991 she taught her students many verses from that poet's work Nācciyār Tirumoḻi, speaking of the emotional tensions of Āṇṭāḷ as she passed from one representative song to another. Her teaching of the verses was interspersed with commentarial explanations. In another interview she also recounted how in a time of personal crisis she was inspired to recite a particular set (7.4) from the Tiruvāymoḻi. This set of verses speaks about the Lord's triumphs. She is convinced that regular recitation of this set of verses brought her the success and victory in a situation over which she had no control.

Kothai Venkatapathy, Sri Rama Bharati, Venkata Varadhan, and the Goda Mandali are all examples from a generation involved in singing the Divya Prabandham mediated through the beauty and richness of singing in ragas. These teachers of the music claim inspiration and intuition and express the passion of their involvement with the sound and the words over and over again. A listenener cannot but be struck with their overpowering enthusiasm and zeal; it is almost as if they are recipients, all over again, of revelation.

This is not to say that all singers of the Divya Prabandham claim divine inspiration; the market is flooded with the sound waves of electronic devotion. The burgeoning of Divya Prabandham singing in classes has accompanied the proliferation of the recited and sung word through cassettes and the radio, a phenomenon that we may call "electronic devotion," or *bhakti.*

FLOODING THE MARKET WITH THE SOUND WAVES OF ELECTRONIC BHAKTI

O ambrosia that never sates,

you make this servant's body,
so much in love with you,
sway

wander like waters
of the sea,
melt, and dissolve.

(Tiruvāymoḻi 5.8.1)

In this verse, which apparently was the first that Nāthamuni ever heard, Nammāḻvār says that his body, racked with his love, sways like the waves of the sea. It was also this verse that eventually led to the revelation of the entire Divya Prabandham.

Since the time that the minstrels sang this first song for Nāthamuni a thousand years ago, the waves of Divya Prabandham singing have been in flood at times and at ebb at others, depending on the political and social situation. In the latter part of the twentieth century there has been a gradual increase in the proliferation of Divya Prabandham songs through the mass media. Every morning, between 6:15 and 6:45, on Madras radio stations there is a half-hour of "integrated" devotional songs—integrated, in that there are songs of devotion addressed to Viṣṇu, Śiva, Christ, and what is called "Islamiya devotional music." There are only two major government-sponsored radio stations (not including the film music station) in Madras and no private radio stations, and until the advent of satellite TV, there was no television show aired that early in the morning. Therefore, most people who tune in their transistors to get the news also get a liberal dose of this electronic devotion. Part of the philosophy behind these broadcasts is the perceived need to encourage a revival of Tamil lyrics and a highlighting of Tamil ethnic pride; the other side is an attempt at giving "all religions" equal time. Many of the motifs that occur in the songs seem generic enough—praise of the Lord; his supremacy; submission to him; and imploring his grace. The Śaiva and Vaiṣṇava verses, however, are both place specific and sing of the glories of a particular location in which the Lord has manifested himself. The supremacy of Viṣṇu and Śiva and the grace of Christ are also proclaimed through these songs.

There has not been any study to assess the impact of these broadcasts, but one may observe a heightened awareness of Tamil works, including the Divya Prabandham and the poems of the Śaiva corpus. For the last two hundred years Carnatic music has largely swirled around lyrics in the Telugu language, and only recently has there been a desire to appreciate, learn, and sing Tamil songs. Veenai Rangarajan, the resident musician of the Srirangam Temple, remarked in an interview that, even a generation back, his father would play more Telugu Kirtanas in the temple during the rituals, but because of popular demand he (the son) now plays a lot of Tamil songs from the Divya Prabandham. One observable result, then, of the frequent playing of Divya

Prabandham songs on the radio and the encouragement of institutions such as the Tamil Isai Sangam has been the increased popularity of and familiarity with the Tamil songs; it has been a way in which many Śrīvaiṣṇavas and people of other communities have rediscovered the beauty of the old lyrics.

With the increasing popularity there is a new demand to listen to the recitation and singing of the Divya Prabandham, and in the last few years there has been a boom in the cassette market. Verses from the Divya Prabandham are recited and sung, and the recitation of the complete Tiruvāymoḻi and singing of the Tiruppāvai have been very popular. The songs are rendered in many ways. When Ariyakudi Ramanuja Iyengar sang the thirty verses of the Tiruppāvai in Carnatic music style in the 1950s it took almost four hours and was treated like a Carnatic music concert, with special time, for instance, for percussion instruments. He sang each of the thirty verses in a separate raga and also spent a considerable amount of time prefacing each verse with a long elaboration and exploration of the contours of each raga.[19]

Now many versions of the Tiruppāvai are sung in less than an hour. There are also cassettes on which the Divya Prabandham is sung in a semiclassical fashion, bordering on film music; other artists, such as Mani Krishnaswami, render the verses in elaborate and beautiful ragas. There are considerable differences in the styles of singing between the different artists and no uniformity in choosing a raga for a particular verse. The renderings range from the mediocre ("tacky" was a description I once heard) to the extremely melodious. For the first time there is a variety of Divya Prabandham performances that are easily available. Many of the cassettes simply have an assortment of songs chosen from the *āḻvārs;* there are others that are thematic and which focus on the verses composed about a certain place. Thus, there are many cassettes containing just those songs composed by the *āḻvārs* on Tiruvenkatam, and these include selections from Tirumaṅkai, Nammāḻvār, and others. In making these selections, the musicians are keeping to traditional categories and are emphasizing the Śrīvaiṣṇava community's esteem for the sacred land where the Lord manifests himself. Even electronic recitation reiterates the importance of territorial theology.

This renewed surge of interest in the Divya Prabandham is looked upon as a mixed blessing by many of the Śrīvaiṣṇava teachers and elders. While they welcome the newfound interest and the popularity of the Divya Prabandham, they are also apprehensive and occasionally alarmed about the electronic means of dissemination, and their objections seem startlingly similar to those voiced when the Divya Prabandham and some commentaries were first printed. The easy availability of the material, they believe, leads to casual reading and listening and possible misapprehension of the material, because there is no live teacher on hand to guide the student through the material. Further, it is argued, one should hear the Divya Prabandham with proper attention and veneration, while one is in the presence of the Lord; that is why the Tiruvāymoḻi is always recited when one is sitting in front of the deity or when one is within the precincts of a temple. Rendering it in ragas diverts the attention from the words to the music, and it now becomes mere entertainment. Now one can pop a cassette into a Sony Walkman and listen to it while otherwise occupied; listening thus becomes secondary because one's mind is often focused on some other activity.

And yet, against these objections, one may argue that in terms of Śrīvaiṣṇava theology the dissemination of the Divya Prabandham has made the Tamil Veda *more* accessible, and this, after all, would have been something the early teachers would have approved of. One may further argue that the early *ācāryas* also found pleasure in interpreting the Divya Prabandham through the music and dance of the time, and the new renderings speak to the aesthetic tastes of the audience today. A new orality has surfaced through the electronic media, one that combines the personal articulation through voice with the impersonal distance of the printed text.

Old forms of recitation exist side by side with new forms of singing the Divya Prabandham. Alongside the tradition of reciting the verses there continues to be the tradition of *interpretation,* through words and through performances, which we will consider in the next two chapters.

7

EXEGESIS AND INTERPRETATION

Oral and Written Commentary on the Tiruvāymoli

INTRODUCTION

> To interpret . . . is to bring out what is concealed in a given manifestation, to make evident what in the manifestation is not evident to the milieu in which the interpreter's audience lives. . . . To interpret verbal utterance is to bring out what the utterance does not itself reveal to a given audience. What utterance reveals calls for no interpretation.
>
> —Walter Ong, "Text as Interpretation"

> Revered people say that a commentary clarifies [the original] and teaches us other things as well.
>
> —Vātikecari Kārikai

In his 1969 classic *Hermeneutics* Palmer shows that the verb *hermeneuein* and the noun *hermeneia,* which are the roots of the word *hermeneutics,* are both connected with the wing-footed messenger god Hermes. Hermes was associated with the function of transmuting "what is beyond human understanding into a form that human intelligence can grasp."[1] Palmer points out the three directions of meaning of *hermeneuein* and *hermeneia* in ancient usage. These were (1) "to say" or to express aloud in words, (2) to explain, and (3) to translate from one language to another. Thus, *interpretation* referred to three rather different matters: an "oral recitation, a reasonable explanation, and a translation from another language." In all three cases, Palmer argues, the foundational "Hermes process" is at work: "something foreign, strange, separated in time, space or experience is made familiar, present, comprehensible; something requiring representation, explanation, or translation is somehow 'brought to understanding'—is interpreted."[2] Comment and interpretation become necessary when an original statement is not self-explanatory.

In this chapter we will study the process of interpretation and the commentarial tradition on the Tiruvāymoḻi. As we saw in the last two chapters, the poem was always recited or sung *orally,* but alongside this there existed a tradition of *explanation,* or commentary, in which several distinctive positions were asserted. Finally, there was a unique kind of *translation* involved: the Tamil poem was said to be equivalent to the Sanskrit Vedas, and this equivalence was portrayed by rendering the meaning of the poem in Sanskrit, *maṇipravāḷa,* and a "newer" (and presumably more easily understandable) kind of Tamil.

Through the elaboration of the commentarial tradition on the Tiruvāymoḻi the Śrīvaiṣṇava community affirmed some distinctive positions, which defined its identity. These positions included the attribution of equal importance to the Sanskrit and Tamil Vedas, the notion of the goddess Śrī as a mediator between a human being and the Lord, and holding the Tiruvāymoḻi to be a text that gives salvific knowledge.

THE IMPORTANCE OF THE COMMENTARIAL TRADITION

In the second chapter we noted that Nāthamuni, who lived around the tenth century C.E., is said to have recovered the Tamil poems of Nammāḻvār and divided them into passages that could be set to music and verses that could be recited. The Śrīvaiṣṇava community understood this to be an act that emphasized the equivalency of the poems to the Sanskrit Vedas; *The Splendor* says that, just as the legendary sage Śrī Veda Vyāsa divided up the Sanskrit Vedas according to the forms of chants involved,[3] Nāthamuni divided the Tamil poems into music (*icai*) and recitation (*iyal*). Nāthamuni is said to have transmitted the proper singing and interpretation of the Tiruvāymoḻi to his two nephews, and *The Splendor* specifically mentions that another disciple called Uyyakoṇṭār was given the task of disseminating the Tiruvāymoḻi and the other works of the *āḻvārs.*[4] There is epigraphical evidence that the Tiruvāymoḻi was chanted in temples at least from 1023 C.E.,[5] and *The Splendor* tells us that Nāthamuni introduced the Tiruvāymoḻi and other Tamil hymns into home and temple liturgies and initiated an annual ten-day Festival of Recitation, which was accompanied by oral and performing commentaries.

The Tiruvāymoḻi was interpreted either by long commentaries or by short summaries. Chronologically, the long commentaries came first, beginning with the recording of the oral commentaries in the late eleventh and early twelfth centuries. The earliest commentary was written by Tirukkurukai Pirāṉ Piḷḷāṉ (late 11th–early 12th c.). This commentary was called the *Āṛāyirappaṭi,* or *Six Thousand-paṭi.*[6] Later commentaries that are considered to be classical by the community are called the *Nine Thousand-paṭi, Twelve Thousand-paṭi, Twenty-four Thousand-paṭi,* and *Thirty-six Thousand-paṭi.* A *paṭi* is a literary unit of thirty-two syllables. Thus, Piḷḷāṉ's commentary has thirty-two times six thousand syllables and was numerically modeled on a Sanskrit work of the same length, the *Viṣṇu Purāṇa.* This self-conscious modeling is, of course, significant in the twofold Sanskrit-Tamil tradition.[7]

Starting in the thirteenth century, there were several short summaries, usually in the form of a poem. These poems were either independent pieces or sometimes part of a longer narrative. Independent pieces include Vedānta Deśika's Sanskrit poem *The Gem-Necklace of Reality in the Tamil Upaniṣad* (Dramiḍopaniṣad Tātparya Ratnāvaḷi) and the Tamil poem *The Hundred Verses on the Tiruvāymoḻi* (Tiruvāymoḻi Nūṛṛantati). Both these works have a similar format: each set of "ten" verses in the Tiruvāymoḻi is summarized by one verse in the poem. Each set of ten verses in the Tiruvāymoḻi is presented as containing a coherent theme, and the main philosophical idea of those ten verses (as perceived by the interpreting poet) is condensed into a single verse.[8] Thus, in these summaries there was a translation either from Tamil into Sanskrit or from "older" Tamil into a more current Tamil of that age.

The longer commentaries, on the other hand, were detailed prose interpretations of the original Tiruvāymoḻi verses, containing several quotations from Sanskrit scripture. Piḷḷāṉ, the first commentator on the Tiruvāymoḻi, elucidated each verse of the Tiruvāymoḻi but frequently wrote a short introduction to each set of ten verses. The comment is not a word-by-word elucidation of the poem (as later commentaries tended to be) but, rather, an interpretation of the verse as a whole, with the commentator supplying a context for the verse.

WRITTEN AND ORAL COMMENT

According to *The Splendor*, it was during the time of Rāmānuja, the most important teacher of the community, that the first commentary on the Tiruvāymoḻi was written, by his cousin Tirukkurukai Pirāṉ Piḷḷāṉ. The writing of a commentary on the Tiruvāymoḻi marks a new epoch in Hindu literature. While commentaries were frequently written in Sanskrit, for Sanskrit literary and religious works, the commentarial tradition in Tamil began only about the eighth century C.E.[9] No Hindu religious work in the vernacular had been deemed worthy of a written commentary, although a strong oral tradition on the Tiruvāymoḻi had probably existed even before Piḷḷāṉ committed one to writing for the first time.

Piḷḷāṉ's first commentary highlighted and articulated certain ideas that challenge traditional norms of the Hindu culture without rebelling against them. The very fact that he, a Brahmin scholar well versed in Sanskrit, wrote a commentary on a Tamil hymn composed by a person believed to have been from the "fourth class" (i.e., a *śūdra*) was an unprecedented act. The writing of the commentary challenges two claims made by the traditional Hindu society: the consideration of Sanskrit as the exclusive vehicle for revelation and theological communication and the importance of the hierarchical class system, which denied salvific knowledge to the *śūdra*. This latter point is openly refuted by Piḷḷāṉ's assumption that Nammāḻvār is the ideal devotee who is always at the Lord's feet, whose name, in fact, is synonymous with the Lord's grace. As we saw in chapter 2, the close connection between Nammāḻvār and divine grace is articulated by a ritual seen in Śrīvaiṣṇava temples and shrines. The silver crown, which is engraved with the feet of the Lord and which is placed on the head of every devotee, is called Śaṭhāri, a name of Nammāḻvār. The first written reference to this ritual, significantly enough, is in Piḷḷāṉ's commentary.[10]

Piḷḷāṉ wrote his commentary in *maṇipravāḷa*, a new hybrid language of communication used in Śrīvaiṣṇava circles. The Tamil of Nammāḻvār was translated and explained in a new "situational language." *Maṇipravāḷa* means "gems and corals" or "pearls and corals" and refers to a combination of Sanskrit and Tamil. Unlike other forms of *maṇipravāḷa*,[11] the Śrīvaiṣṇava variety always retained Tamil grammar and endings, though the sentences were heavily interspersed with Sanskrit words. The language of the commentary itself gave the message effectively, proclaiming the equivalency of the Sanskrit and Tamil languages and literatures. This style of communicating—in speech and writing—flourishes even today in the Śrīvaiṣṇava community.

Why was the commentary committed to writing in the late eleventh century C.E.? The oral commentarial tradition must have become popular by the time of Yāmuna (ca. 10th C.E.) who was Rāmānuja's teacher's teacher. His opinions have been preserved in the longer written commentaries on the Tiruvāymoḻi.[12] We may speculate about the reasons why Rāmānuja permitted the writing of the first commentary. It is possible that Rāmānuja wanted the opinions of the earlier *ācāryas* to be preserved for posterity, and committing the texts to writing ensured that they would not be forgotten. He may have also believed that the comments and opinions of earlier *ācāryas* would add to the flavor of the community's understanding of the poems. The poems were meant to be relished, enjoyed, and experienced; hearing the anecdotes and earlier interpretations (some of which were at variance with one another) would encourage the listeners to participate in the meaning of the poems without feeling confined to hold onto the interpretation they had just heard.

According to *The Splendor,* there had been an earlier incident in Rāmānuja's life which, we believe, may have led to his decision to record the commentary. Apparently, while learning the meaning of the Tiruvāymoḻi from Tirumālai Āṇṭāṉ, Rāmānuja disagreed with his teacher's interpretations of several verses and offered alternate explanations. After Rāmānuja offered a different interpretation for Tiruvāymoḻi 2.3.4 Āṇṭāṉ ceased his instruction, saying that these were mischievous explanations, which he had not heard from *his* teacher, Yāmuna.[13] The stalemate was resolved by another disciple of Yāmuna, Tirukkōṭṭiyūr Nampi, who reconciled Āṇṭāṉ and Rāmānuja by proclaiming that he had heard the alternate interpretation from Yāmuna. What is interesting to note is that Rāmānuja's position had to be vindicated by another teacher's recollection of Yāmuna's commentary; there was no text with which to check it.

The Splendor goes on to say that at a later time Tirumālai Āṇṭāṉ again hesitated at a certain interpretation, but Rāmānuja said that he was a disciple of Yāmuna, like the legendary Ekalavya was a disciple of Droṇa, a student who learned from a master in spirit, without actually ever being in his presence.[14] So, even when there was no witness to attest that Rāmānuja's opinion had been stated earlier by Yāmuna, the community assumed that whatever Rāmānuja said would have been said by or at least permitted by Yāmuna. *The Splendor*'s account of Rāmānuja's learning the Tiruvāymoḻi gives us a glimpse of the transmission of the poem, and at this stage it still seems to have been on the model of a "private tuition" and not a public oration to a Śrīvaiṣṇava audience. The commentarial tradition certainly did become that in later years, and we hear of large audiences listening to the *ācāryas'* exposition of the Tamil poems.[15]

Rāmānuja's permission to allow the commentary to be written, therefore, may have stemmed from his desire to preserve all possible alternate opinions in writing, so that later generations may know that these opinions, and others, *within reason,* were admissible. Similarly, by not writing the commentary himself, Rāmānuja made sure that the line of commentaries on these hymns which were meant to be "experienced" and enjoyed by all would keep growing. Rāmānuja's comments were considered authoritative and would have been held to be the final word on a topic, and it seems probable that the teacher wanted to encourage a chain of commentaries, rather than establish one set of "correct" interpretations. The Tiruvāymoḻi has inspired a long line of commentaries in which the community relives and reexperiences the emotions of the *āḻvārs.* Sanskrit literature, on the other hand, is perceived as embodying one truth for all time: following Rāmānuja's commentary on the Bhagavad Gītā and the *Brahma Sūtras,* no Śrīvaiṣṇava has written another commentary on them.[16] Usually, commentaries preserved the correct interpretations and the right opinions on a text; interestingly enough, the commentaries on the Tiruvāymoḻi preserve a diversity of opinions. It is important to note, however, that the diversity of the opinions did not at any time involve important theological issues pertaining to the supremacy of Viṣṇu, his auspicious nature, and other doctrines cardinal to the community but, instead, usually reflected the particular flavor of each teacher's enjoyment of the poem.

Despite the writing of the commentaries, it seems clear that the community was and remains one in which oral comment was primary. It is clear that in the past not too many people had access to the written commentaries, and interested disciples were always taught the commentary orally. The function of the written commentaries, therefore, was probably to serve as a teacher's guide, inspiring new oral commentaries. The written commentaries seem to have served not so much as firm boundary fences but as elastic parameters.

THE QUESTION OF AUTHORITY

In the thirteenth century the community believed that the Tiruvāymoḻi contained sacred knowledge and that only "worthy" souls could receive such instruction, in the form of a commentary. A thirteenth-century commentary gives this process of oral transmission a name; it is called the way of individual instruction (*orāṇ-vaḻi*).[17] In keeping a close watch on *who* received this information, the community affirmed that, while members of all castes and both sexes could hear the commentaries on the Tiruvāymoḻi—and thus the belief that the poem is meant for *all* people—a teacher could withhold instruction depending on his perception of the disciple's worthiness. Even the scribe who copied the commentary had to prove himself worthy of the knowledge he had to record: the story of Nañjīyar (a late-twelfth-century teacher) and his scribe-disciple Nampiḷḷai is instructive. This story, as translated here, is recorded in *The Splendor:*

> Nañjīyar, by the grace of [his teacher] Bhaṭṭar composed a commentary on the Tiruvāymoḻi. The commentary was the size of the *Śrī Bhāṣya* [Rāmānuja's Sanskrit commentary on the *Brahma Sūtras*]. Holding the manuscript,[18] he asked . . . Is there anyone who can write this [neatly]? His disciples answered "Nampūr Varadarājaṉ from the south bank comes here often; he writes well."
>
> Nañjīyar invited Varadarājaṉ and asked him to write a syllable. . . . Seeing it, [Nañjīyar] thought, "His writing is as beautiful as a pearl, but still, this is a commentary on the Tiruvāymoḻi and [now] it is to be written by a stranger. How can I ask him to write it just because his name is sacred? [Varadarājaṉ is a name of Viṣṇu.] This commentary ought to be written by a specially knowledgeable person." While he was skeptical [about the scribe's worthiness], Varadarājaṉ, understanding Nañjīyar's mind, said, "Can you not guide me, your servant, and make me acceptable to your heart?" Nañjīyar was overjoyed [at the scribe's humility and perceptiveness] and immediately adopted him [as a disciple], graciously initiated him with the five-fold sacrament [as befits] one who had submitted himself to God, and taught him the

> scriptures. . . . He taught the *Nine Thousand-paṭi* commentary [on the Tiruvāymoḻi] once, fully, to Varadarājan̲ and said, "Write it thus, without deviating from it." He delivered the manuscript to Varadarājan̲'s hands. . . .
>
> When Varadarājan̲ was crossing the Kāveri river, he came to a place where he had to swim for a short distance. He tied the manuscript to his head but as he swam, a wave hit him and swept the book (*grantham*) away. When Varadarājan̲ came to the other bank, he was devastated: "The manuscript is gone! What shall I do?" He procured blank palm leaves that were joined together for writing and wrote down well the meaning that Nañjīyar had graciously [revealed] to him. Because he was a Tamil scholar . . . in some places he brought out a special meaning by using felicitous and majestic words. Having written [the commentary] he gave it to Nañjīyar, who opened up the sacred text and read it. He saw that though his opinions were given, the words were particularly fitting in several places and special meanings had been given. His heart was elated; looking at Varadarājan̲, he said, "This is excellent—but how did it come about?" Varadarājan̲ was frightened and remained silent. Nañjīyar reassured him and said, "Speak the truth!" Varadarājan̲ told him [what had happened] . . . and concluded "and so . . . the waves made your book sink. I wrote this because you had gone through the whole [text] with me once."
>
> Overjoyed, Nañjīyar . . . realizing his [scribe's] wisdom, embraced him and said "You are our son. . . ." Since Nañjīyar had called him "our son" (*nam piḷḷai*), Varadarājan̲ was called Nampiḷḷai after that day.[19]

It is clear from the first part of the story that Nañjīyar believed his scribe should understand the material and be initiated to the proper study of the text prior to his reading it and copying it. Reading a commentary on the Tiruvāymoḻi (in the process of copying it) was obviously not the correct way of receiving salvific knowledge; the transmission of such knowledge had to be through *oral discourse.*[20] Because the matter discussed was of utmost importance, the teacher had to ensure that the pupils understood the verses, and, as in all oral utterances, meaning was negotiated in the discursive process. In oral discourse the commentator interpreted himself as he proceeded, shaping his commentary to fit the audience on hand.[21] The second part of the story shows that Nañjīyar was not upset with his scribe upstaging him and highlighting certain meanings; rather, the student's innovation was rewarded.[22]

In the past students listening to this comment wrote it out, with (and, occasionally, without) the teacher's permission. *The Splendor* narrates a story connected with Nampiḷḷai's (Varadarājan̲'s) life. When he became the next teacher, succeeding Nañjīyar, he gave several oral commentaries on the Tiruvāymoḻi. With his permission one of his students, Periyavāccān̲ Piḷḷai, wrote a commentary that was equivalent in length to the Rāmāyaṇa.[23] This commentary was apparently based on the oral discourses that Nampiḷḷai gave to his students. Another disciple, Vaṭakku Tiruvīti Piḷḷai, is said to have heard the commentary during the day and wrote it out at night, without telling his teacher. Vaṭakku Tiruvīti Piḷḷai gave it to his teacher, Nampiḷḷai, who read it and was happy with it but said that, since the commentary had been written without his permission, it could not be recognized as an authorized work. Nampiḷḷai took the original and locked it away. A disciple who heard about this incident prayed to the Lord that the commentary should be brought to light, and, according to *The Splendor,* the Lord at Srirangam instructed Nampiḷḷai to *teach* from the new commentary of his disciple. Nampiḷḷai obeyed the Lord, and that version became the most famous of all the Tiruvāymoḻi commentaries.[24]

A footnote has to be added to this emphasis on oral commentary and strict control over what was committed to writing. While the process of orally transmitting commentary from teacher to disciple still continues within the community, it is obvious that there has been a major change in attitude in the twentieth century. This is evident in the decision to publish and bring to public attention all the classical medieval commentaries as well as the modern ones. For the first time in Śrīvaiṣṇava history these sacred matters (*bhagavad viṣayam*) are available (for reading, at any rate) to anyone who chooses to buy the texts. The writing of a commentary on a sacred text and its publication, with the knowledge that it may well be read by "outsiders" without an authorized person to interpret it, is a phenomenon we encounter in the twentieth century and represents a distinct break from earlier days. There has been no self-conscious statement made about this change in attitude, and the impact of non-Śrīvaiṣṇavas commenting on sacred matters is an issue still to be assessed.

Despite the conscious decision to *write* commentaries, the Śrīvaiṣṇava tradition has had a strong oral base and maintains that oral interpretation is the only way of communicating a commentary if the purpose is to obtain salvific knowledge. Both oral and written commentary share certain features: in each there is a desire to proclaim the equality of both Tamil and Sanskrit Vedas; there is an emphasis on cardinal doctrinal positions that have defined the Śrīvaiṣṇava community's identity; and, by the incorporation of large stretches of Rāmānuja's words in the commentary, there is an effort to show correspondence between the Tiruvāymoḻi and Rāmānuja's philosophy. The language used in both written and oral commentary is *maṇipravāḷa,* and here the medium itself was the message: a harmonious combination of Tamil and Sanskrit.

CASTING LIGHT UPON THE SOUNDS OF TAMIL REVELATION

There is only one woman who is known to have written a commentary on the Tiruvāymoḻi, but this is rather different in style from the earlier commentaries. This commentary was written by Tirukkōnēri Dāsyai, and for centuries it has been marginalized by the Śrīvaiṣṇava community.[25] Entitled "The Garland of Words" (*Tiruvāymoḻi Vācakamālai*), the commentary focuses on only a hundred verses of the Tiruvāymoḻi; these are considered to be the "fragrant blossoms" and are woven into a verbal commentary. The author sees the entire poem as elucidating the meaning of the very first verse, and so she weaves phrases from the first verse into the comments on the later ones. Like a flower garland in south India, which is held together with twinings of fragrant herbs and silver threads, she weaves the first verse around the poem, holding it together. She is also the only commentator to illustrate her work with drawings, pictorially depicting important themes of the poem.

Each time that Dāsyai uses the words of the first verse to interpret the meanings of the later verses she teases out a new meaning, gives a different nuance, offering the reader a breathtaking kaleidoscope of linked images and pictures. The word *radiant,* for example, is used as an adjective for the Lord's feet in the first verse; in subsequent verses the author uses the word to indicate the Lord's glory, which is like the "brilliance" of a million suns, or she refers to the "glow" of human devotion, the "fire" of divine passion, a "beacon" of divine grace, the "search light" of human quest, and so on. While her delight in this word play makes her commentary unique, it is important to note that the techniques of using a word or phrase and interpreting it in dozens of ways is an integral part of singing and dancing in the Indian tradition. A singer may repeat a phrase from the Tiruvāymoḻi several times, exploring the nuances of a raga; a dancer may interpret a phrase in many ways, each time bringing new associations to the original meaning. Dāsyai seems to have applied a performing art technique to a verbal commentary; thus, her "Garland of Words" links the performances to verbal commentaries. The colophon at the end of her text says clearly that she finished writing it in the Tamil month of Mārkaḻi. It is in this month that the Festival of Recitation, which includes the performance of the Sacred Utterance, takes place, and it seems clear that the verbal commentary was being written as the author was witnessing the performative ones.[26]

THE COMMENTARIAL AGENDA

Commentaries on the Tiruvāymoḻi were given to groups of students, and, in the process of commenting, the teacher drew from the earlier ones he had studied but paraphrased them in his own words. Generally, commentaries were written or recorded after a teacher had spoken about a particular verse several times. Both oral and written commentaries share common features, and here I shall focus on some of these similarities, looking for my examples to the first commentary on the Tiruvāymoḻi written by Piḷḷāṉ.

The commentarial tradition allows for the *elaboration of doctrine* and the strengthening of the notion of the Dual Vedānta. The language of the Tiruvāymoḻi itself can be understood easily; the concept that has to be communicated to the audience is something that was already present in Nāthamuni's incorporation of the hymn in liturgy—that this poem was equivalent to the Sanskrit Veda. One of the principal tasks of the commentarial tradition seems to have been the establishment of this concept. The commentaries are directed to an audience that is familiar with both the Sanskrit Vedas and Tamil verses. The lengthiest comments occur either when there are issues of doctrinal importance to be proclaimed or when there are parallels in Sanskrit literature; we see important examples in Piḷḷāṉ's comments on Tiruvāymoḻi 1.1.7 and 4.10.1.

The commentator perceives these verses as proclaiming: (1) the relationship between Viṣṇu and the universe as analogous to the relationship between a human soul and the physical body, and (2) the supremacy of Viṣṇu. Here, there are long lists of quotations from Sanskrit Vedas and later literature; the written commentary records and preserves these lists of quotations, thus reiterating the notion of the Dual Vedānta.

There is also extensive *incorporation of Rāmānuja's formulaic phrases* and lines in almost all the long commentaries. This is particularly seen in Piḷḷāṉ's commentary; reading it, one gets the distinct impression that here is a disciple who has listened to his teacher for many years and one who is eager to show that his commentary is close in spirit to his master's thought. He uses formulaic phrases, especially those describing qualities, auspiciousness, and purity of the Lord, in his paraphrase and condenses Rāmānuja's lengthy discourses into brief theological platforms. In the following example, the commentary on the first verse of the Tiruvāymoḻi, phrases used both by Rāmānuja and Piḷḷāṉ are given in italics, and details are given in the notes:

1.1.1

Who is he
who has the highest good
　　cutting down all other heights,
who is he
who bestows wisdom and love,
　　slashing ignorance,
who is he
who commands the tireless[27] immortals?

worship his radiant feet
　　that quell all sorrow,

and rise,
O mind.

Piḷḷāṉ's *Six Thousand-paṭi* commentary:

The *āḻvār* with his holy soul "experiences" the supreme person as he really is. This is the supreme person who has *transcendent, extraordinary, divine ornaments, weapons, consorts and attendants*[28] and *whose sports is the creation, development, etc. of this universe.*[29] The *āḻvār* speaks as he experiences the love that arises from his being

> with the Lord. [The *āl̲vār* says], "[The Lord] is wholly opposed to all fault, and [is characterized] by the statement 'He who has the bliss a thousand times that of human beings (*Taittirīya Upaniṣad* 2.8.1).' [The Lord] is an immense ocean of *infinite bliss that is multiplied a thousand fold*[30] and other countless *auspicious attributes*.[31] He who has this bliss and other auspicious attributes, further has that great quality, like gold having a fragrance, of making himself known to me, without reason, such that there is not even a trace ("*whiff*") *of ignorance*.[32] [He arouses in] me unsurpassed *bhakti* toward his sacred feet. This Lord who has all auspicious attributes shows his generosity to Śeṣa, Garuḍa, and other innumerable divine beings who are naturally and wholly without fault and *who have unflickering wisdom*.[33] His flowerlike feet have the inherent nature of dispelling all sorrows of his devotees. Serve these feet at all places, times, and conditions [as befits] a servant and live." Thus speaks [the *āl̲vār*] to his holy soul.

In oral discourses also one frequently encounters the incorporation of formulaic phrases seen in the writings of Rāmānuja. In 1988 I recorded a discourse on the life of Nammāl̲vār. The orator, in the first five minutes of discourse, used thirteen Sanskrit phrases seen frequently in Rāmānuja's writings and ten from the Tamil poems of the *āl̲vārs*.[34]

Piḷḷān̲ and later commentators *elucidated the verses with categories not intrinsic to the poems* but which were borrowed from Sanskrit literature. Such extrinsic categories included *bhakti yoga,* "the Way" (*upāya*), and "mediator" (*puruṣakāra*). Where the poem merely hints at a topic, the commentators use formulaic phrases from Sanskrit to explain the idea. Thus, if the poet mentions Śrī (the consort of Viṣṇu) in the verse, the commentators take it as a signal for "divine intercession," as the following example makes clear:

Tiruvāymol̲i 6.10.10

> O [Lord] on whose breast
> resides the lady of the flower who says:
> "I cannot move away from him even for a second!"

Piḷḷān̲'s *Six Thousand-paṭi* commentary:

> . . . I, your servant, who am without refuge, without any other goal, having the divine Mother *as the mediator,* took refuge at your sacred feet. . . .[35]

A mere mention of Śrī is interpreted as mediator, and her position as one who intercedes between human being and God is seen to be indicated by this verse. Like Piḷḷāṉ, later commentators also take this verse to be one in which the poet formally seeks refuge from the Lord.

Variations in opinion and particular incidents connecting the verses with the earlier teachers are narrated to make special points. *The Thirty-six Thousand-paṭi,* the thirteenth-century commentary on the Tiruvāymoḻi, records many instances of earlier conversations and discussions on the meaning of a certain word or phrase.

> Empār [Rāmānuja's cousin] would say "The Lord of all, has three kinds of souls as his servants. . . . The liberated souls and the *eternally* liberated ones[36] are blissful and make [the Lord] happy; the bound souls are not blissful, but still make him happy. All [categories of souls form] part of his play. Piḷḷai Tirunaṟaiyūr Araiyar asked Empār: Why should [Nammāḻvār] who has obtained "wisdom and love" (Tiruvāymoḻi 1.1.1) petition "take me as yours," instead of saying "[the Lord] will do as he pleases"? Empār replied: "Listen; It is like Śrī saying 'I cannot move away from him even for a second' (Tiruvāymoḻi 6.10.10), when in fact, she *never* parts from him. She is never *re*united with him, because she always resides on his breast. Similarly the *āḻvār* is praying for the pleasure of the goal."[37]

In this conversation Empār answers a subtle theological question posed by Araiyar: Why is the *āḻvār* actively *asking* the Lord to do something instead of calmly waiting for the Lord's will to be done? Empār defuses the question by using the analogy of Śrī's inseparability with the Lord, thus implying that the *āḻvār*'s request is almost a rhetorical one.[38]

Improvisation is allowed but only with the usage of standard phrases and techniques. Sometimes, in earlier commentaries, two or more sequential explanations are given, as in the following example. This is a translation from Periyavāccāṉ Piḷḷai's *Twenty-four Thousand-paṭi* commentary on the Tiruvāymoḻi and is his introduction to 2.10:

> Āḷavantār (Yāmuna) would say: [Nammāḻvār] takes refuge with the sacred hill to obtain the goal that he sought in the verse "My father's house . . ." (Tiruvāymoḻi 2.9.1). While that [explanation] exists, Emperumāṉār [i.e., Rāmānuja] would say, "The goal desired earlier would have been obtained in heaven when his body [dies]. But the *āḻvār* does not think [like us]; in his fervor, he says [he

> wants the goal] "quickly" (Tiruvāymoḻi 2.9.1) and "without losing time . . ." (Tiruvāymoḻi 2.9.2). He wishes to experience the [supreme goal] with his earthly body itself.

Here the commentator first records the interpretation of Yāmuna, who had provided the context for Tiruvāymoḻi 2.10. But the later teacher, Rāmānuja, had provided further exegesis, saying that in the following set of verses Nammāḻvār wants to experience the supreme goal in his earthly body and not wait for heaven. Rāmānuja says that in the previous set of verses the poet had craved immediate fulfillment for his desires, and this seems to be achieved now. Rāmānuja was only expanding Yāmuna's line of thinking by giving further reasons (from the poetry itself) about why Nammāḻvār said the ten verses that are being introduced. The commentator who wrote this introduction probably heard these contextual explanations orally from his teacher, Nampiḷḷai, and used the material from earlier oral tradition as part of his own written introduction.

In this example, too, another feature of a commentary is also clearly visible: the commentator tries to connect the verses into a coherent framework and to link sets of poems. He attempts to provide connections that may not be evident in the poem itself.

In oral commentaries today, while the commentator may be familiar with details of interpretation for all the verses, because of time constraints, and to hold audience interest, he may pause only at those words or lines that he thinks are striking and introduce some new examples to make the poem seem relevant. In a sense, therefore, the stages of composition and transmission of the commentary have been collapsed to one event.[39]

In the early commentaries *normative ideas for the ideal Śrīvaiṣṇava* and the ideal community were forcibly stated. In his comment on Tiruvāymoḻi 3.5.4, for example, Piḷḷāṉ says:

> He is Śrīdhara ("The supporter of Śrī"); he is so called, because to unite with the Lady Nappiṉṉai, he subjugated the seven bulls. His passion caused his red lips to glow.
>
> What is the use of people being born amidst Śrīvaiṣṇavas if they do not become excited by the wondrous love that is born out of thinking of the [Lord's] passion [for Nappiṉṉai]? . . .

A Śrīvaiṣṇava is exhorted to visibly show his or her fervor, his or her joy, in contemplating the Lord's qualities. In a later comment Piḷḷāṉ addresses another issue that he and later commentators believe to be very important: a Śrīvaiṣṇava is told to be the servant of other Śrīvaiṣṇavas:

> This set of ten verses says that the supreme goal is to be the slave of any Śrīvaiṣṇava, *whosoever* he may be, if that Śrīvaiṣṇava has been conquered by and is a slave of the Lord's innumerable qualities. . . . For all those who learn this set of verses, all obstacles that may lie in their path to be a slave (*śeṣa*) of the Lord's devotees will vanish. (*Piḷḷāṉ's Six Thousand-paṭi* 3.7.11)

The *whosoever* is an important caution, a direct statement warning one not to discriminate on the basis of caste. An ideal Śrīvaiṣṇava is to be a servant of all other devotees of Viṣṇu, not withstanding caste, social, or financial status.

The history of interpretation, both oral and written, for this sacred poem in the Hindu tradition still continues. Nammāḻvār, like the poets described by Socrates in Plato's dialogue the *Ion,* is himself a "messenger of the gods."[40] Like Hermes, this poet is a "go-between" from God to human being in the Śrīvaiṣṇava community; his enunciation of the poem, his "simply saying . . . or proclaiming is an important act of 'interpretation.' "[41] Nammāḻvār is thus an interpreter in a primary sense, for before him the words were not yet said. Nammāḻvār asserts in one memorable verse that the Lord speaks through him; in this sense the poem is taken to be revelation. For the Śrīvaiṣṇava the Tiruvāymoḻi, then, is an interpretation of the ultimate unspoken truth.

The commentator who recites these words and then elucidates them in Sanskrit and Tamil is a part of the long interpretive tradition that goes back to Nammāḻvār. From Nammāḻvār to the twentieth-century commentator each tries to express the truth, *utter* it as he or she *sees* it. From their insight words are articulated, and the process of explanation, of making relevant in an understandable language, is set in motion. Seeing the truth and orally expressing it become two interconnected parts of the interpretive process. This uttered word, this spoken word, empowers the written word of the commentator. The written commentaries in tandem with the oral discourses have fostered the commentarial tradition for several centuries, but, within the Śrīvaiṣṇava community at least, the explanation of the written forms has not displaced the oral nature of the hermeneutical process.

8 RECREATING HEAVEN ON EARTH

Ritual and Performative Commentaries on the Tiruvāymoḻi

The name of the most important temple town of the Śrīvaiṣṇava community, Srirangam, translates as "sacred stage" or "sacred arena." But, unlike the dynamic Śiva, who is the dancer in the city of Chidambaram, here the manifestation of Viṣṇu, who is known as Ranga-natha (Lord of the stage), reposes in tranquility on his serpent couch. He is not the performer but, rather, the audience, entertained by the recitation and the dance of human beings. Srirangam, during the Festival of Recitation, becomes the cosmic stage, and here Nammāḻvār's passion and ascent to heaven are enacted annually. Through song and dance this place is affirmed to be *bhūloka vaikuṇṭha,* or heaven on earth.

Śrīvaiṣṇava hagiographical literature also describes Srirangam as heaven on earth. According to *The Splendor,* when Rāmānuja entered Srirangam and was greeted by members of the Śrīvaiṣṇava community it seemed as though the servants of the Lord in heaven were welcoming a liberated soul to heaven.[1] The mythical portrayal of heaven (*vaikuṇṭha*) seems similar to the physical description of Srirangam: an island garlanded by a river. Srirangam, which is near the town of Tiruchirapalli, is circled by the Kaveri and Kolladam rivers, and it is said to resemble *vaikuṇṭha,* or heaven, circled by the Virajā River. The rivers form clear boundary markers—separating earth from heaven, the outside world from the realm of the Śrīvaiṣṇava community. On the days of the Festival of Recitation one is in a liminal state, for only during those ten days are the northern gates of the temple, known as the "gates of heaven," opened, and the distinction between the earth and heaven is said to be removed; heaven and earth become contiguous with each other. Heaven comes to earth; the Lord, who cannot be grasped or perceived by the senses, is seen by all; and the unheard sound resonates through the articulation of the Tamil Veda. Revelation is simultaneously visual and aural, as the devotees see the Lord enshrined in the Hall of the Thousand Pillars and hear the words of the Tiruvāymoḻi. At the end of the ritual the Lord grants salvation to Nammāḻvār; at the end of the sacred time, when heaven has descended to earth, Nammāḻvār, the human being, ascends to heaven.[2]

The celebration of the Lord's splendor and glory, along with his close relationship to his devotees, is seen in the rituals of the Śrīvaiṣṇava Temple. The Festival of Recitation on the "sacred stage" is such a celebration of the Lord's glory, as made manifest in the words that he himself spoke (as the Śrīvaiṣṇava commentators write) through his devotee Nammāḻvār.

THE FESTIVAL OF RECITATION

In the eleventh century C.E. the Śrīvaiṣṇava community introduced the Tiruvāymoḻi into the temple and home liturgies and began to comment on it—orally at first, and through the performing arts, then later in writing. A full recitation with verbal and performative commentaries is held during the Adhyayana Utsava, the annual Festival of Recitation. These ritual contexts comment upon the Tiruvāymoḻi and inform us about the poem and the community—perhaps more so than even a verbal commentary. *The Splendor* tells us that Nāthamuni introduced the Tiruvāymoḻi and other Tamil hymns into home and temple liturgies and initiated an annual Festival of Recitation, which lasted twenty-one days. The whole festival is one of rejoicing and splendor, celebrating the quest of Nammāḻvār, and every devotee, for union with the Lord.

The Festival of Recitation takes place in the month of Mārkaḻi (15 Dec.–13 Jan.) in all Śrīvaiṣṇava temples—or, at least, as many as can afford it. Over twenty-one days the 4,000 verses composed by the *āḻvārs* are recited. During the first ten mornings the first 2,000 verses of the *āḻvārs* are recited and explained with oral and performative commentaries. This is followed by ten nights during which the focus is on the 1,102 verses of the Tiruvāymoḻi. (The Tiruvāymoḻi is usually counted as the fourth thousand in the corpus of hymns composed by the *āḻvārs*.)

On the twenty-first day there is a fast-paced recitation of 1,000 verses of the *iyaṟpā* section (the third thousand) of the Tamil hymns. The program for twenty-one days starting with the new moon includes: (1) the recitation of poems, (2) processions of the festival image through the streets, (3) the dressing up of the festival image in various costumes,[3] (4) enactment of particular episodes from the *āḻvār* poetry or the epics by special actors called *araiyars* in Srirangam, Srivilliputtur, and Alvar Tirunagari,[4] and (5) enactment of particular verses from the *āḻvār* poetry. On each day the processional image of the Lord used for celebrations (*utsava mūrti*) is dressed up in special costumes, and Viṣṇu is worshipped in his other manifestations.

It seems fairly obvious that the Tiruvāymoḻi gets the most time during the festivities (about one thousand verses over ten days, while the other three thousand are compressed into eleven days). According to one traditional source, the whole festival was started by Tirumaṅkai Āḻvār just to declare that the Tiruvāymoḻi was a Veda.[5]

The crowds pay special attention to attires of the Lord, and a special favorite with the pilgrims is the Lord dressed as a woman, an enchantress, or Mohini; "truly," they say, "tonight, the Lord is more beautiful than the Goddess (Śrī) herself." It is also possible that this festival may reflect one of the earliest instances of ritual enactment of episodes from the epics in the temple context. (As early as the fourth-century Tamil epic *Cilappatikāram,* the *rās līlā* was enacted by young girls, but this was not in a temple context.) Unlike in northern India, where the enactments of the epics are called *līlā* (play), here they are part of the larger festival, or "*utsava*." The enactment of particular verses by Nammāḻvār or myths that are alluded to in the Tiruvāymoḻi are called *araiyar cēvai,* that is, "service (*cēvai;* Sanskrit: *sevā*) by the *araiyar*."[6] The recitation and enactment of the verses is considered by devotees as a service to God and the community. While *līlā* in the Śrīvaiṣṇava context indicates God's celebration of his own glory, *sevā,* or *cēvai,* is the human celebration of God's dominion.

The recitation of the Tiruvāymoḻi begins formally on the *ekādaśi* day, that is, the eleventh day after the new moon of Mārkaḻi. In Srirangam preparations for this ritual are actually started a full month in advance, in the Tamil month of Kārtikai (15 Nov.–14 Dec.). During this month a "divine proclamation" (words spoken by one of the temple priests) is issued to the temple scribe—who is also the accountant[7]—

and he is asked to write an invitation, which is issued to Nammāḻvār. The invitation is supposed to be announced by the Lord through the voice of a priest:

> It is the month of Kārtikai, and as we are seated in the Pavilion of the Handsome Bridegroom, on the Cera Pandyan throne, above the couch of Harihararāya and below the canopy of pearls, listening to the poems of Tirumaṅkai Āḻvār, the chief of the temple servants, and other Vaiṣṇavas have come, and beseeched us to honor Nammāḻvār once again. Hence, we are sending the cloak that I have worn, sandalwood fragrance, and flower garlands [as marks of my favor] to Nammāḻvār, through my emissary.
>
> *Write* it! *Read* it aloud! Read it again!

Notice the importance on writing and reading the invitation aloud. This invitation is tied to the head of the "chief of the temple servants" and in earlier days was sent to Nammāḻvār's birthplace, Alvar Tirunagari. The poet (in his image form) was formally invited to come to Srirangam and witness the performance of the Tiruvāymoḻi. According to the Chronicles of the Srirangam Temple, the image of Nammāḻvār was brought to Srirangam from Alvar Tirunagari for this festival until the time of Rāmānuja. Apparently, bad weather prevented it one year, and after that time the local Nammāḻvār image in the Srirangam Temple has been used for the festivities.

After this day in the month of Kārtikai, the regular schedule of recitation (discussed in chap. 4) is suspended and is not resumed until the end of the Festival of Recitation. The Festival of Recitation begins on the day of the new moon in the month of Mārkaḻi. For the first ten mornings two thousand hymns of the *āḻvārs* are recited by the *araiyars*, and selected verses are also enacted. The Tiruvāymoḻi recitation begins on the eleventh day (*ekādaśi*) after the new moon; it is on this day that the gates of heaven will be open. On this eleventh day, during the bright half of the moon in Mārkaḻi, the heaviest crowds of the year are expected at the Srirangam and most other Śrīvaiṣṇava temples. In recent years there has been extensive television coverage of the moment when the Lord passes through the gates of heaven. Beginning on this day, the northern doors of the Srirangam Temple, the gates of heaven (*vaikuṇṭha vācal* or *paramapada vācal*), are opened, just prior to the recitation of the Tiruvāymoḻi. These doors are kept closed for the rest of the year and kept open only during the ten days of Tiruvāymoḻi recitation and interpretation; for these ten days heaven is contiguous with earth.

In Srirangam, for the ten nights of the festival, the processional image of Viṣṇu is brought through the gates of heaven, taken to the temple tank and then brought to the Hall of a Thousand Pillars.[8] In the Parthasarathi Temple at Triplicane, Madras, the Lord and Nammāḻvār are taken in a procession around the temple, with Nammāḻvār going in front. The image of Nammāḻvār faces the Lord, and the priests carrying the palanquin on which Nammāḻvār is borne go in front of the Lord, but it seems as though Nammāḻvār is walking backward. The Lord, it is said, loves Nammāḻvār so much that even during the procession he cannot bear not to see his devotee's face. The street processions with the deity and Nammāḻvār occur before the recitation of the poem. The priests in the Triplicane Temple usually recite a Sanskrit poem called "Upadeśaratnamālai" written by Maṇavāḷa Māmuṉi in the fourteenth century C.E. The Tiruvāymoḻi is never recited outside the temple limits; because it is the Veda, it is sacred and must be recited with proper attention. In the Triplicane Temple, after the procession, the two images are brought into the temple and kept in a large hall, which, unlike Srirangam, does not have a thousand pillars.

In Srirangam the festival image of the Lord is called "the handsome bridegroom" (*aḻakiya maṇavāḷaṉ*). During the ten days that the recitation of the Tiruvāymoḻi takes place, he goes in a procession to the Hall of a Thousand Pillars; this generally begins around noon. A few minutes before noon there is an *aruḷappāṭu* (commandment or summons) to the *śrī pāda thānkis* (bearers of the sacred feet), the name given to the group of palanquin bearers. They reply, "Nāyantē; nāyantē" (At your call), put on their turbans, with right hands covering their mouths respectfully, a picture of total humility, and go in a single file into the closed shrine. At noon sharp the doors to the main shrine are flung open. (Local residents of Srirangam never tired of telling me how everything takes place at the correct time.) This Lord is a *king* (Raṅga-rāja), and punctuality is important in the royal court.

At noon, when the doors open, the bearers emerge with the Lord on a palanquin. A gold-plated palanquin called *tōḷukku iniyāṉ* (that which is sweet to the shoulders) is used for the trip to the Hall of a Thousand Pillars and a silver-plated palanquin for the trip back at night. The Lord is covered with different jewels and a fancy new head covering each day, and the local people could always identify the special names given to the clothes he was wearing that day. When the Lord emerges from the main shrine his jewels are covered with a shawl and are not visible. The palanquin bearers together walk like a lion (*simha gati*) and stride out in majesty. They make a swift right turn, move down the steps, and go around the main shrine. The crowds follow the handsome bridegroom as he takes his two-hour journey to the thousand-pillared hall. This hall is only a five to ten–minute walk away under normal circumstances, but it takes the procession a full two hours to reach it, because there are frequent stops under flower canopies. The Lord's procession is led by a young man wielding a whip; he slashes it on the ground every now and then to make way for the Lord, shouting, "*Echarikkai*" (Warning! or Caution!). The *bhaṭṭars* (priests) traveling with the procession recite a Tamil poem composed by Piḷḷai Perumāḷ Aiyaṅkār in the fourteenth century. This is a poem that has not been published but one that has been passed on by oral tradition.

After circling the main shrine the Lord comes out to the third enclosure of the temple. He makes a semicircle around the main shrine and stops under a stone pavilion. It is here that the Virajā River (which in Hindu mythology encircles heaven) is supposed to flow underground. The Lord stops here for a few minutes and hears opening lines from the Sanskrit Vedas. While the entire celebration is called Festival of Recitation, and the Sanskrit word *adhyayana,* "recitation," is generally used for the study of the Sanskrit Vedas, there is very little recitation from the Sanskrit Vedas which actually takes place. It is possible that in earlier days there may have been more elaborate recitation of the Sanskrit scriptures, but it now lasts barely a few minutes. The reciters of the Sanskrit Vedas are honored in the place where the Virajā River is said to flow underground in Srirangam. As we noted in chapter 3, in the Parthasarathi Temple at Triplicane, Madras, at times there have been very few reciters of the Sanskrit Vedas, and so people from other cities have been invited to join the celebrations.

The crowds following the Lord in Srirangam now stay back. The priests carry the Lord a few yards and come to a gateway. Beyond this gateway is a threshold, and then comes the *paramapada vācal* (gates of heaven), which are closed. The Lord enters the first gateway, and this is closed as soon as he enters the threshold; the Lord is locked between two gateways for a few minutes. Here the priests remove the shawl surrounding the Lord, and he emerges, radiant in his jewels. The doors are flung open, and the Lord passes through the gates of heaven. The Lord's jewels are hidden under a thin shawl when he emerges from the main shrine, and it is only as he passes through the gates of heaven that the shawl is removed and the Lord is seen in his radiant splendor. The allegorical explanation given to me was this: the Lord is like a human soul on his/her way to heaven; after having bathed in the river Virajā the soul's radiance is revealed.

The gates of heaven are about forty feet high. The threshold is decorated with paintings of the Lord and Nammāḻvār. After passing through this gateway the Lord turns right (east), goes under several flower canopies, by the side of the "lotus lake of the moon" (*Candra Puṣkarini*), turns right (south), going parallel to the thousand-pillared hall. He passes in front of the shrine of the Lord of heaven (Paramapada Nāthar) and under a special stone pavilion. There are three such pavilions in the temple, all fifteen-feet square with pillars in the four corners. The pillars are rather unusual; one main pillar is flanked by several small slim pillars, and, according to Sri Nadhamuni Araiyar, the primary *araiyar* of Srirangam, there are hidden pillars inside the main one. He says that the main pillar is the Veda, the Tiruvāymoḻi, and the slim pillars are the Vedāṅgas, the other Divya Prabandham works.

After stopping under this stone pavilion the Lord proceeds straight down to the "outer sands" near the thousand-pillared hall. Here, seated in palanquins, are Nammāḻvār, Tirumaṅkai Āḻvār, and Rāmānuja, facing in the direction from which the Lord is going to come, waiting to have a sight of his arrival. When the Lord passes through the four-pillared stone pavilion he hurries to meet his devotee, Nammāḻvār. Meanwhile, male Śrīvaiṣṇava devotees have assembled by the side of the thousand-pillared hall and are reciting a poem composed by Parāśara Bhaṭṭar in the twelfth century. This hymn, *Śrī Raṅgarāja Stava,* is in praise of the Lord in Srirangam, and the poet likens Srirangam to Vaikuṇṭha, the heavenly abode of Viṣṇu.

Here, in the outer sands, near the Hall of a Thousand Pillars, the images of Nammāḻvār, Tirumaṅkai Āḻvār, and Rāmānuja are waiting for the Lord. The bearers of Nammāḻvār, Tirumaṅkai, and Rāmānuja stand up, holding them aloft. The Lord comes in haste, and the bearers of Nammāḻvār hurry forward, leaving Rāmānuja and Tirumaṅkai behind. This is to show the special passion that the Lord and Nammāḻvār have for each other and their eagerness to be with each other. They break into a run, and there is excitement among the devotees. Suddenly, Nammāḻvār pauses and seems uncertain, not knowing where to go. It is as though he is suddenly conscious of his unworthiness; at this point the Lord's haste increases, and he runs to his devotee, as though he were saying "I'll never let you go." Sri Nadhamuni Araiyar, while reflecting on the daily meeting (Sanskrit: *saṁśleṣa,* literally, "union") between the *āḻvār* and the Lord, enacted during the ten days of Tiruvāymoḻi recitation, described Nammāḻvār's position as comparable to "a fish caught in the jaws of a crane; the Lord will never let go the devotee whom he is going to enjoy."

The *āḻvār* and the Lord meet each other; Rāmānuja and Tirumaṅkai are now brought up and greet the Lord. The procession, led by the Lord and followed by Nammāḻvār, Tirumaṅkai, and Rāmānuja, now winds its way directly in front of the thousand-pillared hall. Here the *āḻvārs* are waiting in two long parallel lines for the others to arrive. Nammāḻvār, Tirumaṅkai, and the Lord go to the southern side and face north; the Lord stands on the fourth side of the rectangle, facing south. The Lord and his devotees face one another, forming a closed circle ("rectangle," literally). Here two or three *araiyars* are waiting for the Lord and stand near Nammāḻvār.

The Lord faces his court of devotees. Each one of the *āḻvārs* is formally commanded to appear with the priest, shouting the name of the *āḻvār* and adding *aruḷappāṭu*" (summoned). The first commandment is for Nammāḻvār. Finally, the *araiyar* is called with a different *aruḷappāṭu* each day (e.g., "Tiruvāymoḻi viṇṇappam ceyvār aruḷappātu"; [Those who will be offering the Tiruvāymoḻi are summoned!]). The *araiyar* goes forward, as a representative of the *āḻvār.* beating his cymbals and with gestures illustrating the first lines of the hundred verses to be chanted for that day. The *araiyars* meet the Lord then lead the way, reciting the formulaic phrases of the Lord, known as *koṇṭāṭṭam* (celebration). They use a special gait, moving back and forth, beating their cymbals in rhythm to their phrases of praise. The Lord and the crowds follow, go through the thousand-pillared hall, and circumambulate the "sacred canopy of gems" (*tirumāmaṇi maṇṭapa*). The Lord is then installed under this sacred canopy.

The sacred canopy is on a raised level, a stage; this, after all, is Raṅga-nātha, "the Lord of the stage." It is about 2:30 P.M. by the time the Lord is installed under the sacred canopy. All the *āḻvārs* and *ācāryas* are brought into the hall and face the Lord, who is installed about 150 feet away. The *āḻvārs,* with the exception of Āṇṭāḷ, the only female saint, and some *ācāryas* are arranged as in three sides of a rectangle, the Lord being the fourth side. Āṇṭāḷ is not brought out to hear the recitation of the Tiruvāymoḻi. During the month of Mārkaḻi her Tiruppāvai is being recited in almost every Śrīvaiṣṇava home in south India and broadcast over many radio stations, yet she is not brought in to the court of the male *āḻvārs.*[9] Nammāḻvār sits with the other *āḻvārs* but has the prime position, directly facing the Lord.

The Hall of a Thousand Pillars is decorated for the festival with leaves, flowers, and, in recent years, neon lights. According to the Chronicles of the Srirangam Temple, this hall was built by two brothers, Kampaya Dandanayakka and Kariyamanikka Dandanayakka, who were generals in the Hoysala army. Kampaya was the commander in chief for the king, Ramanatha (1263–95), and so the hall can be dated to the thirteenth century at least.[10] In the Śrīvaiṣṇava's perception there is no doubt that this hall represents heaven (minus the neon and tube lights). The Kaushitāki Brāhmaṇa says that the supreme realm has a thousand pillars (*sahasra sthūṇa*) and that these verses are quoted or paraphrased by Śrīvaiṣṇava teachers.[11] This large hall has no side walls but is supported by the pillars. The handsome bridegroom is kept under the great sacred canopy of gems, which is also said to be like the one in heaven.[12] Here for the next ten nights the audience will be treated to an exhaustive interpretation of the Tiruvāymoḻi.

While the Festival of Recitation is conducted in many Śrīvaiṣṇava temples, the *araiyar cēvai,* or "the service (rendered by) the *araiyar,*" takes place only in three places. The principal performers of this *araiyar cēvai* at Srirangam, Srivilliputtur (the birthplace of Āṇṭāḷ), and Alvar Tirunagari[13] belong to families that have been associated with the temples for several centuries. Only male members of these brahmin families have the authority to perform the interpretation of the Tiruvāymoḻi;[14] they trace their art to the time of Nāthamuni in the tenth century C.E. and their rights back to the eleventh century. They are called *araiyar,* a Tamil word with multiple meanings.[15] *Arai* may mean "to say" or "to declaim," but the word is generally taken to mean "king." The *araiyar* is said to be the monarch of the *āḻvār* verses; indeed, for the duration of the performance he assumes the roles of the *āḻvār* as well as the roles assumed by the *āḻvār*. A chorus of Śrīvaiṣṇavas recite at the side in Srivilliputtur and Alvar Tirunagari, but not in Srirangam. The *araiyar cēvai* may only take place in front of the Lord (the processional, or "festival," image) and nowhere else.[16] When I questioned Sri Nadhamuni Araiyar about the ban on recording the *araiyar cēvai* he replied simply: "This service is only meant for 'our Lord' [*Nam perumāḷ*, a name of the Lord in Srirangam] and 'our *āḻvār*' [*Nam āḻvār*]."[17] The Lord listens to his own poem, for, according to tradition, he himself uttered the words through the saint Nammāḻvār. Nammāḻvār made that bold claim himself in Tiruvāymoḻi 7.9.1,[18] but here, during the Festival of Recitation, the authors (the deity and the saint) see the poem recited and performed.

Traditionally, recitations of the Tiruvāymoḻi begin with the chanting of laudatory verses (*taniaṉ*) composed between the eleventh and thirteenth centuries C.E. The verses celebrate the *āḻvār* and the poem, but in this performance the laudatory verses are omitted. It is said that the *araiyar* is the *āḻvār* and that reciting verses praising himself would be immodest. It must be noted, however, that this logic does not hold for the recitation of the commentary during the *araiyar cēvai,* in which the *āḻvār* is praised by the commentator. In the Chronicles of the Srirangam Temple it is noted that the *araiyar* is the limbs of the *āḻvār,* the limbs with which he can act. In his performances the *araiyar* impersonates the Lord's action during his incarnations.[19]

On most days the *araiyar cēvai* is scheduled to begin around 4:00 P.M., but it was usually closer to 5:00 P.M. On some days it was much later—7:00 P.M. on the seventh day, 8:30 P.M. on the eighth day, and 1:30 A.M. on the last day. The performance begins with the reading of the introduction to the Tiruvāymoḻi commentary (the *Thirty-six thousand-paṭi*)[20] written by Vaṭakku Tiruvīti Piḷḷai in the thirteenth century. This is followed by the *araiyar cēvai,* which is typically divided into several parts: praise and celebration (*koṇṭāṭṭam*), singing the one song, interpretation through mime and dance, recitation of a commentary,[21] and a final set of lines praising the Lord. After this performance and verbal exposition the rest of the Tiruvāymoḻi is recited.

The first verse of the Tiruvāymoḻi is interpreted through dance on the first evening. All the *araiyars* recite together, while only one *araiyar* does the dance. The *araiyar* dances, using facial interpretation (*abhinaya*), some footwork, and gestures to make his point. There are repetitions of phrases, and a single line may be repeated and elaborated several times, in a manner akin to modern south Indian Carnatic musical performances. The *araiyar* conveys the depth of the *āḻvār*'s emotion or the philosophical import of the verse by going back to a phrase and expressing it in different ways, and it is here that we begin to understand what the community means when it calls the poem "a text that is to be experienced" (*anubhava grantha*). The classical commentaries sometimes alluded to the many interpretations of a line given by the teachers; here the performer achieves a similar effect by dancing out the same line several times.[22] The performance is sometimes called a "visual poem" (*dṛṣṭi kāvyam*).[23] While *The Splendor* and the commentaries on the Tiruvāymoḻi refer to several incidents from which we gather that many, if not all, verses of the Tiruvāymoḻi were thus interpreted, now only 10 out of the 1,102 songs are given the "full-service" interpretation with song, dance, and prose comment,[24] and they are fairly representative of the many themes of the Tiruvāymoḻi.

After the dance and mime the commentary for that individual verse is recited from memory. There is a prompter at hand with the palm leaf manuscript to remind the reciter if he misses a word or so. The commentary is recited with emotion and expression; this is not just an intellectual interpretation of the poem. In January 1990, while an *araiyar* recited the commentary on Tiruvāymoḻi 3.3.1 (see app.), his eyes filled with tears at three different times, and the audience was moved by his emotion-charged rendering of the commentary. It is important to note, however, that this commentary is memorized and chanted; this is *not* like other oral commentaries, in which the written ones served as inspiration for the orator, who then had the freedom to improvise within certain parameters, using standard jargon. Here the *araiyar* keeps to the text at hand but is still totally involved emotionally in its meaning, and there is high drama that is almost tangible in the Hall of the Thousand Pillars.

What is interesting is that, while the dance and the singing can be seen by all, in Alvar Tirunagari the commentary alone is read softly with a screen drawn to hide the speaker; this is considered to be "sacred" and is to be made available only to a small Śrīvaiṣṇava audience close at hand. It is remarkable that there is a sudden concern that the Tiruvāymoḻi is to be orally interpreted and explained only to a worthy audience, one that is fit to hear it with faith, and not to the hoi polloi.

The explanation that I have heard—and which seems to be fairly common[25]—is that, since this deals with sacred matters (*bhagavad viṣayam*), it ought to be communicated only by a master to student, orally, and not broadcast to a general audience. This aspect of the ritual seems to be a relic of a time when the elucidation of the Tiruvāymoḻi was jealously guarded and carefully transmitted only to those who had a desire to learn. The interesting feature is that the *performative* aspect of the commentary is considered to be available for all, while the *verbal* commentary and the meaning that is articulated through words is reserved only for the faithful.[26] By safeguarding the commentary, the community affirms the importance of the text as a work that leads one to salvation. While the Tiruvāymoḻi is sometimes portrayed as an "accessible" text (as contrasted with the Sanskrit works, which are "inaccessible"), in actual practice the accessibility is only for Śrīvaiṣṇavas, although it must be admitted, for Śrīvaiṣṇavas of every stripe, without consideration of caste or sex. In Srirangam, however, the commentary is recited loud and clear, and everyone can hear it. While only the *araiyars* recite and sing in Srirangam, in the other places a chorus of Śrīvaiṣṇava devotees join them in the recitation for the day. The *araiyars* join in toward the end and conclude the services for the day.

While the depiction of the various emotions are carefully rehearsed and very little improvisation takes place today, there is evidence to show that eight hundred years ago there was a considerable amount of audience participation. During a Festival of Recitation an *araiyar* was elaborating a line of Kulacēkara Āḻvār's poem. In this line the poet, identifying himself as an angry cowherd girl (*gopi*), a girlfriend of Krishna, said, "I shall give vent to my anger." The *araiyar* depicted emotions of rage, showing how "she" would hit Krishna and claw at him. Empār (Rāmānuja's cousin), who was sitting in the audience, thought that this was not a fitting interpretation. The anger would be lost on Krishna, who would actually *enjoy* the cowherd girl kicking, hitting, and scratching him. Empār's suggestion, therefore, was that the *araiyar* (impersonating the *gopi*) should show her anger not by hitting and screaming but by feigning indifference and hiding her face from Krishna. By not showing her face to him, her anger would be justly, and effectively, communicated to Krishna, who could not survive without her. From these incidents it seems clear that members of the audience would suggest alternative ways of interpreting a verse, and, apparently, at least in all the cases reported, the *araiyar* accepted the suggestion with good grace.[27]

In Alvar Tirunagari, every evening for the duration of the Tiruvāymoḻi recitation, there is an enactment of the Lord showering his grace on Nammāḻvār.[28] Nammāḻvār's head is made to bow deep and touch the feet of the Lord. This ritual is called *tirumuṭi cēvai,* literally, "service with one's head," but generally taken to mean "display of grace by the Lord placing his feet on the sacred head."[29] Thus, throughout the days of recitation of the Tiruvāymoḻi the liberation of Nammāḻvār through the Lord's grace is stressed.

On the seventh night the image of Nammāḻvār is dressed as a beautiful woman (*mohana alaṅkāram*), pining for her beloved. In Tiruvāymoḻi 7.2.1–11 Nammāḻvār (in the guise of a girl) speaks of his longing for the Lord at Srirangam, and these verses are recited on the seventh night. The Lord is carried and held in the priest's hand (*kaittala cēvai*) for a few moments; meanwhile, the *araiyars* stand in front of Nammāḻvār and chant the eleven verses. There are enormous crowds to see this ritual. In recent years these moments are televised and later broadcast to a statewide audience.

The final emancipation of Nammāḻvār is enacted on the tenth and last day of the recitation (during the *cāṟṟumuṟai* ritual),[30] when the last twenty verses are recited. In Tiruvāymoḻi 10.9.1–11 Nammāḻvār speaks of the ascent of Śrīvaiṣṇava devotees to heaven and of their being greeted by the servants of the Lord. On this day Nammāḻvār's image is not dressed in the usual silk clothes and gold ornaments. Rather, he comes attired in simple white garments, a *tulasi* garland, and twelve *nāmams* (the Śrīvaiṣṇava sectarian marks) painted on his body. The Lord is brought from the innermost shrine (*garbha gṛha*) into the thousand-pillar hall and offered large amounts of food, which are later distributed; Nammāḻvār is brought in with umbrella, fans, and other royal honors.

The ceremony begins as usual, with the temple priest speaking for the Lord and issuing commandments to all the *āḻvārs* and the early *ācāryas* to be present and to be seated; then, at a late hour (it was 1:00 A.M. in Srirangam), the recitation of Tiruvāymoḻi 10.1 begins. In Srirangam, the *araiyars* stop with 10.8.11 and take a long break before the salvation drama of the last twenty verses is enacted. During this interval large quantities of food, endowed for this ritual by various patrons over the centuries, are offered to the Lord and distributed to various participants in the Festival of Recitation.

The salvation drama begins when the *araiyars* come to Tiruvāymoḻi 10.9, which speaks of the final ascent to heaven; in Srirangam it is 6:00 A.M. before this is begun in front of tens of thousands of devotees. The verses of 10.9 and 10.10, the last twenty in the entire Tiruvāymoḻi, are recited twice for emphasis. In the Parthasarathi Perumal Temple (Triplicane) the image of Nammāḻvār is carefully carried by the temple priests, *arcakas,* and they slowly circumambulate the deity. Two priests lead the way, carrying flaming torchlights. They are followed by *arcakas* carrying Nammāḻvār. These priests have scarves tied around their mouths so that their earthly breath does not touch Nammāḻvār. Nammāḻvār is also accompanied by other priests; one fans him, and one carries an umbrella behind him. The gait of the priests is slow and deliberate, and the circumambulation finishes with the end of the ten verses (recited twice for emphasis) describing Nammāḻvār's ascent to heaven. At the end of these ten verses Nammāḻvār is made to bow before the Lord, and curtains are drawn hiding the Lord and the saint from the audience. The priests cover Nammāḻvār with *tulasi* leaves, which are sacred to Viṣṇu; five minutes later, as the curtains are drawn apart, the priest waves a radiant flame (*dīpa ārati*), and the audience can only see a mound of *tulasi* leaves covering the image of the saint. The covering of Nammāḻvār with leaves indicates his liberation.

The last ten verses are now recited, and in the Triplicane Temple (not Srirangam) the congregation joins in with the chorus and the *araiyars.* The chanting of the last verse of the Tiruvāymoḻi is followed with the very first verse of the whole poem, thus coming full circle. The reason for this is in the format of the poem itself; it is composed in the form of an *antāti* (end-beginning), with the last word of the first verse being the first words of the next one, and so on. Thus, the last words of the last verse are also the first words of the first verse of the Tiruvāymoḻi. The linking together of the verses is clear when one recites or hears the poem, and the last verse leads one back to the first verse, forming a garland of words for the Lord.

A representative of the Śrīvaiṣṇava community then goes up and requests the Lord to return Nammāḻvār to them and recites verses from the *Śaraṇāgati Gadya,* a prayer written by Rāmānuja. The lord's reply, spoken through a priest, thunders forth: "We give him back to you."

The request and its affirmation are repeated three times, at which point the saint and the deity are covered with a curtain again. The *tulasi* leaves are removed, and Nammāḻvār is returned to humanity as the audience and the *araiyars* recite the poem composed by Maturakavi Āḻvār, the disciple of Nammāḻvār. Śrīvaiṣṇavas believe that the Lord took up Nammāḻvār with his earthly body into heaven but that Nammāḻvār returns to be the teacher of human beings.[31] While achieving salvation, he remains as an indispensable link between human beings and the Lord. Liberated from mortal life, he is yet one with the living people, drawing them to the feet of the Lord, where he abides. Through his presence and by the sacred words that he spoke—words that are considered divine yet spoken in a human voice (*tiru vāy moḻi*)—he binds the devotee to the Lord and becomes the person in whom the divine and the human realms intersect.

Maturakavi Āḻvār is considered to be the first disciple of Nammāḻvār. While Maturakavi was the only person in hagiographical accounts to learn from Nammāḻvār, in a wider sense the poet is considered to be a teacher of *all* Śrīvaiṣṇavas, reconciling them with God. He is a teacher and a mediator, ending the separation between the human being and the Lord. By becoming the master for Maturakavi Āḻvār, he becomes the spiritual teacher of Nāthamuni and the rest of the Śrīvaiṣṇava community. Thus, the ritual of Nammāḻvār's emancipation ends not with his being at the side of the Lord but, instead, with his return to humanity. This particular role of Nammāḻvār's mediation is brought out rather explicitly in a ritual that takes place the day before his own salvation.

On the last day of the "Ten Nights" of chanting Tiruvāymoḻi an elaborate drama is enacted by the *araiyars* in Alvar Tirunagari, the birthplace of Nammāḻvār. This performance is not directly connected with any Tiruvāymoḻi verse but is said to portray Nammāḻvār's role as mediator and teacher. The ritual is called *praṇaya kalaham* and depicts a lover's quarrel between Viṣṇu and his consort Śrī.[32] The festival image of the Lord is taken out during the day, presumably, for a day without his wife watching over his shoulder. When the Lord comes in later that evening he finds the doors of the temple locked. He then comes in through another entrance, a side door near Rāmānuja's shrine. Śrī is waiting here and confronts him, wanting to know where he has been all day, and a quarrel ensues. The *araiyars* vocally assume the roles of Śrī and Viṣṇu, stand by the images, and communicate the messages of the deities to each other. Viṣṇu says that he was out hunting all day and has now brought flowers (*pārijāta*) for his wife. Incensed, Śrī asks him to leave, saying that she is not falling for *that* line again. The *araiyars* sing and act out three verses (two from Tirumaṅkai Āḻvār and one of Nammāḻvār's [6.2.1]) in which the poets show their anger against the Lord. Subsequently, Nammāḻvār enters the scene. Śrī is persuaded to give up her anger at the Lord *because of Nammāḻvār;* the divine pair are reconciled and exchange garlands.

This rather curious ritual is difficult to interpret in a consistent way but presents several possibilities. The classical Śrīvaiṣṇava position reported by Venkataraman briefly: "Thus Nammāḻvār establishes his role as a teacher."[33] According to this traditional view, Śrī's grace and mediation is necessary for a human being's salvation, and Nammāḻvār teaches us that divine justice is not divorced from divine grace—that the two are inseparable. Another way of interpreting this ritual is to see Śrī as representing a human soul, and the mask worn by Śrī is that of a classical heroine who is bereft of her lover. Śrī, and the human soul, are reconciled to the Lord by Nammāḻvār. Thus, Nammāḻvār is a mediator even between the Lord and Śrī. In Srirangam this ritual takes place in spring, and the reconciliation is supposed to take place because Śrī respects Nammāḻvār as if he were her father, and so does his bidding.[34] It is this multivalency of symbols that makes the drama rich in meaning.

The *araiyar* expresses the *āḻvār*'s emotions through mime and dance, but in some significant rituals, such as the granting of salvation to Nammāḻvār, it is Nammāḻvār's image (*arcā*) and not the *araiyar* which plays the role of the poet. It is important to note that both the *araiyar* and Nammāḻvār's image share the main role in the course of the ten nights of recitation. The actors are the *araiyars* and the images of the *āḻvār,* the Lord and Śrī. The *araiyars* and Nammāḻvār assume roles; the *araiyars* act out the parts of Nammāḻvār and the characters that Nammāḻvār assumes in his poems. Nammāḻvār speaks as a lovesick girl, the girl's mother, or friend, and the *araiyar* enacts all these roles, conveying the depth of the *āḻvār*'s love for "her" beloved. While reciting the poems of Tirumaṅkai Āḻvār, the *araiyar* also assumes the role of a Gypsy fortune-teller, who looks for omens to tell the girl that the Lord will come to be with her soon. At crucial moments, however, as in the granting of liberation to Nammāḻvār, it is the image of Nammāḻvār that is used. This prominence given to the *arcā* is a distinctive characteristic of Śrīvaiṣṇava worship and ritual; the Lord is fully, completely, present in the *avatāra* seen in the temple (*arcāvatāra*). The divine presence is in both the *mūla vigraha,* the immovable primary image in the innermost shrine of the temple, as well as in the festival image, the *utsava mūrti.*[35] At any time of the year the Lord is said to be present in the Śrīvaiṣṇava temple; he is fully completely there as he is in heaven, and the temple precincts are a piece of heaven on earth. While all Śrīvaiṣṇava temples are transhuman in this way, the temple at Srirangam is considered to be *the* Temple. This temple is called Bhūloka Vaikuṇṭham, "Heaven on Earth."

THE SACRED ARENA

Śrīvaiṣṇava theologians use the words *nitya vibhūti* (the realm of continuous glory) to describe heaven, where the Lord dwells permanently, and *līlā-vibhūti* (the glorious realm of play) to speak of the created realm. Rāmānuja uses the terms *bhoga upakarṇa* and *līlā upakarṇa* ("instrument of enjoyment" and "instrument of play," respectively) to speak of heaven and earth. While both heaven and earth are enjoyed by the Lord, the difference seems to be in the nature of their permanence. Both are real, but, while heaven is continuous and eternal, "the instruments of his cosmic play, though real, being cognizable through valid means of cognition, are subject to change and therefore not abiding."[36] While all Śrīvaiṣṇava temples are part of heaven, it is Srirangam that is particularly held to be so, and it is during the rituals that this notion is explicitly emphasized.

Srirangam is an island in the middle of the river Kaveri, near the city of Tirucchirapalli, and the temple here seems to have been compared to heaven more often than any other by the Śrīvaiṣṇava teachers. Parāśara Bhaṭṭar claimed that the river Kaveri was like Virajā, which surrounds heaven, and that by bathing in it, one's sins were destroyed. The supreme land of Viṣṇu, he said, is on earth, and we may point to Srirangam and say "Lo, it is here!"[37]

It is in this sacred land that the festival takes place; then the gates between heaven and earth are opened, and all of humanity, by crossing the threshold, may hear the sacred words in the presence of the Lord, gain salvific knowledge, and be liberated. The whole festival promotes the idea that the Tiruvāymoḻi is a text that grants salvific knowledge and one that has the ability to transform earth into heaven. By focusing on the salvation that is assured for Nammāḻvār, it promises salvation to all human beings who listen to him. The *araiyar* acts as Nammāḻvār, portraying his emotions vividly, making the meaning accessible through song and dance. Like a good actor, his task is to include the members of the audience in the emotional drama, and involve them in the poet's quest for salvation. By assuming the identity of these characters, the *araiyar* shares with the audience the cosmic drama of liberation. The audience participates in this pilgrimage, identifying with the *araiyar*—and, through him, with Nammāḻvār—and conveys meanings and emotions that are perhaps not possible through an oral discourse.

A story in the *Thirty-six thousand-paṭi* commentary makes this point. Nañjīyar (early 12th c.) is quoted as saying that, though he had studied the Tiruvāymoḻi three times under Tirunaṛaiyūr Araiyar, he learned more about the poem when he saw his teacher so moved by a verse that he wept while trying to interpret it.[38] What is even more interesting is that the reference here is to the *araiyar*'s real emotion and not to mime or skillful acting on his part. Perhaps the distinction between total participation and acting is lost in some cases—in a Geertzian sense the actor becomes Rangda; the actor becomes the character he plays.[39] The intensity of emotion that is available through identification seems to be the ideal that the Śrīvaiṣṇava *araiyar* strives for. The audience is drawn into the emotion of the *āḻvār* and journeys with him through his moments of despair and celebration. It is in this participation that revelation is experienced by the devotee in the city that is, in fact, called the "sacred stage" (*Śrī-raṅga*). Here there is an ultimate role reversal: through their enjoyment of and participation in Nammāḻvār's poem the *araiyar* and the Śrīvaiṣṇava community become the actors, and the Lord of the stage (*Raṅga-nātha,* the name of Viṣṇu in Srirangam) becomes the audience, enjoying the community's enjoyment of the poem, which he spoke through Nammāḻvār. Revelation is not frozen in myth with the Lord speaking through Nammāḻvār; for the Śrīvaiṣṇava it appears to be ongoing, occurring whenever there is an inclusive participation of the devotee in the unfolding of the poem. Along with the reiteration of the Tiruvāymoḻi as a salvific text, perhaps it is this notion of ongoing revelation which is the dominant message that comes through in the ritual commentary on the poem.

The recitation and interpretation of the Tiruvāymoḻi locate the deity and the devotee within the paradigmatic pilgrimage of Nammāḻvār's search for union with the Lord and the perceived fulfillment of his desire. The verbal and ritual comment *create* those significant moments in the life of the community when the devotee participates in the poet's quest for the Lord and celebrates the assured nature of the Lord's grace, which is seen through his revelation of the sacred word. By the revelation of the divine word through a human poet the divine mercy of the Lord is understood as being extended to all human beings. By chanting that divine word every day, and by acting it out annually in the Festival of Recitation, the devotee participates in the Lord's granting of salvation to the poet and, in fact, to the entire community of Śrīvaiṣṇava devotees.

The recitation and dramatic interpretation binds the devotee to other worshipppers who participate in the liturgy and also links him or her to the chain of earlier religious teachers who rejoiced in chanting the holy word. It creates an extended family of Śrīvaiṣṇava devotees, stretching vertically through a line of past *ācāryas* and horizontally in the present, encircling all participating worshippers.

Through the recitation of the text and the exposition through ritual commentary heaven is invoked on earth. The recitation of the holy word in the divine presence of the deity, in the temple or the home shrine, is itself an occasion for rejoicing. This is not considered as a pale imitation of future happiness. For the Śrīvaiṣṇava it is one way of experiencing heaven on earth.[40] While the text of the verses (Tiruvāymoḻi 10.9 and 10.10) indicates that Nammāḻvār *ascends* to heaven in his physical body (verses that are acted so vividly in the *araiyar cēvai*), the opposite, in fact, seems true for the Śrīvaiṣṇava devotee. For the devotee heaven *descends* to earth, and Srirangam becomes the arena in which to experience the sacred presence of the divine. The visual perception of the Lord is as important as hearing the sacred word; they both translate as partaking in divine grace. The Lord is said to actually be present in the words of Nammāḻvār; we may find him, says Parāśara Bhaṭṭar, on the banyan leaf (during dissolution), in the Vedas, close to the breast of Śrī, and *in the words of Nammāḻvār*.[41]

During the Festival of Recitation it is easy to understand why Srirangam is hailed as heaven on earth by pilgrims. According to the Śrīvaiṣṇavas, the revelation of the holy word in the Veda—Sanskrit or Tamil—seems homologous to the manifestation of the deity in the temple. The Lord in his true form is said to be imperceptible to human eyes, but, because he loves human beings, he is said to manifest himself on earth and make himself visually perceptible here. Parāśara Bhaṭṭar put it this way:

> [We] hail the Lord of Srirangam
> as he who has no beginning.
> Like the revealed words [he appeared on his own];
> and the stain of human beings does not touch them [or him].
> They fulfill all desires, but their intent
> is to bestow liberation (*sāyujyam*).
> They remove all doubts.
> The Lord of Srirangam is our refuge.
> (*Śrī Raṅgarāja Stava*, pt. 1, 44)

This comparison between the Lord, who is said to have manifested himself in image form, and the Vedas, which are revealed, synchronizes with the classical Hindu notions of sound and music: there is ethereal sound, which cannot be perceived by human beings but which nevertheless forms the basis of the entire perceptible universe. In contrast to this imperceptible form is the *ahata nāda*, the "struck note," which, unlike its eternal prototype, resonates and is made audible to ordinary mortals.[42] We may say that according to the Śrīvaiṣṇava, just as the imperceptible deity makes himself accessible (in sacred places) by manifesting himself in a *visible* manner to human eyes (sometimes seeming to be the very embodiment of *śrngāra rasa*),[43] he, out of his mercy, reveals the sacred word and makes it *audible* to human beings. For the Śrīvaiṣṇava divine presence in visual form and in sound simultaneously creates the experience of salvation—on earth, as it will be in heaven.

In Śrīvaiṣṇava theology the Lord's play is manifested and perceived at the intersection of the divine and the earthly realms. Inasmuch as there is such an intersection in the entire cosmos, because the Lord pervades all that he creates, all of creation is his sport, his *līlā*. The cosmos is a celebration of the Lord's glory and, therefore, an expression of his *līlā*. In the thought of north Indian theologians the Lord's *līlā* is perceptible at those points in time when the Lord descends to earth and is here. In his *avatāras* his actions are inscrutable and mysterious to human beings and, therefore, seem to follow a different drumbeat, or at least a different melody from the magic flute, and Vallabha, Caitanya, and others celebrate these descents of the Lord. But the Śrīvaiṣṇava community rejoices in the ascent—or the transformation—of the earthly realm into the divine realm. With the gates of heaven being open during the ten days of Tiruvāymoḻi recitation the sacred land of enjoyment is contiguous, spatially and temporally, with the land of play.

9 REFLECTIONS

Ricoeur has observed that a community's "identity relies on the identity of the text, as distinct both from nonsacred texts and from other sacred texts," and adds that, "if these two boundary lines should disappear, then the identity of the community would also disappear."[1] The discussions in this book have primarily focused on the second boundary that Ricoeur has referred to: How does the Tiruvāymoli̲ differ from other sacred texts for the Śrīvaiṣṇava, and how does the identity of the community impinge on its perception of the unique nature of the Tiruvāymoli̲ and its author?

The Tiruvāymoli̲, a poem that reverberates with rich imagery, symbolism, and passion has been learned by heart, recited, studied, enacted, sung, performed, enjoyed, revered, and commented upon orally, in writing, and through ritual, for over a thousand years. It is seen as being authored by Nammāl̲vār, God, and, ultimately, like the Sanskrit Vedas, it has no author. It is the vernacular Veda, and, by reciting it, singing it, interpreting it for the Lord, who has made himself visible in a shrine, the Śrīvaiṣṇava is hearing and seeing the sacred and participating in the ongoing process of revelation. Because it is considered to be the essence of the Sanskrit Veda, and revelation in both languages is important, the Śrīvaiṣṇavas make a unique claim to the heritage of *ubhaya vedānta,* or a dual theology.

REVELATION

Showing the equivalency of the vernacular Veda to the Sanskrit one preoccupied the discourse of the early Śrīvaiṣṇava teachers. They demonstrated at great length and considerable ingenuity that the contents of the Vedas and the Tiruvāymoḻi were similar. The physical structure of the Tiruvāymoḻi, with about a thousand verses, was considered to be similar to the thousand branches of the Sāma Veda; there was also numerical correspondence, with the four works of Nammāḻvār being considered as the essence of the four Vedas. By the fifteenth century the equivalency of the Sanskrit Veda and the Tiruvāymoḻi were affirmed in many ways. The Śrīvaiṣṇava teachers emphasized the auditory and visual modes of revelation in the Sanskrit and Tamil Vedas. They also affirmed the eternity of the Tiruvāymoḻi, its beginningless and endless nature, which was similar to some earlier notions of the Sanskrit Veda. Thus, neither Nammāḻvār nor God are authors of the Tiruvāymoḻi; rather, the words are eternal, following a cosmic sequence and order. The words are preordained, and Nammāḻvār is no more the author of them than the creator god Brahmā is of the Sanskrit Vedas. These notions, however, draw attention away from the humanity of Nammāḻvār, the exuberance of his devotion, and the passion of his search for a union with the Lord, a passion that is preserved in the drama of his salvation presented in the ritual.

The Śrīvaiṣṇavas also reinforced the revealed nature of the Tiruvāymoḻi by their understanding that, like the Veda, Nammāḻvār himself had no real beginning or end. Nammāḻvār is either an incarnation of Viṣṇu or his celestial commander in chief, Viśvaksena, and thus removed from the human experience. Just as the Vedas are not touched by human beings and are therefore perfect, Nammāḻvār is portrayed in biography as not touched by worldly substance—he does not imbibe any food or drink, does not marry, and does not work or communicate in any form—and is therefore considered beyond the touch of human beings. In affirming this, the Śrīvaiṣṇava tradition has given him an exalted position, rather different from that of the other incarnations of Viṣṇu. Krishna and Rama ate, drank, married, and acted human, but Nammāḻvār is more like an image incarnation (*arcāvatāra*). He remains silent until his yogic meditation is jolted by the question of Maturakavi Āḻvār, the paradigmatic seeker. To this seeker the seer Nammāḻvār gave the Sacred Utterance.

Nor was revelation confined to Maturakavi Āḻvār. While the first revelation of the Tiruvāymoḻi came through Nammāḻvār, who *saw* the truth and articulated it through his sacred *words,* a second revelation took place to Nāthamuni, who was given the Tiruvāymoḻi and the entire

Divya Prabandham through a "disembodied voice." But the category of revelation does not seem to be frozen in the past; it is ongoing, experiential, and realized every time one recites the Tiruvāymoḻi with faith. The Tamil Veda speaks to the reciter and the musician; they speak, sing, hear, and see the sacred when they perform in front of the enshrined deity.

Unlike the Sanskrit Veda, whose meaning was not always understood, the Tamil hymns were comprehended, and theology was made accessible in a vernacular language. By incorporating selections from the Tiruvāymoḻi into temple ritual, the Śrīvaiṣṇava community highlighted and articulated certain concerns that collectively challenge the traditional norms of Hindu culture, without explicitly rebelling against them.

The first notion challenged was the claim that Sanskrit is the exclusive vehicle for revelation and religious communication. The recitation of Tamil verses in the temple and home brought the concepts and themes embodied in the verses within the domain of comprehension for all the local devotees—an unusual phenomenon, since *understanding* scripture was seldom primary in the Hindu's interaction with scripture. Renou quotes Kane: "it appears that from the beginning the Veda was confined to memory and that the majority of men cared little to know its meaning."[2] Now, however, through the introduction of the Tiruvāymoḻi in liturgy, verses that were central to a community's perception of itself and a human being's relation to God were made accessible to almost all segments of society. Sanskrit has been a dead, stylized language; worship in the vernacular carried the personal intimate dimension that comes with conversing in one's own mother tongue and allowed for greater devotee participation in the emotional and intellectual content of the ritual. The meaning was accessible even without the commentarial tradition, and many formulaic phrases from the Tiruvāymoḻi have entered everyday life and the commentarial literature.

VOICING THE SACRED WORDS

The recitation and oral transmission of the vernacular Veda is based on an inflexible, fixed, rigid orality, for which the memorization and exact repetition of a word is crucial. Learning by heart is fine-tuned to the point that, given a certain word, a trained reciter can quote every verse from the Divya Prabandham in which that word occurs, almost like the "search" process in computers. Learning by heart is still an important tool in Indian pedagogy; children in English medium schools in India memorize Wordsworth, Tennyson, Shelley, Keats, and large portions of Shakespeare. Frequently, the same children learn Sanskrit and vernacular prayers at home and are trained to value the fixed order of words.

It is in the realm of oral commentary that we see "free orality": here the commentators take an underlying theme on which they base their discourse and ornament it with formulaic phrases from the *ālvārs*, Rāmānuja, and other teachers. There is an interplay between creativity, rigidity of doctrine, and fidelity to the verse that is being interpreted. Although the canon of the Divya Prabandham is closed, there is no sense of closure for the commentarial tradition, which is seen in oral and written forms. Oral commentarial discourse flourishes, and, given its popularity, there seems no danger of its dying out. It must be noted, however, that, while the recitation of the hymns in the daily ritual provides a situation in which the devotee can participate directly in the communication of the original poet with God, in the oral or written commentary the participation in the poet's experience is more indirect and mediated.

Although some concern has been expressed by Śrīvaiṣṇava elders on the proliferation of *ālvār* hymns through cassettes, there seems to be no objection to the printing and making available of the commentarial literature. These commentaries, which revealed the various meanings of the verses of the Tiruvāymoli, were closely guarded, and, as we saw in chapter 7, were only revealed to those worthy of receiving them with piety. Even the scribe had to be initiated into the community with a sacrament before he had the authority to *listen* to the commentary and then copy it from an existing manuscript. This concern for worthiness and jealously safeguarding the meaning of the verses cannot exist in an environment in which print is all important. The important Śrīvaiṣṇava theologians of this century, including Sri P. B. Annangaracariar, Sri Uttamur Viraraghavachariar, the *Andavan* (the pontiff of the Munitrayam Matha), and Sri Ramadesikachariar of Uppiliappan Cannati, Karpangadu Swamigal, have all written commentaries, and Sri Krishnaswami Iyengar at Puttur Agraharam, near Srirangam, is publishing all the major commentaries. This flurry of publishing activity has been unprecedented and opens up the whole commentarial tradition to a non-

Śrīvaiṣṇava audience, including members of the academic community in India and other countries. This shift from a commentarial tradition that was primarily oral to one found on the printed pages of a book is analogous to the shift from reciting and singing the hymns from temples to broadcasting them over electronic media.

The recitation of the Tamil Veda has been done by men and women of all castes, and has contributed to a vociferous revolution within Hindu society. By incorporating the verses of Nammāḻvār, who was apparently born in a low caste, and by acknowledging him as the ideal devotee of Viṣṇu, the Śrīvaiṣṇava tradition questions the hierarchy of the caste system, which denied salvific knowledge to the *śūdra*. Class hierarchy, at least at certain moments of Śrīvaiṣṇava history, is rejected in favor of devotee/faith hierarchy and the potential equality of all devotees. This is a significant stance taken by the Tamil devotees of Viṣṇu and one that is magnified in medieval poems and movements all over India. The extent to which this rejection of caste hierarchy has been followed, the rationale behind glorifying low-caste devotees, and the differences between theological discussions and practice is still to be studied and evaluated carefully.

Historical evidence tells us that women and members of the lower castes recited in the temples. As we see from the family history of Sri Vipranarayana of the Nammāḻvār Shrine, members of the scheduled caste have taken pride in flawless recitation over the centuries. The title "servants of the servant of the Lord," which I have used for the section describing their recitation, was drawn directly from observing their liturgy: unlike the brahminical recitation, in which the first verse always recited is Periyāḻvār's benediction for the Lord, they begin their rituals by reciting the poem that Maturakavi Āḻvār wrote in praise of Nammāḻvār. Thus, they do not have to verbally articulate that they were primarily devotees of Nammāḻvār; their ritual makes it very clear.

There are also role reversals with interesting sociological implications involved in the study of the vernacular Veda. Some brahmin reciters believe that it can be learned only after a boy is invested with the sacred thread, because this is the Veda containing salvific knowledge, and one is to be "twice born" before one studies it. Women have also learned the poem, without the benefit of the sacred thread, but that has not been commented upon. Because the Tiruvāymoḻi contains salvific knowledge, the scheduled caste community in Bangalore also has ceremonies of thread investiture, and the men wear it. Because they have the authority to study the Tamil Veda, which is equal, if not superior, to the Sanskrit one, they are also taught the Sanskrit Vedas. In this context it is hard to accept Renou's statement that "within a group as much linked to the Vedānta as were the Śrīvaiṣṇavas, the Tamil sect of the Tengalai appears to have equally renounced the [Sanskrit] Veda."[3] Far from renouncing it, all Brahmin reciters as well as Śrīvaiṣṇavas of the Nammāḻvār Shrine (who, in fact, belong to the Tengalai subsect) learn at least some parts of the Sanskrit Veda.

Sanskrit and Tamil Vedas are recited every day in the temples, making the worshippers aware of the dual heritage of scripture from both languages. The dual heritage is also seen in verbal commentarial literature on the Tiruvāymoḻi, which is in *maṇipravāḷa,* a hybrid language of Sanskrit and Tamil, and here the medium itself is the message: the two languages have equal prestige, and the sacred words in both languages are of equal status.

The power of the Vedic mantra is seen also in the Tiruvāymoḻi, and, like the Vedic mantra, it is transformative and transactive in function. Above all, it is salvific in nature.

SEEING AND HEARING THE DIVINE

While on one level it is believed that reciting the sacred text will lead to salvation, on another, especially in the Nammāḻvār Cannati, there is the belief that salvation is already attained. In other words, recitation is not seen as a means to a life with Viṣṇu but as a goal in itself, and the Tiruvāymoḻi is quoted as an authority for this. Nammāḻvār and many *āḻvārs* had spoken about seeing the Lord in the temple as their goal; seeing and reciting the sacred on earth are actions perceived as indicative of salvation that has already been achieved for them.

Reciting the sacred word while visualizing the Lord enshrined in a temple or home seems to be the principal way through which the Śrīvaiṣṇava experiences revelation. In the articulation of religious experience the Hindu tradition has pressed the language of many senses into use: we have been primarily concerned with vision and sound in this book, but the notion of taste is also predominant. Nammāḻvār has used the analogy of swallowing, eating, and taste to talk of his mystical experiences[4] and modern commentators do not hesitate to use these images in talking of the Divya Prabandham. Consider, for instance, the single quotation given on the Cover of *Divya Prabandha Icai mālai* (Garland of Divya Prabandham Music). The quotation that appears on this music book focuses on *vision;* it is a line from Tiruppāṇ Āḻvār's Amalanātipirāṉ, "My eyes that have seen the Lord . . . will not *see* anything else." A few pages into the book the author says: "The pictures of several *arcās* [the form of the Lord enshrined in the temple] will provide a dazzling sight in this book. This book will contain two hundred verses that have been set to music; the verses are on twenty sacred places and [altogether] will provide a way to obtain a *feast* for the *eyes* and *ears*."[5] The intertwining of both vision and sound is seen in the word used for both activities in the Śrīvaiṣṇava parlance: both seeing the Lord and reciting the holy word are called *sevā,* "service."

FROM SACRED STAGE TO A SECULAR STAGE

The art of recitation and singing has moved from the sacred stage (srirangam) to a secular platform in the twentieth century. With the movement from the temple hallways to the secular forum the visual perception of the Lord, which is supposed to accompany the aural recitation, is lost. This movement is significant because, for the first time since their composition, the verses are being rendered in front of a purely human audience; until now the primary audience at temples and at homes had been the Lord. It is also important to note that, because the recitation and singing was done in front of the deity, the human audience both listened to the sacred word and simultaneously had a vision of the Lord.

Between the sacred stage and the secular platform is another arena, one in which parareligious performances take place, and perhaps one in which the Divya Prabandham will become popular over the next few years. This, in its present form, is a late-twentieth-century urban phenomenon. The groups that sing devotional songs are called *bhajana maṇḍalis* (devotional song circles), and there are literally dozens of them in the city of Madras alone.[6] Many of these groups, though not all, primarily have women as members. They learn to sing as a choir, and, whereas north Indian songs were popular in the 1970s, the Divya Prabandham and some other Tamil works on Murukaṉ devotion have now become popular. A full study of this phenomenon and its impact on

Tamil ethnic pride, especially in terms of caste issues, is yet to be done. As positive reinforcement, there is always a possibility of the good groups being auditioned for radio, and the really good *maṇḍalis* being chosen for the weekly television program on devotional music called "Garland of Song." So, at this point of time, the popularity of the hymns seems to be at an unprecedented high, even among non-Śrīvaiṣṇava groups.

RITUAL: REVELATION AS DÉJÀ VU?

> the performance of an oral epic . . . can serve also simultaneously as an act of celebration, as *paideia* or education for youth, as a strengthener of group identity, as a way of keeping alive all sorts of lore—historical, . . . religious—and much else.[7]

While the performance of an oral epic is different from the Tiruvāymoḻi in many respects, it also shares many of its characteristics. The performance is, of course, beautiful and moving, but it is not simply aesthetic; there is celebration, education, and certainly a considerable strengthening of group identity.

The Śrīvaiṣṇavas hold that the Lord *actually* incarnates himself in a temple and is as fully present there as he is in heaven and listens to the hymns. In recitation the devotee participates in the erotic and mythic structure of the poem; central to the experience of the Śrīvaiṣṇava liturgy, at home and in the temple, is the participation of the devotee in the passion and submission of the poet by reciting his words.[8]

At the same time the divine origin of the word is also upheld. As we saw earlier, on one level the Śrīvaiṣṇava community believes that the Lord composed the poem and the poet only "voiced" the divine word (the poem itself makes this internal claim to revelation). The devotee who recites these words participates in a paradigmatic circle of praise: Viṣṇu uttered the Tiruvāymoḻi through the poet, who sang it in praise of Viṣṇu; every Śrīvaiṣṇava reciter *is* this poet, communicating God's word back to him. According to the Śrīvaiṣṇavas, the revelation of the holy word in the Tiruvāymoḻi is homologous to the manifestation of the deity in the temple. The Lord in his true form is said to be imperceptible to human eyes, but, because he loves human beings, he is said to manifest himself on earth and make himself visually perceptible here. According to the Śrīvaiṣṇava, just as the imperceptible God makes himself accessible (in sacred places) by manifesting himself in a *visible* manner to human eyes, he, out of his mercy, reveals the sacred word and makes it *audible* to human beings. For the Śrīvaiṣṇava divine presence in visual form and in sound simultaneously creates the experience of salvation. By understanding Śrīvaiṣṇava ritual recitation, we are able to appreciate the faith that some Hindus have in the salvific power and divine grace that are extended through the divine word.

I went to the *araiyar cēvai* expecting to see and hear just another style of recitation. On the third day one of the *araiyars,* Sri Sampathkumaran, recited the verbal commentary after interpreting the verse through dance and facial expressions. He recited the verbal commentary from memory, and his brother stood near him, with a palm leaf manuscript in hand, ready to prompt him if he hesitated. A temple servant stood at the side holding a flaming fire torch over the manuscript, a service left over from the pre-electricity days. As the *araiyar* recited the commentary for Tiruvāymoḻi 3.3.1 (see app.), he was so moved by the words that he openly wept at three different occasions, pausing each time to compose himself. The audience was swept along in the experience, and some of its members wept with him. I was caught unawares; it was an experience I had least expected, and I left the performance that night with an indelible impression of the power of the sacred word that is enunciated with feeling.

From witnessing the *araiyar cēvai* and after talking to the *araiyars* in Srirangam, it seemed clear that it was not just another performance, not just another recitation. It is a communication of the *āḻvār*'s words to the Lord, which the Śrīvaiṣṇavas are privileged to hear and witness and participate in. Inasmuch as it is a personal communication, one can enjoy, participate, and rejoice in it, but the *avaiyar cēvai* is not an art form that the *araiyar* wants to be taught to, analyzed, or critiqued by people outside the community. The *araiyar* talks and communicates with God, and the Śrīvaiṣṇavas can witness it; the *araiyar* will not allow it to be recorded on audio- or videotape because it would be an intrusion on this privacy. While the *araiyar* whose performance I witnessed did not use this analogy, it seemed as inappropriate to record aspects of his performance as it would a personal conversation. This is for the "family" to enjoy and experience; without the presence of the Lord this conversation would be meaningless. One looked at the *araiyar*'s expressions and heard the tone and meaning of his words, the rhythm of his cymbals. And frequently, one looked at the other side to see the camphor lamp being waved in front of the Lord and had a *darśan* of him while hearing the sacred word. The cymbals and words on one side, the lamp and the deity's form on the other: together, through sound and sight, word and form, by having the inaudible and the invisible be accessible to the ear and the eye, there seemed to be an apprehension and communication of reality and truth in those few hours by and within the Śrīvaiṣṇava community congregating in the sacred arena, in the Hall with a Thousand Pillars.

While the poem of Nammāḻvār affirms his ascent to heaven, the Festival of Recitation declares his presence on earth. After the enactment of Nammāḻvār's liberation, a devotee from the congregation petitions the Lord to return Nammāḻvār to humanity. The Lord's reply is spoken through the priest addressing the community: "We give him, We give him, We give him [back to you]." Thus, while the poem makes no reference to the continued presence of Nammāḻvār on earth—it ends with the assured nature of his salvation—the ritual affirms Nammāḻvār's return to humanity. Nammāḻvār, whose origin is perceived as *not* human, stays with human beings, and his continued presence is requested and affirmed, year after year. Like the Vedas, which have no origin but which exist among human beings, Nammāḻvār continues to live among his devotees. The living word is enshrined in his presence, and the continued presence of the word and Nammāḻvār in the Śrīvaiṣṇava community is affirmed through the festival and, in fact, every act of recitation.

Appendix

TRANSLATION OF THE TEMPLE TIRUVĀYMOḺI SONGS Translated by Vasudha Narayanan, A. K. Ramanujan, Francis Clooney, and John Carman

1.1

1.1.1

Who is he
    that has the highest good
    cutting down all other heights
who is he,
    who bestows wisdom and love
    slashing ignorance?
who is he,
    who commands the tireless[1] immortals?

worship his radiant feet
    that quell all sorrow,

and rise
O mind.

1. *Ayaṛvu arum*. The word *ayaṛvu* may be translated as "fatigue, forgetfulness, or sorrow." All these meanings are given by Uttamūr Viraraghavacariyar in his commentary on this verse. This phrase is quoted frequently by Piḷḷāṉ and is used to describe the "immortal ones" who serve Viṣṇu.

1.1.2

The inmost mind
cleansed of all things foul

flowering, rising upward,
cannot measure him or know him;

the senses cannot know him;
yet he is bliss most complete:

unparalleled in present, past
and in times to come,

he is my life and breath
and there is no one higher
than him.

1.1.3

"He doesn't have that; he has this,"
such thought he eludes

in earth and sky, he has forms,
this formless one;

in the midst of the senses,
he is not of them;

unending, he pervades,
he is the Good
and we have reached him.

1.1.4

We here and that man, this man,
        and that other in-between,
and that woman, this woman,
        and that other, whoever,

those people, and these,
        and these others in-between,
this thing, that thing,
        and this other in-between whichever,

all things dying, these things,
        those things, those other in-between,
good things, bad things,
        things that were, that will be,

being all of them,
he stands there.

1.1.5

Each according to his understanding,
each in his own way,

each man reaches his own god's feet:
and these gods, they lack nothing,

for the Lord has arranged it
that each man will attain

according to his destiny.

1.1.6

He stands, he sits, he lies down, he wanders;
he doesn't stand nor sit nor lie down nor wander—

any thought that he is any of these states
he eludes

Yet he is always one changeless quality,
our Lord who is forever firm.

1.1.7

Becoming all things,
spread on the certainties of sky, fire,

wind, water, and earth,
he is in each of them;

hidden, he pervades
like life in a body,

yet according to the sacred word
all flame
he is the one

who devoured them all,
this god.

1.1.8

This supreme God
beyond the gods' understanding,

first one of the skies
and everything beginning there

who devoured them all—

as Araṉ, he once burned
the demons' three cities;

as Ayaṉ, he brought
understanding to the gods;

he destroys,
then creates the worlds

and dwells in all of them.

1.1.9

Say he is, then he is:
his forms are these forms.

Say he is not, then
these nonforms are his formlessness.

If he is and is not,
if he has both qualities,

these forms and nonforms
are his form and formlessness.

In both states, he pervades
and he is without end.

1.1.10

Pervading every drop of the cool wide sea
and spread over this round wide earth,

all lands and all of space,
missing not a spot,

hidden in every open shining space,
he pervades everything everywhere,

the steady one
who once devoured everything.

1.1.11

These ten verses out of the thousand
full of good sounds and sense

spoken by Kurukūr Caṭakōpan̲
about the feet of the great one

who stands in space
in fire air water earth

in sound strength force grace
and sustenance

will bring you release.

1.2

1.2.1

Leave it all
and having left it,
leave your life with the Lord
who owns heaven.

1.2.2

Less than a lightning flash
are bodies inhabited by lives.
Just think on this
for a moment.

1.2.3

Pull out by the roots
these things called
"you" and "yours."
Reach God.
There's nothing more complete.

1.2.4

His form is not
what is nor what is not.
He is the Good without limits.
Cut your bonds and embrace him.

1.2.5

Cut your bonds,
your life-breath
will reach heaven.

Destroy your bonds,
wish for lasting things,
let go, and hold fast
to the Lord.

1.2.6

The Lord too has no bonds.
He exists as everything.

Losing your bonds,
lose yourself in his fullness.

1.2.7

Behold his beauty,
his wealth.
And seeing it
lose yourself in it.

1.2.8

Think on thought,
word, and deed,

these three ways
you have,

and undo them
to lose yourself

in the Lord.

1.2.9

Move to his side.
Weaknesses will flee.

When your body falls,
think of him.

1.2.10

Good without measure,
dazzling goal.

Without end,
his glorious fame.

Reach Nāraṇa<u>n</u>'s
secure feet.

1.2.11

Consider carefully
these ten

from the rich garland
of a thousand:

these words of Caṭakōpa<u>n</u>
from beautiful Kurukūr

studded with lakes.

2.10

2.10.1

Before the growing glow of youth begins to fade,
and your limbs become feeble,

if you reach the temple,
        where the dark Lord,
        whose splendor ever grows,
        dwells with love

Māliruñcōlai,
hill surrounded by luxuriant young groves

Rare fortune is yours.

2.10.2

Heed not the charms of lovely young women!
Praise the temple of the handsome Lord
        whose conch roars with might.

Praise Māliruñcōlai
whose peak is awash with moonlight
and arise
That is your reward.

2.10.3

My heart! there is nothing to gain
by performing wasteful deeds.

Reach yonder hill:
near Māliruñcōlai
surrounded by thick enchanted forests.

This is the temple,
where he who has the hue of stormy cloud,
delights to dwell.[2]

This is the right thing to do.

2.10.4

So that our strong bonds of attachment
caused by previous deeds[3] may be cut;

So we may serve him and live,
the powerful [one],
who held aloft the great mountain,
abides in this temple,
Māliruñcōlai, drenched in rain.

Reach that sacred hill:
that is the righteous way.[4]

2.10.5

Do not add to your sins with your gathered strength:
Reach the slopes of the outer hill.
Māliruñcōlai,
surrounded by sparkling clear mountain springs.

This is the temple of the Lord
who uses his discus
in righteous wars.

That is the way.

2. Tamil: *purintu,* "desire"; also "shine."

3. *kar(u)ma vaṉ pācam,* "strong bonds of Karma."

4. *Tiṟam,* "path, fortune, excellence, upright."

2.10.6

Think of the way;
Avoid what is base.
This is the temple of him
    who ate the butter
    from the hanging jars.
Māliruñcōlai
Hill where the doe is close to her fawn.

This is the way:
Thinking of it is good.

2.10.7

Think good thoughts; do not sink in hell.
He who bored through
and raised Earth long ago,
has long dwelt in this temple.

Māliruñcōlai
Here the moon cuts through impurities[5]

Approach it in the right manner, reach it,
    and you shall be secure.

5. This line can also read "where the moon cuts through impurities."

2.10.8

Be strong, don't waste your strength day by day.
This is the temple of the marvelous cowherd,
    who makes you strong.
Māliruñcōlai
where the celestials come
to circle him in adoration.
Circle, come near him everyday;
    it is the right way.

2.10.9

Think of the right way; don't drown in powerful sins
This is the great temple where the Lord
    who killed demon woman lives.
This is Māliruñcōlai
here herds of young elephants gather together.

Be firm in your desire to adore him:
        success will be yours.

2.10.10

Deeming it as success.
don't cheat and gamble,
This is the temple desired by the one
who, long ago, expounded the Vedas.

This is Māliruñcōlai
where lovely peacocks dwell in
Enter the hills
covered with buds just ready to blossom:
        this indeed is wealth.

2.10.11

These ten verses from a thousand
        spoken without delusion
        by truthful Caṭakōpaṉ
        from the fertile town of Kurukūr

to illumine the glory
of him who created this world
        as his wealth

will at last unite you
with the feet of the gracious Lord.

3.3

3.3.1

Staying with him at all times
without a break,
we must serve him faultlessly,

our Lord who's a flame of beauty
on Vēṅkaṭam Hill
among deep-voiced waterfalls,

our father, our father's father,
father of our father's father!

3.3.2

Our Lord who was before the father
of our father's father's father

dwells in Vēṅkaṭam Hill
looking splendid with the flowers

showered by heaven's gods
and the king of heaven—

our Lord of endless fame,
dark and beautiful as a rain-cloud.

3.3.3

Our Lord of marvels
with eyes beautiful as red lotuses,

mouth red as a berry,
body dark as blue sapphire,

he dwells in Vēṅkaṭam Hill
with its springs clear and full;

his long-standing virtues numberless,
he is the Lord of the gods of heaven.

3.3.4

When I say he's the Lord
of the gods of heaven,

would it be praise enough
for our Lord of Vēṅkaṭam?
for my Lord, flame of flames,
who loves me though I'm low
and empty of virtues?

3.3.5

When I say, he's the flame
worshipped by all the worlds,

the very first of images,

would it be praise enough
for our Lord of Vēṅkaṭam,

whose virtues are without a flaw,

ambrosial essence of all the Vedas
that Vedic experts know.

3.3.6

When debts burn
and bodies deeds
ripen and fall away

they'll do only things
that are good for them,

once people carry out the duty
of saying "I bow to you,"

to the Lord who lives on Vēṅkaṭam Hill.

3.3.7

That Vēṅkaṭam Hill
where the gods of heaven

and their king
bear great flowers, holy water,

lamps and incense,
and bow down in unison and rise—

that great hill
will make us equal to him
and bring us release.

3.3.8

He who once lifted the hill
to save his people from the cold rains,

the Lord who once measured the worlds,
the one beyond,

has settled here in Vēṅkaṭam—
if one worships just that great hill

our deeds will come to an end.

3.3.9

Old age that slows one down,
birth, death, and disease,

he'll show the way to end them; all,

that Cowherd on Vēṅkaṭam Hill,
his feet like lotuses
opening just now—

to those who hold him
in their words and in their hearts.

3.3.10

Before the appointed span of your life
narrows its bounds
and wears you down,

go to the foothills of Vēṅkaṭam
with dense groves and lily ponds,
where the Lord lies
on the hooded serpent.

3.3.11

Caṭakōpaṉ of Kurukūr
with its tall groves

has sung a thousand
incomparable verses

about him who crossed the earth
pacing with his feet:

and anyone who knows these ten
out of the thousand

will live a full life
praised by the world.

4.10

4.10.1

When there were no gods, no worlds, no life,
        when there was nothing,

He created the four-faced one, and with him
        the gods, the worlds and life.

When this Original God stands in Tirukkurukūr
        where jeweled terraces rise like mountains,

how can you run after other gods?

4.10.2

He who first created the very gods

who you seek and worship,
who first created even you,

The First One with timeless glory
He loves to dwell in this temple

in Kurukūr, surrounded by palaces
        and towers:
O people of this world, sing it,
        dance, spread out, and spread the word.

4.10.3

You know how the other day
he created the various gods,
the many sprawling worlds;

how he then swallowed, hid,
and spat them out;

how he strode across the worlds;
how he dug them

Yet you're muddled,
O masses and worldlings.

There are no gods
who are not part of him,
the Lord at Kurukūr,

to whom they all
bow their heads.

Now you can talk.

4.10.4

He is the Lord of Śiva, of Brahmā,
of all the other gods you speak of.

Look: he once freed Śiva
from the skull stuck on his hand.

The Lord stands in Kurukūr,
surrounded by splendid majestic towers.

What would they gain,
these followers of the Liṅga Purāṇa,

by speaking ill of him?

4.10.5

He is you:
        you devotees of the Liṅga texts.

He is you:
        you Jainas, Buddhists, you crafty debaters.

He is your various gods,
        and that's no lie.

He flourishes in Kurukūr,
        where rich fields fields of paddy
fan him like yak tails.

Praise him.

4.10.6

He made you praise and worship other gods,
and set you apart,

For if all of you had reached heaven,
there would be no more earth.

Today he has cleared your minds.

Having now seen the magic of the mighty Lord
who stands in Kurukūr

where rich paddy grows in wet fields
and lotuses thrive,

come to know him, know him
and run to him.

4.10.7

Running, rushing into several births,
singing and dancing in worship
for other gods in a myriad ways,

you've seen it all.

Celestials gather and praise
the First One at Kurukūr
with the soaring bird on his flag.

Enter his service.

4.10.8

Markaṇḍeya the sage served the Lord,
entered his service and saw him;

the naked god saved the sage's life
through the grace of Nārāyaṇa.

The first of gods stands in Kurukūr
where the tall screw pines with blossoms

white as cranes
fence the city

and you talk of other gods.

4.10.9

Neither the much-vaunted six systems,
nor others like them,
can see or gauge

the elusive First One
who stays at Kurukūr
surrounded by cool fertile fields
of paddy.

Be wise and be mindful of this
if you wish to be saved.

4.10.10

With all the gods, all the worlds, and all else
as his flawless form,

he stands radiant in Kurukūr, abundant with fields
of red paddy and sugarcane.

He is the dancer with the tall pots
who once came down
as a little dwarf:
serve him.

4.10.11

Anyone who masters these ten verses
from the thousand

sung with passion by the poet of Kurukūr,
Māṛan̲ Caṭakōpan̲,

with a *makil̲* garland fragrant
on his chest,

who reached by his service,
the Lord of the wheel,

will find the City of Heaven, Vaikuṇṭham,
and much else
near at hand
and will never return.

5.8

5.8.1

O ambrosia that never sates,

you make this servant's body,
so much in love with you,
sway

wander like waters
of the sea,
melt, and dissolve.

O Tall One
in sacred Kuṭantai
where lush fields of paddy
move like yak tails
over the rich waters,

I saw you, my Lord,
radiant and reclining
in a lovely posture.

5.8.2

My Lord, O white image,
my ruler

You assume any form you wish,
O handsome bull

In sacred Kuṭantai
where large red lotuses
open their eyes
on the rich waters,

you close your eyes like flowers.
What am I to do?

5.8.3

What am I to do? Who will protect me?
What are you doing
with me?

I want nothing
that anyone other than you
can fulfill.

O you who rest in Kuṭantai
surrounded by walls
with lovely work on them,

glance at me: grant
that I, your servant, shall pass
all my livelong days

holding your feet.

5.8.4

O Lord, whose glory spreads as far as seers can see.
You are incomparable.

Your body contains
all worlds.

You rest in Kuṭantai
full of virtuous people.

Restless to see you,
I scan the skies,

I cry, I bow.

5.8.5

I cry, I bow,
I dance about to see you.

I sing, I call.
Because sins cling to me

I look this way and that,
I hang my head in shame.

Lord, you rest in Kuṭantai
rich in fertile fields.

O Lord with eyes like red lotuses.
Find me your worshipper
a way

to reach your feet.

5.8.6

Find me a way. Cut through
my ancient deeds, good and bad

Even though I know
how to reach your feet,

how long am I to be away
filling pits
that cannot be filled?

You sleep in Kuṭantai
which glows with people
of long-standing fame,

O King of celestials,
O music of lutes,
O nectar, fruit of wisdom,
best of lions!

5.8.7

Best of lions,
my golden fire,

dark cloud
with flaming eyes,

mountain of coral
all ablaze,

Father with four shoulders,
by your grace, you took me on
for inseparable service,

O Dark One of Kuṭantai,
I cannot stand it anymore:
Give me your feet

and end this cycle of births.

5.8.8

Whether you end my sorrow or not,
I've no other support,

O Lord of the wheel with the curving mouth,
miraculous one who sleeps in Kuṭantai,

when my body goes limp and self falters,
you then must will that I do not weaken

my grip on your feet.

5.8.9

O Lord who consents
to keep me
at your feet,

Leader of leaders among gods
who do not falter,

O primeval image,
you lie still

with the world adoring you
in Kuṭantai

where great glowing gems
cast rainbows.

Come here,
so I may see you.

5.8.10

You do not come
and then you come inside my heart
without a form,

O Lord of marvels
becoming a magical image,

ambrosia that never sates

tasting sweet in this servant's self,
ruling me so my unending sins
come to an end:

Lord of Kuṭantai city,
though bound to your service,

will I still go astray?

5.8.11

Those who can babble
till their confusion clears,

these ten verses out of a thousand
(softer than the melody of a flute)
spoken by Caṭakōpaṉ of Kurukūr
who took as his refuge

the feet of that Lord
who sucked out the breast
and devoured the life

of that demon-woman
with bones
tough as a cross-bar:

they will be loved
by the doe-eyed women.

6.10[6]

6.10.1

O big-mouthed fellow who once ate the world,[7]
Lord with unending fame,

6. Śrīvaiṣṇava commentators see this set of verses as central to the Tiruvāymoḻi. Nammāḻvār is portrayed as seeking refuge with the Lord at Tiruvenkatam in 6.10.10. Commentators see this to be a paradigmatic act of *prapatti,* or "surrender to the Lord."

7. The myth of the Lord eating the world is seen in the Mahābhārata and the Viṣṇu Purāṇa. In the Tiruvāymoḻi, Nammāḻvār uses the myth to show the unity of the world and the Lord.

image of light,
surrounded by everlasting splendor

O Tall One,
your servant's life and breath

My Lord of Vēṅkaṭam Hill,
that sacred mark on the brow of the world,

summon me so that I,
descendant of an old clan of your servants,

may come and reach your feet.

6.10.2

O you who holds the sacred wheel of raging fire
that breaks down, burns to ash
razes to the ground
entire clans of wicked demons,
King of the gods,

O Lord of Vēṅkaṭam Hill
where lotuses red as flames
grow on muddy banks and in pools,

show me your grace
so that I, your servant
who loves you without end,

may reach your feet.

6.10.3

As if grace found its color
your color is the color of a lovely cloud,

Lord of miracles,
ambrosia that seeps sweetness into my heart,

commander of the gods,
Lord of Vēṅkaṭam Hill

where clear waterfalls crash
spilling gems, gold, and pearls,

O Master, just say, "Ah, there he is!"
and bring me to your feet.

6.10.4

Demons who can't say, "Ah! Ah!"
in compassion

torment the world,
and your bow rains arrows of fire
on their lives,

O husband of the great goddess Tiru,
O god of Vēṅkaṭam Hill
that gods and sages love,

Unite with me, so this sinner
may deserve your feet
covered with flowers.

6.10.5

The other day,
with your bow you knocked down
seven trees, close together;
O First One,

you crawled between two giant trees
twined together,
and split them

Lord of the Vēṅkaṭam Hill
where rogue elephants herd
like dense clouds,

lord of the strong bow called Cārṅkā,
when will the day come
when I, your servant,

will reach your feet?

6.10.6

"When will we ever see the twin lotus feet
that once paced the worlds?"
ask the hosts of immortals

as every day they praise you,
standing, waiting,

serving you
with body, speech, and mind.

O Lord of Vēṅkaṭam:

When will the day come
when I, your servant,
will reach truth

and touch your feet?

6.10.7

Ambrosia that I, your servant,
love and long for,[8]

God of gods
with the ferocious bird
on your banner,

your lips are luscious like fruit,
O antidote to sins
that multiply like weeds,

My Lord of Vēṅkaṭam Hill,
even though I've done no penance
to see your feet,

I cannot wait a second
to see them.

8. The words translated as "love" and "long" are *mēvu-tal* and *amar-tal*. Both words mean "desire"; *mēvu-tal* also means "to eat, to love or to be united with." Commentators usually paraphrase it as "to enjoy."

6.10.8

"Even though we've done no penance
to see your feet, yet we cannot wait
to see them,"

say the subtle blue-throated god,
the perfect four-faced one
and Indra,

joined by women with sparkling eyes,
they come desiring you,
O Lord of Vēṅkaṭam.

Come then, as you once did, Māl,
dark and entrancing, O come to me,
your servant.

6.10.9

You seem to come but you do not.
When you seem not to come, you do.

Eyes like red lotuses, lips like red fruit,
O four-shouldered one, ambrosia, my life,

Lord of Vēṅkaṭam Hill
where glowing gems make night into day,

I, your servant, cannot bear
even for a second to be away

from your feet.

6.10.10

O you, on whose breast
dwells the lady of the flower
saying: "I cannot move away from him
even for a second!"

Unmatched in fame,
Owner of the three worlds!
My Ruler!
O Lord of the sacred Vēṅkaṭam
desired by the peerless immortals
and crowds of sages!
I, your servant, who is without shelter,
sat at your feet and entered you.

6.10.11

"Come sit at my feet, enter me
and live, O Devotees" says the Lord,
offering them grace

and about him, Caṭakōpaṉ of Kurukūr
where paddy fields are plentiful
composed a thousand songs

that will end all cycles of birth:
anyone who holds onto anyone
who holds onto these ten verses

on the sacred Hill of Vēṅkaṭam
will be enthroned
in the high heavens.

7.2

This is the only set of verses in the entire Tiruvāymoḻi that is dedicated to the most important of all the Śrīvaiṣṇava temples—Srirangam. Śrīvaiṣṇava teachers who lived in this holy city held this set of verses to be extremely important, and Naṁpiḷḷai (thirteenth century C.E.) is said to have claimed that the songs addressed to other holy places were really just ancillary to this set addressed to Srirangam. "All thousand songs of the Tiruvāymoḻi were addressed to the sacred feet of the 'Great Lord' [at Srirangam] and then set apart as ten verses each for Tirumokkur, Tiruvenkatam, and so on. Like the food that is offered in a platter to the Lord [at Srirangam] and is then distributed all other songs [of the Tiruvāymoḻi] have been measured out to the Masters of the other holy places."[9]

The recitation of this set of verses is accompanied by high drama in Srirangam. Nammāḻvār is dressed as a lovesick girl *(nāyaki)* this evening. The (male) Śrīvaiṣṇava devotees who are waiting in the sands outside the thousand-pillared hall for the Lord to come from the main shrine usually chant Parāśara Bhaṭṭar's *Śrī Raṅgarāja Stava*. On this day they recite poems, not in honor of the Lord, but those praising his consort Śrī's grace. These

9. Naṁpiḷḷai, qtd. in Vaṭakka Tiruvīti Piḷḷai's *Īṭu* (Thirty-six Thousand-paṭi) for TVM 7.2.11.

poems include Bhaṭṭar's *Śrī guṇaratna kośa* ("A treatise on Śrī's jewel-like qualities") and Kurattāḻvāṉ's *Śrī stava* ("A prayer to Śrī"). While it is not articulated thus, it seemed to me that by reciting these poems, they are highlighting the role of the Goddess' grace and contrasting it with the Lord's slowness in rescuing Nammāḻvār. The Lord has listened to these pitiable lines spoken by the poet and not yet offered salvation to the poet, and so Śrī's grace seems to be sought.

The most exciting ritual of the evening is called *"kaittala cēvai,"* the vision of the Lord being carried in the priests' hands and coming forward, almost as if he wanted to approach Nammāḻvār. Nammāḻvār, dressed as a woman, is held aloft on one side of the thousand-pillared hall, and the *araiyars* representing the *āḻvār* recite these verses. Across the hall, on the stage, the Lord is lifted from his place under the "Sacred Canopy of Gems" and is held high in the priests' hands *(kaittala)*. While the verses talk of the poet coming near the Lord (7.2.10), the ritual highlights the Lord appearing in front of the devotee. The preceding rituals of the afternoon, when Śrī's grace is sought, when juxtaposed with this Lord's approach to Nammāḻvār, makes it seem through the ritual—if not from the verses themselves—that it is by the Goddess' intervention that the Lord softens and appears before Nammāḻvār.

Even though this service lasts only five minutes, it draws extremely large crowds—the hall is filled up completely about an hour and a half before the ritual, and even the special tickets sold for the occasion do not guarantee a good view.

Later that evening, while reciting 7.2.5, there is an enactment of the story of Prahlāda and Viṣṇu's incarnation as "man-lion" *(nara-siṁha)* to protect his young devotee.

The mother says:

7.2.1

Night and day, her eyes know no sleep.
She splashes her tears with her hands.

O conch, O wheel, she cries and folds her hand
O Lotus Eyes, she cries
and grows faint.

How can I survive without you? she asks,
and searches the earth, groping with her hands.

O Lord of Tiruvaraṅkam
where red *kāyal* fish dart in the waters,

what are you doing with her?

7.2.2

What are you doing, my Lotus Eyes? she asks,
her eyes brimming with tears.

What shall I do, O Lord of Tiruvaraṅkam,
where the waters come in waves? she cries.

She sighs and sighs hot sighs.
She melts and says, "*Come O past deeds,*
        come face me!"
O Lord dark as a cloud, is this fair? she asks.
You once made this world, swallowed it,
spat it out, measured it—

how will it all end for her?

7.2.3

Without a jot of shame she cries,
O Lord dark as sapphire!

Infatuated, she scans the sky and says,
her heart melting,
Lord who once all alone
        devoured the lives of all the terrible demons!

Unseen by any eyes, O Kākutta, O Kaṇṇaṉ! she cries,
Show me your grace and the way to see you.

O Lord of Tiruvaraṅkam,
surrounded by flags and strong walls,

what have you done to her?

7.2.4

Where she puts them
her hands and legs stay put;

rising, she wanders bewildered;
folds her hands in worship.

She says, "*Love is hard,*"
and swoons.

"*O Lord, dark as the sea,*
look, you're cruel," she exclaims

"*O Lord with the whirling wheel*
in your right hand, come close,"

she begs over and over,
quite lost.

O learned one, Lord of Tiruvaraṅkam
lush with waters,

what do you think you are doing with her?

7.2.5

She thinks. She falls in a swoon.
She recovers. She folds her hands.

O Lord in Tiruvaraṅkam! she exclaims.
She prays. With eyes raining tears,

she calls and calls again: *Come, O come!*
And she faints.

O you who tore the demon's body[10]
in that twilight, pure ambrosia

10. At this point the *araiyars* pause and act out the drama of Narasiṁha Avatara, Viṣṇu's incarnation as a man-lion.

who once churned the ocean of waves

you have made her lose her mind,
this young thing who only thought

of meeting you and reaching your feet!

7.2.6

O you who have made me lose my mind
and held my heart captive, she says.

Great Lord of miracles, she says.
You red-lipped jewel, she says.

You who dwell in Tiruvaraṅkam
surrounded by cool waters, she says.

Leader of the celestials, O you
with blazing sword, mace, conch, discus, and bow, she says.

You who use the hooded serpent for a bed,

You do not show your grace to her
sinner that I am.
This is my lot.

7.2.7

You allot happiness and sorrow, she says.
Refuge of those without refuge, she says.

You hold the wheel of time, she says.
O Lord dark as the sea who lives on the sea, she says.

Kaṇṇaṉ! she cries.

Fish frolic in the cool waters that circle
your Tiruvaraṅkam, she says.

O Lord of the sacred river, says
my tender little girl,

her large lovely eyes flooding
raining down with tears.

7.2.8

O scion of the gods of heaven, she says.
You lifted the mountain and saved the cows, she says.

She weeps, she bows, and her breath is hot
enough to set her soul on fire.

O Lord dark as collyrium, she says.
She rises, raises her eyes, stares long

without blinking, and asks,
Where can I see you?

O Lord of Tiruvaraṅkam
surrounded by waters and flourishing gardens

what can I do for my poor daughter
who is as lovely as the Goddess?

7.2.9

O you wear the Goddess on your chest, she says.
O you, you are my soul, she says.

*husband of the Earth Goddess whom you scooped up
and rescued with your sacred tusks,*

*Lover of the cowherd girl you took that day
after taming the seven angry bulls*, she says.

O Lord who has taken Tiruvaraṅkam in the south
for your temple,
I do not know what end awaits her!

7.2.10

I do not know what end awaits me, she says
Master of the three worlds, she says

O Lord who wears fragrant koṇrai *blossom
on his matted hair*, she says.

Four-faced god, she says,
chief of the handsome gods of heaven, she says.
O Lord of rich Tiruvaraṅkam, she says.

Coming as one who could get nowhere near his feet,
she came close to the Lord dark as a cloud,

and reached his feet.

7.2.11

Dark as a cloud is the Lord,
and Caṭakōpan̲ who reached his feet,

who wore his grace on his head
and was lifted up,

who lives near Porunal, river
of flowing clear silken waters,

who comes from lovely Kurukūr
surrounded by rich gardens of flowers—

he made a word-garland of a thousand verses
and anyone who knows these ten

about the feet of the cloud-dark Lord
will live immersed in a flood of bliss,

surrounded by celestials in the heaven
of the Lord dark as a cloud.

8.10

8.10.1

All that I did
was think of serving
the Towering Lord.

But then, he,
stealthily cut through my confusion

and ended my evil ways
Thinking of this good fortune,
can I, a wicked sinner, ever exist
unless I am united
with the feet of his servants?
Ah! can I ever let them go,
even if I were to get
the wonderful three worlds?

8.10.2

Even if I were to obtain the three worlds,
or become my pure self itself,[11]

would that come close to the happiness, the fortune
that I, a sinner, get right here

by bowing before the sacred feet
of those who, holding their heads high,

triumphantly serve, the feet of the Lord,
whose sacred form resembles a storm cloud,
and whose ankles are adorned with beautiful flowers?

11. Śrīvaiṣṇava commentators take this line to indicate the state of *kaivalya* (alone), a goal that human beings can attain, instead of *mokṣa* (liberation), which would be a communion with the Lord and other devotees in heaven. There is no progression from *kaivalya* to *mokṣa*; it is said to be a state in which one is lost in the bliss of enjoying one's own soul. While *kaivalya* is freedom from the shackles of earthly life, it is portrayed as a state that is of less value than *mokṣa*.

8.10.3

The sacred dwarf, Lord with red lotus eyes,
raised his small [but] great body
and all at once,
these three worlds were filled with him!

Would it be right for me, a sinner,
to reach his great, good feet
which are like fresh, fragrant flowers,

when his servants,
the small [but] great people[12]
who rule me, wander here on earth?

12. "Small-great" people (*ciṟu mā manicar*); a frequently used phrase in the Śrīvaiṣṇava community to refer to devotees who may be physically small but great in piety.

8.10.4

What do I lack if I wander here
by the grace

of my Lord with a radiant form,
coral lips, eyes red as lotus,
who in the past
swallowed this great earth
and then spit it out—
following the right path with
a mouth to praise his ever-increasing glory
a mind in which his form dwells
conquering the senses
hands to hold flowers so fit for him?

8.10.5

If hastening to worship
receiving grace
I were to be caught up
in the swirling floods
of brilliant light
and ever-growing joy
beneath the exquisite flowerlike feet
of the Wondrous One,

would I enjoy it all as much as
being born
in a lowly transient body
learning of his glory
and rendering in words,
I enjoy the flowing ambrosia of poetry?

8.10.6

The Lord
struck the dark elephant
peerless in its ferocity,
its face crimson with rage

Lord who has a golden wheel in his hand
Lord who rules the wandering bird
which destroys and consumes
the lives of tall demons
with glowing red hair and fiery eyes.

Can obtaining liberation from the three worlds

even come close to the enjoyment
of his great and magnificent glory?

8.10.7

He manifested himself
such that his glory,
mighty and incomparable,
will flourish forever.

He, the first seed of the sage,
the great Brahmā,[13]
He causes the three worlds to sprout

Rather than reach his feet,
soft as buds divine
incomparable, great, and blissful,

may it come to pass
that we have the great joy
of being one, forever,
with his servants.

8.10.8

Creating the cold waters of the ocean
he spread forth his feet
his shoulders and hair
without number
beyond compare;
Reclining, he appears
like a grove of flowers
and wish-fulfilling trees;
a mountain of gems
emitting the light of many suns.

May it come to pass
that we are ever with
crowds of his devotees.

8.10.9

He is the image of dexterity
destroying the strong deeds

13. "Great Brahmā" is the translation of *mā piramā* (Sanskrit: *mahā brahmā*). Commentators take this as a reference to the Para Brahman (Supreme Brahman), the transcendent reality, who is to be distinguished from the creator demigod Brahmā.

Vaṭakku Tiruvīti Piḷḷai, in his *Īṭu* (Thirty-six Thousand-paṭi) commentary gives a homely example to explain the reason for creation. The transcendent, ultimate reality, the Supreme Brahman, he says, became the "three-way" cause for the entire universe because of his care for human beings. While the Supreme Brahman is as detached as a "sage," he is *also* as caring as a mother who constantly thinks of her offspring, who is a foreign land. The Lord, therefore, gives rise to creation.

of the congregation of his devotees—
the Lord who wields a wheel, conch, sword,
bow, mace, and other weapons in war.

Ever youthful, father of the handsome love-god,
who holds five arrows.

May it come to pass that
I, destitute one, have the fortune
of being among the devotees,
of the devotees of the devotees,
of his faultless servants.

8.10.10

Age after age, and in every age
may it come to pass,
that I have as my rulers,
the servants of the servants,
of the servants,
of the inseparable servants[14] of the Lord—
my Lord, whose body has the hue
of an exquisite *kāyam* blossom;
my Lord, who has four shoulders,
and whose hand holds the golden wheel.

May I, a lonely person,
have the good fortune
of being in the clan of those
who serve these servants.

8.10.11

Caṭakōpaṉ from beautiful, cool Kurukūr,
spoke[15] about Kaṇṇaṉ who has eyes
[soft] as a water lily—
who fills and pervades the three worlds
where there is established order.

Those who are skilled in
these ten out of a thousand
will live happily at home, in comfort,
with agreeable wives and children.[16]

14. The commentator Vaṭakku Tiruvīti Piḷḷai identifies three kinds of servants from this set of songs and correlates them with the brothers of the Lord Rāmā in the epic Rāmāyaṇa. The "inseparable servant" mentioned in this verse is said to be exemplified by Lakṣmaṇa, who accompanied Rāmā everywhere and served him continuously. "Those [devotees] who, with triumph, are immersed, head-high, in serving the feet of the Lord" (8.10.2) is seen as a description of Bharata, who followed Rāmā's wishes and acted as a regent for the kingdom while Rāmā was in exile for fourteen years. The "faultless servant" mentioned in 8.10.9 is considered as highest praise, describing Śatrughna. Śatrughna was devoted to Bharata, who was a devotee of Rāmā.

15. At this point Vaṭakku Tiruvīti Piḷḷai comments that the Tiruvāymoḻi is like the Veda, which is self-manifested. The commentator goes on to compare the Sanskrit Veda to the *paratva* (supreme, transcendent) aspect of the Lord and the Tiruvāymoḻi to be his *avatāra* (descent; incarnation) form.

16. Examples of such wives and children are given by Vaṭakku Tiruvīti Piḷḷai. Several Śrīvaiṣṇavas (whom later accounts identify as Rāmānuja and party) stopped in the house of Celva Nampi in Tirukkottiyur, on the way to Tiru Anantapuram (modern Trivandrum). Celva Nampi was not in town, but his wife had their abundant grain pounded, cooked, and served to guests. When the husband returned and asked where the grain was she replied: "I have sown the grain which will grow in heaven!"

9.10

Nammāḻvār is described in the introduction to the commentaries as a being so detached that even if the seductive heavenly dancer Urvashi, whom ordinary people crave to meet, were to appear, he would address her as his mother. For Nammāḻvār there was to be no other love but God.

Vaṭakku Tiruvīti Piḷḷai cites paradigmatic Śrīvaiṣṇava devotees such as Toṇṭanūr Nampi and Eccāṉ, of whom we know very little, except that they "subsisted on service to other devotees," as the kind of ideal progeny that one will have if this set of verses is recited.

9.10.1

Approach the Entrancing Lord,
worship him and rise!
Your deeds will be destroyed.
Night and day,
place lotus flowers at his feet.
He, who rests on the banyan leaf
in the waters,
now dwells in Tirukaṇṇapuram,
where the waves crash against the tall walls
that surround the city.

9.10.2

Worship him with flowers
        that drip nectar
Place within yourself
Tirukaṇṇapuram[17]
encircled by walls
        that rise to the stars[18]
and fields near ponds
        inhabited by crabs.[19]
O servants,
        adore him every day
        and rise.[20]

9.10.3

O servants of the Lord!
If you want your sorrow gone,
adore him alone, place flowers
        not wilted by the wind, on him—
who is the ruler of this planet,
Lord of the immortal ones,[21]
who abides in Tirukaṇṇapuram,
        encircled by flower gardens where bees sing.

17. The Tamil words could possibly be translated as "place yourself within Tirukaṇṇapuram," but this interpretation is not seen in traditional works. Most commentators take the line "place Tirukaṇṇapuram within you" to mean "meditate on the sacred city of Tirukaṇṇapuram."

18. Or "walls made of silver." The Tamil word *veḷḷi* may mean either "silver" or "stars," and commentators give both interpretations for this line. They say that it is Nammāḻvār's love *(prema)* that makes him describe the walls as being constructed of silver.

19. *Naḷḷi* has been translated as "crab," following the commentators who explicitly say that it refers to a female crab. The Tamil lexicon cites this verse as one of the authorities for the meaning of the word.

20. "Adore him and rise" *(toḻutu eḻu)* is a phrase that Nammāḻvār uses in the first verse of the Tiruvāymoḻi.

21. A line taken to indicate the Lord's dominion over two realms: the created universe, which includes this earth *(līlā vibhūti)* and heaven *(nitya vibhūti)*. See Periyavāccāṉ Piḷḷai's and Vaṭakku Tiruvīti Piḷḷai's commentaries on this verse.

9.10.4

Adore him, the nectar,
with flowers that do not fade,
the bridegroom of young Pin̲n̲ai[22]
who has the glance of a fawn.

The Lord, who favors
Tirukaṇṇapuram
city surrounded by fortressed walls
that soar through the firmament,[23]
is our refuge.

9.10.5

Refuge of all those who reach his feet,[24]
Lord who gives Vaikuṇṭha when they die.
He who rules the earth
from Tirukaṇṇapuram
surrounded by fortressed walls
is all love[25] for his loved ones.

9.10.6

Beloved of those who attain his feet,
is the Lord who tore the
red-gold body of the demon.[26]
The beloved one of Tirukaṇṇapuram
encircled by fine walls
with golden turrets
is the True One, for all time,
for those true to him.

9.10.7

True to all who desire and adore him;
False to all who adore him outwardly.
Dear to all who embrace the body
of the Master of Tirukaṇṇapuram
where fishes frolic in flooded fields.

9.10.8

Dear to all those who reach his feet;
their bonds will be broken
He will destroy their births and rule.

22. Periyavāccān̲ Piḷḷai and Vaṭakku Tiruvīti Piḷḷai refer to Nappin̲n̲ai, a consort of Krishna, a "mediator" *(puruṣakāra)* between the human beings and the Lord. One is urged to seek the Lord as a refuge with Nappin̲n̲ai as the mediator.

23. The commentator Periyavāccān̲ Piḷḷai says: "Just as these walls are like a fortress to him, he is a fortress to you."

24. Commentators say that the *āl̲vār* spoke about acts of *bhakti yoga* in the earlier three verses, but that here the act of surrender, or *prapatti*, is described.

25. Periyavāccān̲ Piḷḷai and Vaṭakku Tiruvīti Piḷḷai say that the Lord and love are inseparable, so one cannot say that "he has love," because that indicates a theoretical distinction between the Lord and love. Rather, the Lord is completely love; it is as if love itself has assumed form.

26. A reference to Viṣṇu's incarnation as a man-lion to kill the "golden" *(hiraṇya)* demon.

Worship every day the unique feet
of the One who dwells in the highest place,
he who is in Tirukaṇṇapuram[27]
encircled by tall fortressed walls
of gold and gems.

27. The commentators say that
this city is like heaven; everything
there is present here.

9.10.9

As one worships his feet every day
bonds will be broken;
sorrow will not come near,
what then do I lack?
Those who reach the First One
of Tirukaṇṇapuram,
city desired by those
whose tongues utter the Vedas,[28]
there is no suffering.

28. Periyavāccāṉ Piḷḷai and Vaṭakku Tiruvīti Piḷḷai say that
"those whose tongues utter the
Vedas" is a reference to people
like Tirumaṅkai Āḻvār. According
to Śrīvaiṣṇava tradition, Tirumaṅkai Āḻvār is said to have sung the
Tiruvāymoḻi in front of the Lord
at Srīrangam, and the Tiruvāymoḻi is considered to be the Tamil
Veda.

9.10.10

There is no suffering; what then do I need?
The Lord oṅ whose sacred chest
dwells the lady of the lotus
is in Tirukaṇṇapuram
that is surrounded by rising walls
set with precious stones.
Say the name of this city[29] every day,
and no suffering will come near us, ever.

29. This is the last of the three al-
ternatives to reach God, mentioned in the introduction to this
decad. It was said that one can
reach the Lord through *bhakti*
yoga or, if unable to do those
acts, by *prapatti* by saying some
"words." Saying out loud with
one's tongue, *Tirukaṇṇapuram,* is
said to be this last way to reach
the Lord; if one does not have the
strength to get involved with
bhakti yoga or *prapatti*, one can
always reach him through "only
words" *(ukti).*

9.10.11

O you who want to break
the hold of deeds
and stop them from coming close,[30]
worship the feet of the Lord,
singing and dancing these ten
of the thousand Tamil songs[31]
sung by Caṭakōpaṉ who hails from Kurukūr,
a city with lofty mansions.

30. "Close" is the translation of
patu. The Tamil lexicon cites this
verse as the authority for such an
interpretation for the word.

31. "Just as a flower blossoms
with fragrance, Tamil verses set to
melody, sung with great love as
one falls at the Lord's feet" is considered to be the delicious act
that is enjoined by these verses.
See Periyavāccāṉ Piḷḷai's and Vaṭakku Tiruvīti Piḷḷai's commentaries on this verse.

10.9

The last two decads of the poem are vividly enacted in
Śrīvaiṣṇava temples to show Nammāḻvār's liberation and

return to humanity. While commentators say that Nammāl̲vār is describing the Śrīvaiṣṇava devotees' ascent to heaven, the rituals make it clear that it is Nammāl̲vār's own progress to Vaikuṇṭha, the sacred abode of Viṣṇu. The image of Nammāl̲vār is carried slowly by Śrīvaiṣṇava priests; others carry lighted flame torches to show the way. Nammāl̲vār is taken to the "great sacred canopy of gems" *(tirumāmaṇi maṇṭapa)* while this decad is chanted; the priests then walk around the Lord, who stands under the "sacred canopy" while reciting every verse of 10.10 twice. After the recitation Nammāl̲vār is made to bow at the feet of the Lord and is covered up with *tul̲ai,* or *tulasi,* leaves, signifying his liberation from the mortal world. A Śrīvaiṣṇava then steps up and requests the Lord to return Nammāl̲vār to human beings; the Lord answers through a priest, thundering forth: "We give him back to you." The curtains are drawn, the *tul̲ai* leaves removed, and Nammāl̲vār is slowly carried back to where the other *āl̲vārs* stand, to the recitation of Maturakavi Āl̲vār's Kaṇṇinun̲ Ciruttāmpu (The Short Knotted String). This ritual is known as the "Liberation of Nammāl̲vār" (*Nammāl̲vār mokṣam*). In Srirangam, the recitation of the tenth hundred takes place about 2.00 A.M., but the *araiyars* stop with 10.8. At 6.00 A.M. they resume with 10.9, and Nammāl̲vār's liberation is enacted in front of a crowd of thousands, which has been gathering since 4.30 A.M.

10.9.1

The encircling firmament
and resplendent clouds
beat the sound of joyous drums.
The deep oceans raised their arms
of billowing waves and danced.
The seven worlds, bearing riches,
rejoiced, seeing the devotees
of my father Nāraṇan̲,
whose glory ever rises.

10.9.2

Seeing the devotees of Nāraṇan̲,
clouds in the high heavens rejoiced

and filled auspicious golden jars
with their pure waters.[32]
The oceans, adorned with waters, roared;
the worlds were filled with pennants
made of the tall mountains,
    and all adored [the devotees].

32. In south India honored visitors are greeted with pots filled with water, with which they may refresh themselves. A filled golden jar or pot (*pūrna poṟ kuṭam*, a phrase also used by the *āḻvār* Āṇṭāḷ in Nācciyār Tirumoḻi 6.1) is supposed to be auspicious, a place where the goddess Lakṣmī resides.

10.9.3

The people of the world adored them.
They showered mists of incense
and large [fragrant] flowers,
throwing them in front of the devotees
    of [the Lord] who, long ago,
    measured this earth.
Like music on both sides,
the sages came in front,
saying, "Come: Yonder lies the path to heaven."

10.9.4

Immortals kept coming
in front of Mātavaṉ's devotees,
    [Mātavaṉ,] who wears the *tuḻai*
    dripping with nectar on his head,
and created places to rest.
The brilliant suns with their many [radiant] hands
    pointed the way [to heaven]
and drums with resounding voices
roared with waves in the ocean.

10.9.5

Because they are devotees of Mātavaṉ,
celestial beings came outside saying,
"Come, enter our abodes."
Kinnaras and Garuḍas sang many songs;
and those whose good mouths [recited] the Vedas
offered the [fruits] of their sacrifices to them.

10.9.6

As they offered the sacrifices,
a fragrant mist of smoke wafted,
trumpets and conches blew in unison,

spreading the sounds of music everywhere.
"Rule over the skies, O you devotees
of the Lord with the wheel,"
blessed the [celestial] women,
their brilliant eyes flashing delight.

10.9.7

The clan of servants
of our Kēcavan̲ who lies in the deep sea,
the cowherd of Kuṭantai
whose head glows with the radiance of gems.
were blessed by the women,
while the Winds and the Precious Ones
began to voice their praises in all directions.

10.9.8

Approaching the tall walls and towers
adorned with flags,
the Celestial Ones, with crowned heads
came ahead, row after row,
as [the devotees] entered
the Heavens of Handsome Mātavan̲.

10.9.9

As they entered the portals of heaven,
the celestials said,
"the devotees of the Lord of heaven
are our friends; come enter our place."
The immortal ones and the silent sages of heaven
were full of wonder.
It is the destiny of those who dwell on earth
to enter heaven.

10.9.10

They have entered by [divine] decree
said the good reciters of the Vedas
and, as was custom, washed their feet,
outside their abode;
women with faces [glowing] like the moon
came carrying treasures,[33] fragrant powder,
jars filled [lighted] lamps.

33. *Niti*, from Sanskrit *nidhi*, "treasure." Piḷḷān̲, the first commentator on the TVM, interprets the word as "Śrī Caṭakōpan̲." The name Caṭakōpan̲ (Nammāḻvār) is given to the silver crown in Śrīvaiṣṇava temples, which is engraved with the feet of the Lord. This crown is kept on devotees' heads as a mark of the Lord's grace, and to reiterate Nammāḻvār's inseparability with the Lord's feet the crown is called by his name. Piḷḷān̲ therefore is saying that the greatest treasure of a Śrīvaiṣṇava is the feet of the Lord and association with Nammāḻvār.

10.9.11

As he came and faced [God]
there was a state of infinite bliss
    being with the servants [of God]
    in the great canopy of gems.
Those who can [say] the thousand verses[34]
spoken by Caṭakōpaṉ from Kurukūr
    [city] abundant with gardens
    where bunches of blossoms grow
are silent sages.

34. *Cantas,* from Sanskrit *(chandas).*

10.10

10.10.1

O Sage! O four-faced god! O you with three eyes!
My cruel one, dark as a gem!
O you who steal [my heart]!
Dear life of me, a lonely [soul],
you came and became one with my head;
and I shall not let you go.
Lord,
    don't tantalize me more!

10.10.2

Don't entrance me more!
I swear,
    on the lady whose hair is fragrant with flowers,
    on her, who is like a garland of blossoms
    on your sacred chest!
I take a sacred oath on you,

You loved me,
    and took me without hesitation, so
    my life was one, not different from yours.
O come, beckon me to you!

10.10.3

Now come call me to you, my dark, bewitching gem!
I know not of any pole for my soul to lean on,
    other than you.

O First Cause, from whose navel comes the lotus flower!
[Creator] of Brahmā, Śiva, Indra,
and all others who worship you with ardor!
O Cause of the heavens!

10.10.4

O you who are exquisite fertile cosmic matter![35]
O you who mingled inseparably within it!
O glorious flame of the skies![36]
You are Brahmā and Śiva within [this domain],
O sage who created the divine ones and human beings!
How could you abandon me with my burden
and let me stay here?

35. *Pāle,* "primordial matter or soul"; commentators take it as both and say that it is that which is capable of growth, that which has potential for creation.

36. Commentators take the two words "flame" *(cōti)* and "skies" *(amparam)* to mean fire and ether and as indicative of the other three primordial categories—water, earth, and air.

10.10.5

Just whom can I turn to
if you let me stray outside your hold?
What is mine? Who am I?
Like red-hot iron drinking water
You drank my life to exhaustion[37] and
then became nectar, never ending for me.

37. The Tamil words being ambiguous, the line could read: ". . . like red-hot iron sucking water, / I drank you, my life, to exhaustion."

10.10.6

Becoming nectar that never can end for me,
My love, you dwelt in my soul, within my life,
and ate them as if you could not have your fill.
What more can you eat?
You, dark as a *kāya* flower,
eyes like lotus,
lips, red as fruit,
are the beloved of the lady of the flower,
so fit for you.

10.10.7

My love, you became the beloved
of the radiant lady of the lotus flower.
Like a blue mountain that clutches
and lifts up two crescent moons,
My Father, you, as a resplendent boar,
raised your tusks, carrying Earth.

O you who churned the deep blue sea!
I have obtained you,
would I now let you go?

10.10.8

I have obtained you,
would I now let you go,
my unique exalted life?
You are the two kinds of deeds,
you are life, you are its consequence;
you are in the dense forests [of existence]
in all the three worlds.

O my first matchless seed [of creation]!
Pervading this dense forest,
you are hidden, diffused.

10.10.9

O unique primordial seed,
cause of the three worlds
and everything thereon!
There is none your equal.
You are here, there, on everything;
in life and matter.
You surround all that is
vast, deep, and high,
infinitely.
When shall I reach you,
O First One, O Matchless One?

10.10.10

O supreme cosmic matter,
that surrounds, spreads wide,
dives deep, and soars so high!
O supreme transcendent flaming flower
that encompasses [creation]!
O incomparable blazing fire of wisdom and bliss
that pervades [the universe]![38]

Greater than these was my desire
that was quenched
when you filled and embraced me.

38. This verse is marked by repetition of words. The word *cūḻntu* occurs five times, and I have translated it as "surrounds, encompasses, pervades, filled, and embraced." The word *periya* (big) occurs four times, and I have rendered it as "supreme, incomparable, and great."

10.10.11

Those who know these ten passionate linked [verses][39]
which conclude the thousand passionate linked [songs]
said by Kurukūr Caṭakōpan̲,
whose craving ended,
who attained liberation,
who called on Ari,
[Lord] who destroys desires, who encompasses Ayan̲ and Aran̲,

will be born, so high.

39. The word translated as "linked" is *antāti* (end-beginning). This is the style in which the last word of a verse becomes the first word of the next one.

NOTES

Chapter 1: Introduction

1. The name Nammāḻvār, "Our Āḻvār," is supposed to have been given by the Lord at Srirangam. See Hari Rao, *Koil Oḻugu,* 10.

2. Tamil is "vernacular" only because it is an indigenous language and is a "mother tongue," but it is *not* vernacular in the sense of being "nonclassical." Tamil literature dates back to (approximately) the first century C.E., and the earliest extant poems are sophisticated pieces. In this connection, see Ramanujan, *Interior Landscape,* 115.

3. For further details, see Hardy, *Viraha Bhakti,* esp. 637–52.

4. References are to the section of 100 verses (*pattu*), decad (*tiruvāymoḻi*), and verse (*pācuram*). Thus 7.9.1 would refer to the seventh hundred, ninth decad, first verse.

5. See Hardy, "The Tamil Veda of a Śūdra Saint."

6. In particular, the studies of Renou, Winternitz, and Gonda have been very influential in the latter half of this century.

7. Brown, "Purāṇa as Scripture: From Sound to Image of the Holy Word in the Hindu Tradition," 82.

8. The translator, Sri Satyamurti Ayyangar, interprets the verses in light of the vast exegetical literature, a practice that is lauded by the Śrīvaiṣṇava community, which has long seen the verses through the prism of the five classical commentaries written between the twelfth and fifteenth centuries.

Chapter 2: The Sacred Utterance of the Silent Seer

Epigraph: Vaṭivaḻakiya Nampi Tācar, *The Glory of the Āḻvārs,* v. 838.

1. I have discussed the influence of the classical Caṅkam poems on the Tiruvāymoḻi in "Hindu Devotional Literature" and, with Carman, in *The Tamil Veda,* chap. 2.

2. Books published in India include Damodaran, *The Literary Value of the Tiruvaymoli;* and Balasundara Nayakar, *Īṭṭurai Āṟāychi and Commentary on Tiruvaymoli* (for Agapporul stanzas only). The commentaries on the Tiruvāymoḻi by Uttamūr Viraraghavacariyar and Annangaracariyar also note some of the literary conventions in passing.

Detailed discussions are found in Ramanujan, *Hymns for the Drowning;* Hardy, *Viraha Bhakti;* Narayanan, "Hindu Religious Literature"; and Carman and Narayanan, *Tamil Veda.*

3. "That which is heard." See, however, Aḻakiya Maṉavāḷa Nāyanār's *Ācārya Hṛdayam,* sūtra 45, in which he refers to both Vedas as "sweet to hear" (*śruti cevikkiniya*), and Vaṭivaḻakiya Nampi Tācar's *Āḻvārkaḷ Vaibhavam,* v. 905, in which the Lord makes Nammāḻvār live on earth to give "the *śruti* in Tamil." Nammāḻvār himself refers to the Sanskrit works as *śruti* in Tiruvāymoḻi (henceforth TVM) 1.1.7.

4. *Maṛai* is frequently used by the *āḻvārs* and in the classical Caṅkam poetry to refer to the Vedas. It literally means "mystery."

5. Jaimini composed the sūtras in the second century B.C.E., and Sabara commented upon them around the second century C.E. On the views of Jaimini, see Clooney's book *Thinking Ritually: Rediscovering the Pūrva Mīmāṁsā of Jaimini.*

6. Sivaraman, "The Word as a Category of Revelation," 48 (italics added).

7. Meanings taken from Apte's *Student's Sanskrit-English Dictionary. Puruṣa* is "man," and *a-pauruṣeya* would be "unmanly," or "not of men."

8. The Śrīvaiṣṇava position is summarized by Clooney in "Why the Veda Has No Author," 679–80.

9. *Vedartha Sangraha of Sri Ramanujacharya,* trans. Raghavachar, 180.

10. Raghavachar comments:

> It may appear strange that [Ramanuja] does not take the scripture as springing from God. That position is possible for the *Nyāya* school which claims to have established the existence of God on speculative grounds. But in this school [Śrīvaiṣṇavism] and Vedāntic schools in general, which altogether base their idea of the Supreme on the Vedas, such a course of thought would imply a logical see-saw. "God exists because that is the verdict of the scriptures, and the scriptures are to be admitted, because they form revelations from God."

Raghavachar concludes this discussion by saying that it is in a theistic school that supreme wisdom can properly be spoken of as ever existing. Intro., *Vedarthasangraha of Sri Ramanujacharya,* 10.

11. Raghavachar, Intro., 9.

12. Srinivasa Raghavan, *Sri Vishnu Sahasranama with the Bhasya of Sri Parasara Bhattar,* 259–60.

13. Clooney, "Why the Veda Has No Author," 680.

14. *Cilappatikāram,* bk. 1, canto 10, l. 192. The teachings of Mahāvīra are alluded to (l. 195) as sacred words, *tiru moli,* and the scriptures of the Jaina tradition as Veda (ll. 189–90).

15. Zelliot, "The Medieval Bhakti Movement in History," 153.

16. Ibid., 157.

17. For more details on this concept, see Carman and Narayanan, *Tamil Veda*, esp. chap. 1.

18. Alakiya Maṇavāḷa Nāyaṉār, *The Heart of the Teacher*, sūtra 39, p. 76.

19. Ibid., sūtras 41 and 43.

20. Ibid., sūtra 45. The last phrase in Tamil is "*paṇṭai nirkum muntai alivillā*" (preexistent, without beginning or end).

21. Ibid., sūtra 48 and commentary.

22. Piḷḷāṉ, commentary on Tiruvāymoli 1.1.7. His statement comes after he quotes seventy-three verses from the Vedas and later Sanskrit (*smṛti*) literature.

23. Vaṭivalakiya Nampi Tācar's work, *Ālvārkaḷ Vaipavam* (The Glory of the Ālvārs), has not been utilized by Western scholars in their study of Nammālvār. His biography of the Śrīvaiṣṇava teachers is divided into two large sections, one that focuses on the *ālvārs* and one that describes the lives of the *ācāryas*, primarily Rāmānuja.

Vaṭivalakiya Nampi Tācar's work is in Tamil verse. He was apparently a disciple of one Āttāṉ, who was also known as Rāmānuja Piḷḷai. This Rāmānuja Piḷḷai was the disciple of Maṇavāḷa Māmuṉi (b. 1365), the celebrated Śrīvaiṣṇava teacher. Three versions of this text have been published in the twentieth century, and the most recent one (see biblio. for details) makes use of all the early editions. This one contains 308 verses on Nammālvār, of which 138 summarize the Tiruvāymoli. The treatment of the different sets of "10" verses is somewhat uneven; some sets are summarized in 3 or 4 verses, and sometimes 2 sets are presented in one verse.

24. 4.10.1. In his comment on this verse Piḷḷāṉ, who is normally very sparing in his use of quotation, has a string of seventy-four quotations from the Sanskrit canon, though only some of them are from the Vedas.

25. *Glory of the Ālvārs*, v. 870. The "lotus seat" (*padmāsana*, generally translated as "lotus position") is adopted by a yogic aspirant of supreme knowledge.

26. Ibid., v. 873. The reference is to an incarnation of Viṣṇu as a boar (Varāha) to save the Goddess of the Earth and all beings of the world.

27. Ibid., v. 874–76. The crushing of the Advaitin and Śaivaite beliefs are stated in v. 876.

The phrase "that thou art" (*tat tvam asi*) is from the Chāndogya Upanisad of the Sāma Veda. The seventh-century philosopher Śaṅkara and his followers interpret this phrase as affirming the identity between the human soul (*ātman*) and the supreme spirit, Brahman.

28. Ibid., vv. 904 and 905.

29. Ibid., v. 909.

30. Ibid., v. 910.

31. A reference to the fact that Nammāḻvār was supposedly born in the "fourth" class of society, which had been traditionally prohibited from learning the Vedas.

32. *Glory of the Āḻvārs,* vv. 967 and 968.

33. "Mentally," according to the author of this work, because, according to him, Nammāḻvār never moved from his position under the tamarind tree. The author thus explains the references to other places and Nammāḻvār's travels in the poem by saying that these were mental journeys and not those that took place physically.

34. The exact word is *muniṭṭu* (in front of; through the [good graces] of).

35. *Glory of the Āḻvārs,* v. 997.

36. The meaning of the Tiruvāymoḻi, however, was not given to the uninitiated and, in earlier centuries, to those who (by character or inclination) were not considered to be fit recipients of the Veda.

37. This is a limited analogy, applicable only to the point being discussed. Almost all Śrīvaiṣṇava theologians would agree that both the Sanskrit and Tamil Vedas are as "immeasurable" as the ocean.

38. *Heart of the Teacher,* sūtra 71 and commentary.

39. Ibid., sūtra 72 and commentary.

40. See bibliography, under Vedānta Deśika, *Dramiḍopaniṣad Tātparya Ratnāvaḷi and Sāra,* for publication details. The Tiruvāymoḻi Nūṟṟantāti is frequently added to Teṅkalai versions of the *The Sacred Collect of Four Thousand Verses* and can be read in the edition published by Annangaracariyar.

It appears that almost any work of a hundred verses was considered to be a synopsis of the Tiruvāymoḻi. Recently, the blurb on the dust jacket of a record containing Vedānta Deśika's "Daya Sathakam" (A Hundred Verses on Mercy) declared: "Research scholars have demonstrated that the 10 decads of the Stotra [i.e., the hymn "Daya Sathakam"], deal respectively with the ten hundreds of Nammāḻvār's Tiruvoimozhi."

41. However, while the literature of the community emphasized the philosophical aspect of the poems, the emotional content was retained and reiterated in Śrīvaiṣṇava ritual.

42. The Tiruvāymoḻi and the other works of the *āḻvārs* influence the Sanskrit literature in a remarkable way. See Hardy, *Viraha Bhakti,* for the influences of the Tamil hymns on the *Bhāgavata Purāṇa.*

43. Aḻakiya Maṇavāḷa Nāyaṉar, *Heart of the Teacher,* sūtra 59; Nañjīyar, *Nine Thousand-paṭi Commentary,* on the Tiruvāymoḻi, intro.

44. *Heart of the Teacher,* sūtra 46.

45. Ibid., sūtra 47.

46. Commentary on sūtra 47, p. 85.

47. The date is given by the editor in the Sarasvati Mahal publication of *Nammāḻvār Tiru tāllāṭṭu.*

48. These biographies are comparatively late. There are, of course, several references to Nammāḻvār in earlier works. There are brief references to him in *Rāmānuja Nūṟṟantāti* and a detailed biography in Garuḍa Vāhana Paṇḍita's *The Story of the Divine Sages (Divya Sūri Caritam).* The three texts that I have chosen represent a later and more composite view of the poet's life.

49. *Glory of the Āḻvārs,* vv. 790–95.

50. Ibid., v. 809. The following paragraphs are a summary of vv. 811–16.

51. Ibid., v. 829.

52. Ibid., v. 870.

53. Ibid., v. 113.

54. *The Splendor,* 98. The *Koyil Oḻuku,* or the *Chronicles of the [Srirangam] Temple,* a document that was compiled over several centuries and which sometimes tried to "fill in the gaps" for previous times when entries were not made, gives another version of how the Tiruvāymoḻi came to be held in high esteem as a Veda. According to this work, Tirumaṅkai Āḻvār, one of the twelve *āḻvārs,* petitioned the Lord at Srirangam to have the Tiruvāymoḻi chanted in that temple and to give it equal status as a Veda. The Lord had been pleased with Tirumaṅkai Āḻvār and apparently acceded to the request. In commemoration of this the Tiruvāymoḻi is chanted once a year, over a period of ten nights, starting on the eleventh day after the new moon in the month of Mārkaḻi (15 Dec.–13 Jan.). This festival is called the Festival of Recitation (*adhyayanotsava*), and it is significant that the Sanskrit word *adhyayana* (literally, "learning, study, especially the Vedas"), which is traditionally reserved only for the study and chanting of the Vedas, should be used in this context.

55. *Glory of the Āḻvārs,* v. 897.

56. Ibid., v. 898.

57. Ibid., vv. 904–5.

58. Ibid., vv. 904–9.

59. *The Splendor,* 117–19.

Chapter 3: Reciters of the Sacred Text

1. Meanings taken from Monier-Williams's Sanskrit-English dictionary and the Tamil lexicon. On the use of the word *anusandhānam* as a prefix to a chief reciter and *anusandhikaḷ* for other reciters, see Viraraghavacharya, *History of Tirupati* 2:722 n. 1. The word *anusandhānam* seems to have occurred for the first time in the Tirupati Temple inscriptions, in one dated 17 February 1446

(1.220) and again in 1496 (2.135 [26 Aug. 1496]). See Viraraghavacharya, *History* 2:726.

2. Nammāḻvār frequently refers to his "Tamil verses" and seems self-conscious about the language he has composed in; in addition to the verses cited he also refers to his Tamil verses, or songs, in Tiruvāymoḻi 4.7.11, 4.9.11, 5.1.11, 6.5.11, 7.8.11, 9.8.11, 9.10.11, 10.8.11.

3. Nammāḻvār refers to his verses being sung, in Tiruvāymoḻi 1.5.11, 2.3.11, 2.4.11, 2.6.11, 2.8.11, 4.1.11, 4.7.11, 6.1.11, 6.2.11, 7.1.11, 7.6.11, 8.2.11, 9.2.11, 9.10.11.

4. *Ōtutal*: "recite audibly in order to commit to memory; to recite the Veda with the appropriate intonation" (meanings taken from the Tamil lexicon).

5. See also the discussion on the use of the word *vacana* in chap. 2.

6. The word *kūṟutal*, "to say," is used in 2.5.11; he says that he has "said" *(uṟaitta)* the poem in 3.1.11; *uṟaitta*, 3.6.11, 4.9.11, 5.1.11, 5.3.11, 6.7.11, 7.8.11, 9.7.11, 10.3.11; *connālē*, 3.8.11, 3.9.11.

7. The word *araiyar* is usually taken to mean "king," and the *araiyar* is considered to be the monarch of the verses he recites. *Aṟai* also means "to declaim" or "to say."

8. K. V. Raman, *Sri Varadarajaswami Temple–Kanchi*, 114.

9. Kane, *History of Dharmasastra* (Ancient and Medieval Religious and Civil Law), 2:237.

10. Personal communication, 13 January 1990 and 7 July 1991.

11. Levering, *Rethinking Scripture*, 14. Levering uses the word *transactive* in a more restricted sense; it would apply to those cases in which a person would recite a text and hope to pass the merits on to someone else. While clarifying the concept with Levering, and discussing the Tiruvāymoḻi, she agreed that the instance quoted here would come under the category of "transactive," although she had not specifically included this type of phenomena in her discussions.

12. Although I have heard some *adhyāpakas* split up the words in this verse in the manner that Nadhamuni Araiyar decried, Sri Parthsarathy Iyengar from the Triplicane Temple does not do it. I heard the recording of the Periya Tirumoḻi, which he had made for me, and he carefully pronounced the name Tillai completely, to give the right meaning for the line.

13. His forgetting all else became crucial in the history of the Śrīvaiṣṇava community. According to tradition, in his excitement to undertake the pilgrimage immediately he forgot his appointment with his teacher, Kurukai Kāvalappaṉ, who was supposed to teach him the secrets of yoga. Yāmuna remembered this appointment on his way to Tiru Ananta Puram, but it was too late by that time; his teacher had died. Because of this missed appointment,

the whole tradition of yoga as a way to liberation is said to have been lost from the Śrīvaiṣṇava tradition (*The Splendor,* 137).

14. Venkateswara is the name of Viṣṇu's manifestation at Tiruvenkatam, south India, a place known in ancient Tamil literature as Tiruvenkatam and more commonly as Tirupati today. The temple in Pittsburgh was built with the blessings of and guidance from Sri Venkateswara Temple in Tirupati, India. This is the richest and one of the most famous temples in the subcontinent, and hundreds of songs in the Divya Prabandham are devoted to the Lord here. The songs from the Tiruvāymoḻi (3.3.1–11 and 6.10.1–11) are translated in the appendix. I have discussed the Pittsburgh temple and its rituals in "Creating South Indian 'Hindu' Experience in the United States."

15. A Śrīvaiṣṇava priest is trained to offer worship in temples and to conduct domestic religious rituals connected with weddings, pregnancy, naming of a child, birthdays (especially the important ones, such as sixtieth and eightieth ones for a man), investiture of the sacred thread, and funeral and ancestral ceremonies. The priest usually has to be married before he has the authority to conduct many of the domestic rituals. Apart from learning how to conduct temple worship he usually has to undergo a special initiation, called *dīkṣa,* which gives him the right to enter the sacred chamber in which the Lord is enshrined.

16. This account is based on interviews conducted with Sri Venkatacharlu in the summer of 1988 and with Sri Krishnamacharylu, by telephone, in December 1987.

17. The *sandhya vandanam* is a ritual prayer said by every male after he has received the sacred thread and undergone the initiation, or Upanayana, ceremony. It included the repetition of the *Gāyatri* mantra ("We meditate on the effulgence of the sun; may it illumine our minds") about 108 times, along with ancillary mantras.

18. The Hindu Temple Society of Southern California is located at 1600 Las Virgenes Canyon Road, Calabasas, CA 91302.

19. On the acrimonious legal battles fought about traditional rights in the Triplicane Temple, see Appadurai, *Worship and Conflict under Colonial Rule.*

20. Some orthoprax Śrīvaiṣṇavas respect, but do not venerate, the head of the Kanchi monastery, who follows the nondualistic teachings of the philosopher-teacher Sankara (8th c.). The irony of asking Sri Parthsarathy Iyengar, a pious Śrīvaiṣṇava, to seek the blessings of this Sankaracharya is obvious. Apparently, when Sri Parthsarathy Iyengar approached the Kanchi Sankaracharya with his problem the abbot kept repeating the Lord's name, Nārāyaṇa, for over twenty minutes. Sri P. Iyengar interpreted this as meaning that his project will be successful but that the fund raising will take a long time.

21. Complete details of the funds raised for the regular celebration of

one of the events for which the association is responsible are given in the annual brochure produced by "Sri Udayavar Kaimkarya Sabha" (The Association to Render Loving Service to Rāmānuja). Under the rubric of this association the birth anniversary of Rāmānuja is celebrated every month, and during the annual birthday celebrations a full recitation of the Tiruvāymoḻi takes place.

22. K. V. Raman, *Sri Varadarajaswami Temple–Kanchi,* 135.

23. Ibid.

24. Details of the expenditures connected with the celebration of festivals on important days at the Rāmānuja Shrine in the Triplicane Temple are published in the annual report of Sri Udayavar Kaimkarya Sabha, and the categories given in the text were summarized from the reports for the years 1987 and 1988. Thus, while the recitation is done during volunteered time, the other expenses connected with regular festivals are still borne by the association.

25. On the theological differences between the Vaṭakalai and Teṅkalai Śrīvaiṣṇavas, see my dissertation, "The Śrīvaiṣṇava Understanding of *Bhakti* and *Prapatti:* Āḻvārs to Vedānta Deśika"; and Mumme's fine analysis in *The Śrīvaiṣṇava Theological Dispute.* On the legal feuds in the Triplicane Temple, see Appadurai, *Worship and Conflict under Colonial Rule.*

Chapter 4: Recital of the Divya Prabandham

1. *The Splendor,* 157, 160.

2. I have occasionally seen 4.1 of the Tiruvāymoḻi added to the Temple Tiruvāymoḻi set.

3. These sets are 2.10 (Tirumaliruncolai); 3.3 (Tiruvenkatam); 4.10 (Tirukkurukur or Alvar Tirunagari, Nammāḻvār's birthplace); 5.8 (Tirukutantai or Kumbakonam); 6.10 (Tiruvenkatam); 7.2 (Srirangam); 9.10 (Tirukannapuram).

4. I am indebted to Sri Parthsarathy Iyengar, secretary, Veda Adhyapaka Goshti of the Triplicane Temple, for the details of the daily recitation.

5. While the *āḻvārs* sang about 108 *divya desas,* or "sacred places," two of them are deemed to be outside this earth: one is Vaikuṇṭham, or heaven, and the other is Tirupārkaṭal, or the Ocean of Milk. Many of the temples are in the modern states of Tamilnadu and Andhra Pradesh, and in these temples the songs of the *āḻvārs* are recited regularly. The hymns are not recited in the sacred places in northern India and in many of the temples of Kerala.

6. Tirukkachi Nampi was a nonbrahmin teacher of the *ācārya* Rāmānuja. The poem "Rāmānuja Nūṟṟantāti" (The Hundred Verses on Rāmānuja in the *Antāti* Style), which had been composed by Amutaṉār in honor of Rāmā-

nuja, is recited on Tirukachi Nampi's birthday because he is said to delight in the praise of his disciple.

As a general rule of thumb, during the celebration of the birth stars of the major *ācāryas,* whether they were the teachers or disciples of Rāmānuja, the Rāmānuja Nūṟṟantāti is recited. Since Rāmānuja is the most important teacher in the tradition, it is popularly held that one is saved through one's connection with him.

If the birth star of an *āḻvār* is shared with a teacher, a work composed by the *āḻvār* is recited.

7. The Perumāḷ Tirumoḻi of Kulacēkara Āḻvār has many verses dedicated to Viṣṇu's incarnation as Rāma. Rāma's star in the Hindu calendar is Punarvasu, and, since the poem Perumāḷ Tirumoḻi focuses on devotion to Rāma, it is easy to see why it is recited on that star day.

Empār was Rāmānuja's cousin, and Mutaliyāṇṭāṉ was Rāmānuja's nephew. Both of them were devoted to Rāmānuja, and they are considered to be important teachers in the early Śrīvaiṣṇava tradition.

8. Since Kurattāḻvāṉ was Rāmānuja's disciple, the work in honor of his teacher is recited that day.

9. Maṇavāḷa Māmuṉi, an important Śrīvaisnava teacher, is considered to be one of the principal *ācāryas* of the Teṅkalai sect. He commented upon the works of Piḷḷai Lokācārya and Aḻakiya Maṇavāḷa Nāyaṉār (see chap. 1) and wrote several independent poems. The Upadeśaratnamālai (The Gem-Necklace of Instruction) is seventy-four verses long and is also recited by the Triplicane *adhyāpakas* when the Lord is taken in procession through the streets during the Festival of Recitation in December. This Tamil poem is not part of the Divya Prabandham but is usually appended to Teṅkalai versions of the book. In this poem Maṇavāḷa Māmuṉi praises all the *āḻvārs* and teachers. Sri Parthsarathy Iyengar thought that it was significant that the poem had seventy-four verses. He explained that the Veeranam reservoir (near the birthplace of the first teacher, Nāthamuni) is said to have seventy-four outlets and that there is a Tamil saying that, even if the oceans dry up, the Veeranam Lake will not.

The entire Divya Prabandham is said to have had its debut in this area in the time of Nāthamuni. The Veeranam reservoir was apparently built around the eleventh century C.E. by the Chola king Rajendra (1011–1037). It is over ten miles long and about three-and-a-half miles wide and is the major source of irrigation in the area (Randhawa et al., *Farmers of India,* p. 39; and Francis, *Madras District Gazetteers, South Arcot,* 1: 132–33). The fact that it had four major water weirs and apparently seventy-four other outlets has been significant in the Śrīvaiṣṇava oral tradition. Rāmānuja, before his death, appointed four major teachers and seventy-four "guardians of the throne" to safeguard the Śrīvaiṣṇava tradition. According to the historical evidence, the reservoir was built on the lake, possibly during Rāmānuja's youth (the traditional dates ascribed to him are 1017–1137), and it seems significant that he would use that almost as a model in rendering his community fertile and prosperous. The numerical significance was continued further by Maṇavāḷa Māmuṉi, who wrote seventy-four verses in honor of all the *āḻvārs* and teachers whom he may have considered as life-giving waters of the community.

The initial analogy of the seventy-four verses and the Veeranam Lake was given by Sri Parthsarathy Iyengar in an interview in December 1988. The research on the reservoir and historical information and details on its construction was done by Sri V. R. Rajagopalan, Neelangarai, Madras.

The Upadeśaratnamālai is recited by the Teṅkalai Śrīvaiṣṇava temples. In the temples, where the Vaṭakalais are in charge, Tiruvōṇam (Sanskrit: *Śravaṇam*), the birth star of Vedānta Deśika (1268–1368), is celebrated, and Deśika's works are recited.

10. Viśvaksena is considered to be the "obstace remover" and commander of the Lord's army (Tamil: *cēnai mutali*) in Śrīvaiṣṇava mythology. He has the place of Ganeśa in many households and is propitiated before the commencement of any important activity.

11. Toṇṭaraṭipoṭi Āḻvār composed the Tirumālai in honor of the Lord in Srirangam, and so this poem is recited at the time of the birth star of the Raṅganātha, the manifestation of Viṣṇu at Srirangam.

Chapter 5: Recitation in Nammāḻvār's Congregation

1. I use the term *scheduled caste* to refer to those who have been traditionally known in Western scholarship as "outcaste." Mahatma Gandhi coined the word *Harijan* (children of God—i.e., children of Hari/Viṣṇu), but I agree with Juergensmeyer's assessment that the people known traditionally as untouchables find the word patronizing in tone (*Religion as a Social Vision,* 14). The members of the Gowthamapuram community used the word *Harijan* just one time to describe themselves. The more opaque term *scheduled caste,* which is the federal administrative label, was mentioned a few times. The community never uses the word *untouchable,* and so I have refrained from using the term, though it has some academic currency and does not mask the orthoprax "high-caste" Hindu's attitude with a euphemistic term. Rāmānuja is said to have converted several outcastes to the community and to have called them "those of the sacred clan" (*tirukulattār*), but, since that word has little recognition, I did not use it. The name Dalit has been popular in recent years, but I did not hear the people near Nammāḻvār's shrine use that word at all.

2. The Sanskrit word *sannidhi* means "appearance, receptacle, presence." Śrīvaiṣṇavas use the word to indicate the sanctum of a temple or a shrine. The

word will be translated in this paper as "shrine," or a place in which the divine presence is perceived.

3. My participation and observation took place in May–June 1983 and 1985. I first came into contact with the members of the shrine dedicated to the female *āḻvār* Āṇṭāḷ, through the kindness of Smt. Ranganayaki Sampathkumaran of Bangalore. Mr. and Mrs. R. Sampathkumaran had visited the Antal Shrine in 1981 and presided over the birthday celebrations of Āṇṭāḷ. Sri M. S. Kanakarajan of Vannarpet, Bangalore, who is in charge of that shrine, took me to the Nammāḻvār Cannati.

4. Nonbrahmin ascetics (*saṁnyāsis*) are known as *ekāngis* by the Śrīvaiṣṇavas. They are distinguished from *saṁnyāsis*, who were brahmins prior to their renunciation by at least two outersymbols: the *ekāngis* do not wear a sacred thread, and they do not carry the three staffs (*tridaṇḍa*) bound together. It must be noted that, according to the thirteenth-century biography, *The Splendor*, Rāmānuja said that the Śrīvaiṣṇavas *saṁnyāsis* (in contradistinction to *advaitin* monks) should wear the sacred thread, carry a *tridaṇḍa*, and have a tuft of hair on the head. I have discussed this in "Renunciation in Saffron and White Robes."

5. The *Śrībhāṣya* was written by Rāmānuja, the primary interpreter of Sanskrit scripture for the Śrīvaiṣṇava community. His commentary on the *Vedānta*, or *Brahma Sūtras*, was called the *Śrībhāṣya;* the section that Sri Govindaraja Ramanuja Dāsar has exegeted is called *apaśūdrādikaraṇam* and deals with the question of authority of the *śūdras* to receive *brahmavidya*. This is *Śrībhāṣya* 1.3.33–40.

6. See Govindacharya, *The Life of Ramanujacharya*, 191 and 192, including n. 1. Sri Govindacharya does not report the sources for this discussion. He follows the thirteenth-century hagiography *The Splendor* fairly closely, but this incident is quoted in parentheses and is not found in it. Govindacharya does have an interesting footnote based on a report from the newspaper *The Hindu*, 5 February 1906. In the midst of its editorializing about Rāmānuja's liberal attitude toward the *tirukulattār* the article also mentions the special canopy (*pantal*) erected by the *tirukulattār* of Bangalore to "greet Their Royal Highnesses." It is quite possible that these people in the newspaper article are the ancestors or part of the same congregation as the ancestors of Sri Vipranarayana.

Gnanambal, in her article "Srivaishnavas and their Religious Institutions," also reports Rāmānuja's conversion of the outcastes and his calling them *tirukulattār* (125).

7. Gnanambal briefly mentions the establishment of the shrine (see ibid.). She reports a conversation with one Sri V. T. Tirunarayana Iyengar of Melkote, who is said to belong to the Tiruvāymoḻi Ācārya family (164–65).

This family was one of seventy-four appointed by Rāmānuja as an *ācārya puruṣa,* or *siṁhāsanadhipati,* "guardians of the throne." (On the allegorical significance of the number 74, see chap. 4 n. 9). The *ācārya puruṣas* were spiritual and ritual leaders of the Śrīvaiṣṇava community and could administer the sacrament of surrender to their own family and to others as well. Gnanambal reports that Sri V. T. T. Iyengar's grandfather was one Tiruvaymoli Tirunarayana Iyengar, who died in 1904, and he is probably the "Tiruvāymoḻi Ācārya" spoken of by Sri Vipranarayana and who was the teacher of Sri Parasurama Dasar. Gnanambal says: "in Bangalore itself, Iyengar's father induced the Tirukulattar to form religious associations known as Ramanuja Kootam. It is parallel to the congregational halls among the Christians" (165). It seems probable that she is referring to the community being discussed in this article, but I never heard the name Ramanuja Kootam mentioned. *Ramanuja Kootam* is, however, a generic term for any Śrīvaiṣṇava congregation, and I suspect that it was used in this loose sense by Gnanambal's informant.

8. According to Sri Kanakarajan, who is in charge of the Āṇṭāḷ Cannati, it was a person called Maturakavidasar who established their shrine.

9. In "Srivaishnavas and Their Religious Institutions" Gnanambal gives a slightly different list of the shrines (166). She states that the shrines are: (1) Pan Perumal Sabha, (2) Andal Sabha, (3) Tiruvengadamudaiyan [Visnu] Sabha, (4) Manavalaa Mamuni Sabha, (5) Kannan [Visnu] Sabha, and (6) Alvar Sabha. The last one presumably is Nammāḻvār Sabha. Of these she says that the first two are formed by *tirukulattār.*

10. He also said that there was a controversy about the question of when the twenty-four generations had actually begun. Sri Vipranarayana's father was one Sri Sarangapani Ramanuja Dasar, and he believed that he was the twenty-fourth-generation Śrīvaiṣṇava from Nāthamuni, the very first *ācārya* of the Śrīvaiṣṇava community (10th c. C.E.); others thought that the count began with the time of Sri Maṇavāḷa Māmuṉi in the fifteenth century. In question was five hundred years of Śrīvaiṣṇavahood for the ancestors, and apparently the difference of opinion on this matter was deep enough to cause a rift between some people in his father's generation. The number 24, however, was believed to be correct.

11. Moffat, *An Untouchable Community in South India,* 221.

12. Gnanambal, in "Srivaishnavas and Their Religious Institutions," also says that in the congregations formed in Bangalore there are no idols or ordained priests (165).

13. As noted earlier, the Tamil calendar is lunar and is adjusted to the solar position every few years. One's birthday is calculated by the position of the moon in relation to twenty-eight stars, or constellations. *Vicākam* (Sanskrit: *Viśākha*) corresponds to Scorpio.

14. . . . I saw the sacred feet of Pin̲n̲ai's unique Lord
and wore them as an ornament on my head.

I wore the feet as an ornament on my head,
[the sacred feet] of He who sleeps on the banyan leaf;
He who stands on the hill as the celestials worship,
He who established himself in my mind
and dwells there without moving.

(Tiruvāymoḻi 10.4.3–4)

15. There is no textual authority for this belief, but I have heard this sentiment repeated several times. Sri Saranatha Bhattar from the Venkateswara Temple at Pittsburgh also emphasized that in brahmin families the boy should be invested with the sacred thread before he is taught the Tiruvāymoḻi, the Tamil Veda.

16. *The Splendor* states that Rāmānuja's funeral was attended by nine thousand *upavitdhāri* Śrīvaiṣṇavas (those invested with the sacred thread), twelve thousand converts to Śrīvaiṣṇavism, and seven hundred *jīyars* (brahmin monks) and *ekāngis* (nonbrahmin monks) (321–22).

17. I have identified the quotation as *Tolkāppiyam, poruḷ atikāram*, 9:71. The exact quotation is: *nūlē kaṛakam, mukkōl, manaiyē / ayum kalai, antaṇa-rukku uriyē*.

18. These incidents are those of Jānaśruti (*Chandogya* 4.2.3) and Jabala (*Chandogya* 4.3–4).

19. *Śrībhāṣya* 1.3.33. The actual etymology of the word is unknown, according to the Monier-Williams dictionary.

Chapter 6: The Traditions of Music

1. *The Splendor*, 121–22.

2. Ibid., 180–81.

3. The Chronicles of the Srirangam Temple are published as *Koil Oḻugu*, ed. Hari Rao.

4. Ibid., 40.

5. Ibid., 25–26.

6. Ibid., 38.

7. For an account of the story as is seen in another temple (Melukote, near Mysore), see my article "Arcāvatara: on Earth, as He Is in Heaven."

In the sequel to the Srirangam story the Sultani is said to have followed the Lord. Although the temple servants had had three days' head start, when they came to south India the Sultani's army was close on their heels. At this time they dispersed, and some of them took the Lord to Tirupati-Tiruvenkatam. The Sultani proceeded to Srirangam and, not seeing the Lord there, died out of grief. (*Koil Oḻugu,* 26–27).

8. Inscriptions at the Tirupati Temple talk about some of these women singing songs in praise of the Lord and sometimes in praise of custodians of temples. See Viraraghavacharya, *History of Tirupati,* 2:417.

9. The *Madhurāvijayam,* qtd. in Hari Rao, *The Srirangam Temple,* 5.

10. Hari Rao, *Koil Oḻugu,* 32; also *Srirangam Temple,* 5.

11. *Koil Oḻugu,* 195–99.

12. In conversation with him at his residence, 5 July 1991.

13. Inscriptional evidence at the Tirupati Temple also testifies to the fact that the recitation was done for the Lord (Viraraghavacharya, *History of Tirupati,* 2:723).

14. Sri Venkata Varadhan, while conducting the "Goda Mandali" class, 12 July 1991. He made these remarks before commencing his class, in which he teaches the Divya Prabandham, at the home of Smt. Chitra Raghunathan, 12 Mahalakshmi St., T. Nagar, Madras 600 017.

15. This synopsis is based on extensive interviews and recordings conducted in March 1990 and July 1991.

16. Some of the ragas that seemed unusual were: *antāḷi kuriñji, vīya yāḻmuri, paḻam pañcaram, catari, manōlayam, puranīrmai.* In addition to these he also taught some more familiar ragas: for example, Bhairavi, Bilahari, Hamsanandi, Hindolam, Kapi, Karaharapriya, Mandu, Sahana, Senjurutti, Sindhu, Tilang, Vasantha.

17. Brochure printed by the Pathsala Trust, 51 Alamelumangapuram, Madras 600 004.

18. This was stated in an interview in December 1989. He also writes about this in Sjoman and Dattatreya, *An Introduction to South Indian Music,* 115.

19. The concert was sung over two days to a select audience, which sponsored the event and recorded it on large spools for private home entertainment. It was not commercialized, but pirate versions did get around because it was in high demand. Ariyakudi also popularized the individual verses of the Tiruppāvai by singing them in between larger Telugu songs in his concert.

Chapter 7: Exegesis and Interpretation

I am indebted to Professor Harold Stahmer, University of Florida, for drawing my attention to Ong's article ("Text as Interpretation") and also to Palmer's book on hermeneutics. Research for this chapter was done under a summer stipend from the National Endowment for the Humanities, 1987. Tape recordings of the Tiruvāymoḻi and some commentarial narration was done with financial assistance from the Division of Sponsored Research, University of Florida.

1. Palmer, *Hermeneutics,* 13.

2. Ibid., 15.

3. The division was into *udātta* and *anudātta. Udātta* is "high, elevated; acutely accented," and *anudātta* is "not elevated or raised, accentless [in chanting]." Meanings taken from Apte's *The Student's Sanskrit-English Dictionary.*

4. *The Splendor,* 122, 124. The *Koil Oḻugu,* which purports to be a chronological account of the Srirangam Temple states that Nāthamuni established classes in which the Tiruvāymoḻ was taught (Hari Rao, *Koil Oḻugu,* 34).

5. K. V. Raman, "Divya Prabandha Recital in Vaishnava Temples," 36. Hari Rao also notes the inscriptions in the Srirangam Temple, which record the gifts of the Chola king Kulottunga (1070–1120) for the recitation of the Tiruvāymoḻi (*Srirangam Temple,* 9).

6. I have discussed Piḷḷāṉ's commentary in detail in Carman and Narayanan, *The Tamil Veda.*

7. The later commentaries are also believed to be as long as certain Sanskrit works. The *Oṉpatināyirappaṭi* (The Nine Thousand-paṭi) was the commentary of Nañjīyar and was rewritten by Naṁpiḷḷai, who is said to have lost the original work of his teacher. This work is said to be numerically equivalent to the *Śrī Bhāṣya* of Rāmānuja. The *Iṛupatinālāyirappaṭi* (The Twenty-four Thousand-paṭi, written in the thirteenth century by Periyavāccāṉ Piḷḷai) was said to be as long as the *Rāmāyaṇa* and the *Īṭu-Muppattāṛāyirappaṭi* (The Thirty-six Thousand-paṭi) written by Vaṭakku Tiruvīti Piḷḷai, a contemporary of Periyavāccāṉ Piḷḷai, to be as long as the *Śrutaprakāśika,* the commentary on Rāmānuja's *Śrī Bhāṣya.*

8. As noted in chapter 2, other summaries of the Tiruvāymoḻi are contained in the Tamil poem *Nammāḻvār Tiruttāllāṭṭu* (A Lullaby for Nammāḻvār) and the biographical poem on the *āḻvārs* called *Āḻvārkal vaibhavam* (The Glory of the Āḻvārs).

9. One of the earliest Tamil commentaries was Nakkīrar's commentary on Irayaṉār's *Akapporul,* written about the eighth century C.E. This work was a commentary on the "secular" love poetry of the classical era. For further details, see Zvelebil, *The Smile of Murugan,* 26. For the commentaries on the Tamil grammar *Tolkāppiyam,* see 135. Zvelebil discusses the commentarial tradition in Tamil (247–63).

10. Piḷḷāṉ, *Six Thousand-paṭi,* 10.9.10.

11. Venkatachari, *The Maṇipravāḷa Literature of the Śrī Vaiṣṇava Ācāryas,* 4–5, 167–71.

12. In the later commentaries on the Tiruvāymoḻi, the *Twenty-four Thousand-paṭi* of Periyāvaccāṉ Piḷḷai and the *Thirty-six Thousand-paṭi* of Vaṭakku Tiruvīti Piḷḷai, there are several verses in which the special interpretations of Yāmuna are quoted. There are about thirty-five instances in these two commentaries alone in which the opinions of Yāmuna are quoted. These verses are cataloged in Narayanan, *The Way and the Goal,* 179. Some of these instances are repeated in *The Splendor*.

13. Yāmuna had, according to biographical tradition, summoned Rāmānuja to the temple town of Srirangam to be his disciple. By the time Rāmānuja came to Srirangam Yāmuna had passed away. Later on Yāmuna's disciples taught Rāmānuja the various texts sacred to the Śrīvaiṣṇava tradition.

14. *The Splendor,* 199–200.

15. Ibid., 373. It is said that after an exposition of the *Bhagavad Viṣayam* ("Sacred Matters," a term used for commentaries on the Tiruvāymoḻi) crowds of Śrīvaiṣṇavas were leaving the teacher Nampiḷḷai's room when a Śrīvaiṣṇava king, who was passing by, wondered out loud: "Is this a dispersal of Śrīvaiṣṇavas from Nampiḷḷai's audience chamber or Namperumāl's (i.e., the Lord at Srirangam) [worship] chamber?" Note that the reference is to a *Śrīvaiṣṇava* crowd that has the authority to listen to interpretations of the Tiruvāymoḻi and *not* a general audience.

16. While the Śrīvaiṣṇavas after Rāmānuja did not comment directly on the Bhagavad Gīta or the *Brahma Sūtras*, they commented on Rāmānuja's commentary on these works. Sudarśana Sūri wrote a commentary on the *Śrī Bhāṣya*, which was Rāmānuja's commentary on the *Brahma Sūtras*, and Vedānta Deśika wrote a commentary on Rāmānuja's commentary on the Bhagavad Gīta. These later commentaries only elucidated and elaborated Rāmānuja's commentaries, which were considered to be the authoritative and only correct interpretation of the Sanskrit works. The Bhagavad Gīta and the *Brahma Sūtras*, therefore, have had only one primary commentary within the Śrīvaiṣṇava community. On the other hand, there have been several direct commentaries in *maṇipravāḷa* on the TVM. Most of the *maṇipravāḷa* commentaries are directly about the poem, though there are a few that remark on a commentary. The TVM and the other Tamil hymns were probably at the center of so many direct commentaries, primarily because they were considered to be *anubhava grantha,* or works that could be "experienced" and "enjoyed" directly by the audience.

17. Vaṭakku Tiruvīti Piḷḷai's *Īṭu* (Thirty-six Thousand-paṭi) commentary on Tiruvāymoḻi 6.10.4. The Tamil lexicon derives *ōrāṇ* from *ōr* (one) + *āṇ* (male). *Vaḻi* is "way"; thus, *ōrāṇ vaḻi* is defined as "unbroken lineage from individual to individual." Venkataraman describes *ōrāṇ-vaḻi* as "an unbroken [chain of] transmission from teacher to disciple" (*Araiyar Cēvai,* 26).

18. I have translated the Tamil word *paṭṭōlai* as "manuscript" for conve-

nience. It literally refers to palm leaves with their ribs removed. The other meanings of *paṭṭōlai* are "first draft of petition, especially what is written to dictation"; "edict of royal proclamation"; "consolidated statement of ledger accounts"; "lists, catalogs of articles, inventory."

On the extensive use of writing for lists, inventories, and accounts, see Goody, *The Logic of Writing and the Organization of Society*, 45–86.

19. *The Splendor*, 364–67.

20. Wulff, discussing the transmission of classical music, quotes a south Indian scholar, V. Raghavan: "For when a thing is taken from a book, it is like a faggot without fire, but when the guru imparts it he transmits also a part of his power and grace" ("On Practicing Religiously," 152).

The scribe, however, has evidently moved a long way from his original lowly position, which Staal and Brown have spoken about. For an excellent summary of Staal's position and other arguments detailing the Hindu bias against writing, see Brown's article "Purāṇa as Scripture."

21. Ong, in "Text and Interpretation," says:

> The world of oral utterance is typically one of discourse, in which one utterance gives rise to another, that to still another, and so on. Meaning is negotiated in the discursive process. . . . What I say depends on my conjectures about your state of mind before I begin to speak and about the possible range of your responses. I need conjectural feedback even to formulate my utterance. . . . Oral discourse thus commonly interprets itself as it proceeds. It negotiates meaning out of meaning. (8)

22. Nampiḷḷai became the next formal teacher of the Śrīvaiṣṇava community in Srirangam. He was the scribe—co-author, according to *The Splendor*—but only Nañjīyar's name is associated with the commentary referred to in this story. Nampiḷḷai's students wrote two commentaries on the Tiruvāymoḻi.

23. Periyavāccāṉ Piḷḷai (b. 1228 C.E.) also wrote commentaries on all the other hymns of the *āḻvārs*.

24. This is the *Thirty-six Thousand-paṭi* commentary, which is frequently referred to as the *Īṭu*, or "equivalent [to the original]" (*The Splendor*, 391).

Relatively speaking, Vaṭakku Tiruvīti Piḷḷai fared well in this incident. *The Splendor* also narrates that one Bhaṭṭar, a disciple of Nampiḷḷai, wrote a commentary, which was 100,000 *paṭis*, without his teacher's permission. Nampiḷḷai was angry that the inner meaning of the Tiruvāymoḻi, which he had given *orally*, was now committed to *writing* so that the world may read it. He reprimanded the student and said that the meaning cannot be known without going through apprenticeship as a disciple and experiencing the honorable relationship between teacher and disciple. Apparently, Nampiḷḷai threw away the commentary and let the termites waste it (*The Splendor*, 390).

25. The book remained in manuscript form until 1950, when it was

painstakingly edited by a scholar in the Sarasvati Mahal Library, Tanjore. The book has still not received the attention it deserves.

26. Women are allowed to comment on the Tiruvāymoḻi, but I have not known anyone to do so. I was recently informed, however, about an eighty-year-old woman near Madras who had formally studied both poems of Nammāḻvār and the later commentaries on them, fifteen times under a certain (male) teacher. She is reported to give brilliant oral commentaries on the Tiruvāymoḻi.

27. *Ayarvu aṟum*. The word *ayarvu* may be translated as "fatigue, forgetfulness, or sorrow." All these meanings are given by Uttamur Viraraghavacariyar in his commentary on this verse (*Nammāḻvār aruḷiceyta Tiruvāymoḻi, prabandha rakṣai,* vol. 1).

This phrase is quoted frequently by Piḷḷāṉ and is used to describe the "immortal ones" who serve Viṣṇu.

28. This list is an abbreviated version of Rāmānuja's description of Viṣṇu. See, for instance, *Gītā Bhāṣya,* intro., in *Rāmānujagranthamālā,* 37; Rāmānuja, *Vedārthasaṁgraha,* ed. van Buitenen, par. 127.

29. "Nikhila jagad udaya vibhava ādi līlanāy." Rāmānuja frequently uses this phrase. See *Gītā Bhāṣya,* intro. in *Rāmānujagranthamālā,* 37; *Vedārthasaṁgraha,* in *Rāmānujagranthamālā,* 3.

30. Piḷḷāṉ employs a phrase that Rāmānuja uses in the description of bliss. See *Śrī Bhāṣya* 1.1.13, in *Rāmānujagranthamālā,* 87.

31. "Asaṅkhyēya kalyāṇa guṇa mahōdadhi." Perhaps the most frequently used phrase by Rāmānuja in talking about God. See, for instance, *Gītā Bhāṣya,* intro. *Vedarthasaṁgraha,* 1.

Later commentaries say that Yāmuna, a Śrīvaiṣṇava teacher who lived a generation before Rāmānuja, used to explain the word *uṭaiyavan* ("He who possesses") in the verse with the phrase *anavadhikā atiśaya ādisaṅkhyēya kalyāṇa guṇa gaṇa* (having a host of countless, infinite, wonderful auspicious attributes). Both the *Twenty-four thousand-paṭi* of Periyavāccāṉ Piḷḷai and the *Thirty-six thousand-paṭi* of Vaṭakku Tiruvīti Piḷḷai quote Yāmuna as the oral authority for this frequently occurring phrase.

32. Another phrase used by Rāmānuja. Rāmānuja uses the phrase "without a 'whiff' [*gandha*] of" when he wants to say "without a trace." See, for instance, *Śrī Bhāṣya* 1.1.21.

33. The phrase "unflickering wisdom" is used by Piḷḷāṉ in later comments (5.3.6 and 10.9.10) as well as by Rāmānuja (*Vedārthasaṁgraha,* in *Rāmānujagranthamālā,* 39.

34. The recording was made in August and September 1988 and was a forty-five-minute discourse on the life of Nammāḻvār. The narrator was Sri Saranatha Bhattar, a Vaṭakalai Śrīvaiṣṇava priest at Sri Venkateswara Temple,

Pittsburgh. This preceded the recitation of the entire Tiruvāymoḻi. The narrator only knew that I was interested in listening to the Tiruvāymoḻi and had no prior knowledge that I was going to analyze some features of traditional Śrīvaiṣṇava oral discourse. I would consider this overwhelming usage of Rāmānuja's phrases and other lines from *āḻvār* poetry to be typical of almost all traditional oral commentary in the Śrīvaiṣṇava tradition.

35. Partial translation from Tiruvāymoḻi and *The Six Thousand-paṭi* Commentary on 6.10.10.

36. The Śrīvaiṣṇava tradition counts three kinds of souls: those who are *eternally* liberated (i.e., those who have never been born on earth), those who were once bound to the cycle of life and death but are now liberated, and, finally, those who are now in the realm of life and death.

37. Vaṭakku Tiruvīti Piḷḷai's commentary, *The Thirty-six Thousand-paṭi* commentary on Tiruvāymoḻi 2.9.4.

38. This point of whether one can petition the Lord for salvation or simply wait for him to save us when he so decrees is one that theologically splits the Śrīvaiṣṇava community in the thirteenth century and socially a few centuries later.

39. This process is not too far removed from Puranic transmission, as described by Bonazzoli. See his "Composition, Transmission and Recitation of the Purana-s" (esp. 266–67), in which he discusses a modern work by a Svamin Tapovanam as one that is written in a Puranic style of the *mahātmyas*. Focusing on his formulas, Bonazzoli says:

> These and similar formulas were composed and written by Tapovanam, who was strongly influenced by the purāṇa-s, which he had surely read and heard. It is very improbable that he copied these expressions from the purana-s directly; he most probably had them in his mind and used them because they were fitting his purpose and gave to his composition the flavour of a puranic *mahātmya*. Such formulas formed his luggage of knowledge not because he was a bard but because he was acquainted with puranic literature which contained—in a written form—those expressions. . . . Moreover, even his knowledge of the purana-s could have reached him both orally by listening to them and/or through writing by reading. So here, we have an example of mixed influence, oral and written, from which no conclusion can be drawn whether the formulas, used by him were previously written or oral. This modern example is probably similar to what used to happen in the past, at least at the time of the composition of the puranic texts we possess now. Thousands of Svamin Tapovanams must have existed, who composed . . . collecting matter from previous texts and adding something of their own while keeping the puranic style by using the same kinds of puranic expression slightly modified according to necessity and personal likings.

40. *Hermenes eisin ton theon;* Palmer, *Hermeneutics,* 13.
41. Palmer, *Hermeneutics,* 15.

Chapter 8: Recreating Heaven on Earth

1. *The Splendor,* 181.

2. Some of the details of the ritual context at the Triplicane Temple were kindly provided to me by Sri Ashtagothram Nallan Chakravarthy Parthsarathy Iyengar, Triplicane, Madras. Sri Nadhamuni Araiyar from Srirangam was kind enough, in the midst of his hectic schedule, to spend several hours discussing his family heritage and details of the *araiyar cēvai* in January 1990 and July 1990. Further information was obtained on visits to Sri Parthasarathi Temple (Triplicane, Madras) during the Festival of Recitation (1989) and the Srirangam Temple in Summer 1987, January 1991, and July 1991. Videotapes of the *araiyar cēvai,* the Vaikuṇṭha Ékādaśi celebrations, and other rituals were generously made available by Sri K. S. Veeraraghavan, Neelangarai, Madras.

3. The costumes for the first ten days of the festival at the Parthasarathi Temple in Triplicane are (1) Vēṅkaṭa Krishnan (for the main deity), (2) Vēṇugōpālaṉ, (3) Kālinga Mardanam, (4) Kōtanḍa Rama, (5) Kaṇṇaṉ (Krishna), (6) Paramapada Nātan, (7) Bakāsura vada, (8) Paṭṭābhi Rāman, (9) Rādha Krishnan, and (10) Nācciyār Tirukkōlam (i.e., sacred dress as a woman or Mohini).

4. The *araiyars* reside only in these three temples today. On the fourth day they act out the killing of Kaṁsa; on the seventh, the incarnation as Vāmana, on the ninth day, a Gypsy telling the fortune of the *āḻvār;* on the tenth day, the killing of Rāvaṇa. During the seventh night of the Tiruvāymoḻi recitation the slaying of Hiraṇya is acted out; on the eighth night, an incident from the life of Tirumankai Āḻvār, and on the tenth night, the granting of salvation to Nammāḻvār.

5. *Koil Oḻugu,* ed. Hari Rao, 9–10, 33–35.

6. The word *araiyar* is usually taken to mean "king."

7. The scribe has evidently moved a long way from his original lowly position, which Staal and Brown have spoken about. For an excellent summary of Staal's position and other arguments detailing the Hindu bias against writing, see Brown's article "Purāṇa as Scripture."

The temple accountant in Srirangam was originally a Veḷḷāḷa, the caste into which Nammāḻvār is said to have been born. Although Veḷḷāḷas were considered as *śūdras* by the brahmins, they occupied a fairly high status in the Tamil country.

8. According to one interpretation at least, this journey of Viṣṇu to the Hall of a Thousand Pillars is said to be symbolic. Lord Raṅganātha is said to represent the *mumukṣu,* or the aspirant for salvation, and the details of his

passage to the hall (which is heaven) is considered to have allegorical meaning. It is also seen as an acting out of some lines from Tiruvāymoḻi 10.9, which speaks of Nammāḻvār's ascent to heaven. I have summarized the interpretation offered by Narasimmayyaṅkār in *Vaikuṇṭa Ēkātaci Utsava Vaipavam,* 17–19:

Ritual	*Meaning*
Doors closed when the Lord leaves *garbha gṛha*	Sense organs shut and controlled
Bearers of palanquin glide like serpent	Movement of kundalini
Lord goes through main doorway	Life passes through the hole on crown of head
Lord greeted by nonbrahmin devotees	Soul greeted by Śrīvaiṣṇavas
Lord is greeted with water	Soul is honored by celestials greeting it with water
Lord orders a gateway to be opened	"Visnukhrānti" is opened in the *śuṣumna* (a channel in the human body)
Lord stands in front of "door to heaven," facing north, and orders it to be opened	"Rudrakrānti" breaks
Lord reaches a well	Soul reaches river Virajā
Lord discards a shawl and wears new garland	Soul assumes new body
Lord wears clothes with gems	Soul is radiant in glory
Servants of the Lord lead the way	Radiant residents of heaven lead the way

Ritual	*Meaning*
Female servants wave lamps/jars near the Sacred Canopy of Gems	Women devotees offer light
Images of *āḻvārs* brought near Lord	Soul renders continuous service with other devotees to the Lord

9. Nevertheless, it is interesting that she is not brought to the Hall of a Thousand Pillars. Some devotees today say that it may have to do with vestiges of discrimination against women, but that does not seem to be a probable theory, given her importance and popularity within the Śrīvaiṣṇava world.

10. Hari Rao, *Srirangam Temple,* 4.

11. The Kaushitaki Bŕahmaṇa verse is referred to, for instance, by Vedānta Deśika (13th c.) in *Srimad Rahasya Traya Sāram* (chap. 1, p. 18) and by Parāśara Bhaṭṭar (12th c.) in his *Śrī Raṅgarāja Stava,* v. 38.

The Srirangam hall is called *Āyirakkāl maṇṭapam,* or the "Hall of a Thousand Pillars," but apparently the count comes to a few short of a thousand. So, just for this festival, an extra forty-seven temporary pillars (coconut palms) are added to be sure that this hall resembles, as closely as possible, its prototype in heaven.

12. Narasimmayyankar, *Vaikuṇṭa Ēkātaci Utsava Vaipavam,* 15.

13. It is only in these places that we have a full-fledged *araiyar cēvai* performance. In Melkote, near Mysore, there is a tradition of *araiyar* music, but the tradition of dance came to an end a long time ago. This art, like many others, has been reduced over the years, and today the dances for only a few verses are remembered, and others have been lost.

14. When a man has no male offspring he usually adopts a boy from the family circle and teaches him the art. Women were traditionally not allowed to perform in the *araiyar* tradition. The *araiyar* performances have to be done on certain days of the year, and it is possible that one reason for excluding women had to do with the pollution associated with their menstruation and childbirth days. At these times women were not allowed into the temples. There was a distinct possibility, therefore, that they would not be allowed to participate on key festival days. Another possible reason may have been the connection of the performing arts with the *devadāsi* (temple dancing) tradition, and women of high-class families would have been prevented from learning anything that was associated with suspected prostitution.

There is a revival of the *araiyar* tradition among female dancers today, in the context of classical *bharata nātyam.* Usha Narayanan, a well-known exponent of this *araiyar* art, performs in this style frequently on national television.

The *araiyar* art was performed *only* in front of the deity (the processional image) in the Śrīvaiṣṇava temples, and for the first time since its inception the dances are now performed in secular settings.

15. See Parthasarathi, "Evolution of Rituals," 399 n. 3(c); and Venkataraman, *Araiyar Cēvai,* 1–2.

16. While discussing music, Wulff says: "Indeed, it is ultimately for God and not for an earthly audience that the devotee plays or sings" ("On Practicing Religiously," 157).

17. Discussion with the *araiyar* on 13 January 1990.

18. What can I say of the Lord
who lifted me up for all time,
and made me himself, every day?
My radiant one, the First One,
my Lord, sings of himself,
through me, in sweet Tamil.
(TVM 7.9.1)

19. *Kōyiloluku,* ed. Sri Krishnaswami Ayyangar, 40, 46, 47.

20. A *paṭi* is a unit of thirty-two syllables, and the commentaries are known by the length of *paṭis.*

21. During the first ten days (*pakal pattu*) the commentary read is either one written by the thirteenth-century theologian Periya vāccāṉ Piḷḷai or an anonymous one written by an earlier *araiyar.* The later commentary is anonymous and is simply called *Tampirāṉ paṭi,* "the commentary composed by the master." Venkataraman in *Araiyar Cēvai* does not give a date for this commentary but reports that the Alvar Tirunagari *araiyars* consider it to date back to the time of the first teacher, Nāthamuni (10th c.). He also says that the present manuscript (which has been copied through the centuries) is about 150 years old. He notes that this is close to the commentary of Piḷḷāṉ and that the author claims to have been "a servant" of Nāthamuni (*Araiyar Cēvai,* 74–76). When I interviewed Sri Nadhamuni Araiyar in Srirangam he said that the *Tampirāṉ paṭi* was about forty-five generations old.

During the recitation of the Tiruvāymoḻi the commentary recited is Vaṭakku Tiruvīti Piḷḷai's *Thirty-six thousand-paṭi.* During the recitation of Tiruvāymoḻi 7.2.5 the *araiyars* act out the story of Viṣṇu's incarnation as Narasimha, or "Man-Lion." It is only at this point that they recite the *Tampirāṉ paṭi* commentary; at all other instances they rely on the *Thirty-six thousand-paṭi.*

22. The Tiruvāymoḻi has inspired a long line of commentaries in which the community relives and reexperiences the emotions of the *āḻvārs.* Sanskrit literature, on the other hand, is perceived as embodying one truth for all time; after Rāmānuja's commentary on the Bhagavad Gītā and the *Brahma Sūtras* no Śrīvaiṣṇava wrote another commentary on them. Usually commentaries pre-

served the correct interpretations and the right opinions on a text; interestingly enough, the commentaries on the Tiruvāymoḻi preserve a diversity of opinions. It is important to note, however, that the diversity of the opinions did not at any time involve important theological issues pertaining to the supremacy of Viṣṇu, his auspicious nature, and other doctrines cardinal to the community but, instead, usually reflected the flavor of the teachers' enjoyment of the poem. See also chap. 7, n. 16.

23. Venkataraman, *Araiyar Cēvai,* 9.

24. These are 1.1.1, 2.10.1, 3.3.1, 4.10.1, 5.5.1, 6.10.1, 7.2.1, 8.10.1, 9.10.1, and 10.1.1. Two of these verses (5.5.1 and 7.2.1) are spoken by Nammāḻvār from the viewpoint of a girl. All these verses, with the exception of 5.5.1, are translated in the appendix.

25. See Venkataraman, *Araiyar Cēvai,* 85.

26. In his *Orality and Literacy* Ong says:

> Some non-oral communication is exceedingly rich—gesture, for example. Yet in a deep sense language, articulated sound, is paramount. Not only communication, but thought itself relates in an altogether special way to sound. We have all heard it said that one picture is worth a thousand words. Yet, if this statement is true, why does it have to be a saying? Because a picture is worth a thousand words only under special conditions—which commonly include a context of words in which the picture is set. (7)

Thus, while the performative interpretation is extremely important for the Tiruvāymoḻi, it is important only in the context of the poem itself. In some ritual contexts, such as the one just discussed in the text, the verbal comment is considered more sacred than gestures. Yet there have been other examples in the Śrīvaiṣṇava tradition in which a person has said that he has been more moved by the emotion expressed by his teacher than by the teacher's verbal commentary.

27. This incident is reported by Uttamur Viraraghavacariyar (commentary on Perumāḷ Tirumoḻi 6.8).

28. Venkataraman, *Araiyar Cēvai,* 85.

29. Ibid., 66 and 85.

30. The *cāṟṟumuṟai* ritual is the concluding ceremony in recitation.

31. I have heard this explanation from several Śrīvaiṣṇava teachers. Venkataraman says: "On the eleventh day, Nammāḻvār ascends in his [earthly] body to heaven, is one with the Lord, but tells him, 'I do not want heaven, I only want to live on earth' and comes back to the world. This is done in the *Cāṟṟumuṟai* [concluding] rituals" (*Araiyar Cēvai,* 84).

32. This drama is enacted on the ninth night of the Recitation of the Tiruvāymoḻi only in Alvar Tirunagari. It is conducted during the month of

Citra in Srirangam and not at all in Srivilliputur. The drama is read out in Tirumokkur and used to be acted out in Tirumaliruncolai (ibid., 84). A partial analysis of this festival as celebrated in Srirangam is given by Younger in "Ten Days of Wandering and Romance with Lord Raṅkanātan̲."

33. Venkataraman, *Araiyar Cēvai,* 91.

34. This was stated to me by the *bhaṭṭars* (priests) at the Nammāl̲vār Shrine in the Srirangam Temple in July 1991.

35. Normally the "festival images," or *utsava mūrti,* are beside the primary image in the *garbha gṛha,* but when these *utsava mūrtis* are being taken in a procession some items of *prasāda* are not given in the *garbha gṛha.* At these times, when the *utsava mūrti* is away and is the focus of the liturgy, it is fully considered to be the Lord. During the time that the festival image is in the thousand-pillared hall, the *śaṭhāri* (a name of Nammāl̲vār), which is a little silver crown representing the feet of the Lord and which is placed on the devotee's head, is used only in the vicinity of the *utsava mūrti.* Its use in the *garbha gṛha* is temporarily suspended while the *utsava mūrti* is away. On the distinctive identity of the *utsava mūrti,* see my article "Arcāvatara: On Earth, as He Is In Heaven," 56–58.

36. *Vedārthasaṁgraha,* 168–69, 214.

37. *Śrī Raṅgarāja Stava,* pt. 1, verses 20 and 26.

38. "Nañjīyar said: I have listened to the Tiruvāymol̲i three times from Piḷḷai Tirunaṛaiyūr Araiyar. No word from that will leave me; but all that I think of is his being overcome by emotion while explaining a verse, losing control of himself and [seeing] his eyes filled with tears" (Vaṭakku Tiruvīti Piḷḷai, *Īṭu* (Thirty-six Thousand-paṭi) commentary on Tiruvāymol̲i 6.9.1; *Bhagavad Viṣayam,* ed. Annangarācāriyar, 3:311).

39. On this theme, see Haberman, *Acting as a Way of Salvation.*

40. Consider the following Tiruvāymol̲i verses, which say that singing of the Lord is one way of invoking the golden age on earth:

> Rejoice! Rejoice! Rejoice!
> The persisting curse of life is gone,
> the agony of hell is destroyed,
> death has no place here.
> The [force of] Kali is destroyed.
> Look for yourself!
> The followers of the sea-colored Lord
> swell over this earth; singing with melody,
> dancing and whirling [with joy].
> We see them.
>
> (TVM 5.2.1)
>
> Those beloved
> of the discus-wielding Lord

uproot disease, hatred, poverty
and suffering
which kill and conquer this earth.
Singing melodiously, they jump,
dance and fly all over this earth.
O servants [of the Lord!]
come; worship, and live.
Fix your minds [on him].

(TVM 5.2.6)

41. *Śrī Raṅgarāja Stava,* pt. 1, verse 78.
42. Wulff, "On Practicing Religiously," 155.
43. *Śrī Raṅgarāja Stava,* pt. 1, verse 72.

Chapter 9: Reflections

1. Ricoeur, epilogue, *The Critical Study of Sacred Texts,* 274.

2. Renou, *The Destiny of the Veda in India,* 24. Renou does say that, however, "it cannot, therefore, be said with absolute truth, that the traditional teaching had excluded, even for the *mantras,* all recourse to meaning. But the meaning, in relation to the form, had only a minor importance. This is, over and above everything, quite Indian."

3. Ibid., 2.

4. I have considered this topic in "Looking behind Piḷḷān's Commentary: 'Swallowing' as a Metaphor in the Poem," a chapter in *The Tamil Veda.*

5. *Divya Prabandha Icai Mālai,* 7 (italics added).

6. On the early development of this phenomenon, see Singer, "The Radha-Krishna *bhajanas* of Madras City."

7. Ong, *Orality and Literacy,* 161.

8. I have addressed this issue in *The Way and the Goal,* 143–45.

GLOSSARY

ācārya. A spiritual teacher or preceptor; the head of a spiritual lineage. Also an honorific title for several Śrīvaiṣṇava theologians.

adhikāra. "Authority."

adhyāpaka. A male who is trained to recite the Sanskrit or Tamil Veda at temples.

adhyayana. Recitation of the Veda.

Adhyayana Utsavam. A festival in the month of Mārkaḻi (15 Dec.–14 Jan.) when the Sanskrit Vedas and the Divya Prabandham are recited over twenty-one days. Very little time is allotted for the Sanskrit Vedas in this festival, which begins on the new moon of Mārkaḻi.

advaita. "Nondualism." School of Vedānta founded by the teacher Śaṅkara in the eighth century C.E.

akam. "Inner." Refers to poems of romance and love. One of the two principal genres of Tamil classical poetry.

Aḻakiya Maṇavāḷa Nāyaṉār. Thirteenth-century Śrīvaiṣṇava theologian.

Āḷavantār. Name of the *ācārya* Yāmuna.

āḻvār. "One who is immersed." Title given by Śrīvaiṣṇavas to one of twelve poet-saints of the seventh–tenth centuries C.E. whose four thousand Tamil verses they acknowledge as the vernacular Veda.

araiyar. A performer of the Divya Prabandham, belonging to certain families claiming descent from Nāthamuni's nephews in the tenth century C.E.

araiyar cēvai. "Service rendered by the *araiyar.*" Refers to the performative interpretation of the Tiruvāymoḻi which takes place during the Festival of Recitation (15 Dec.–14 Jan.).

arcā. "That which can be worshipped." Viṣṇu, enshrined in "image" form in Śrīvaiṣṇava temples.

Glossary

arcāvatāra. "The descent as that which can be worshipped." One of the five forms of Viṣṇu in *pañcarātra* theology.

avatāra. A "descent" of Viṣṇu, in an animal or human form.

bhakta. A "devotee" who loves God or a spiritual teacher.

bhakti. "Devotion, love."

Brahmā. The god of creation, who was himself created by Viṣṇu. Depicted frequently as abiding on a lotus flower that rises from Viṣṇu's navel.

cannati. "Receptacle, presence." Shrine.

cāṟṟumuṟai. "The method of conferring." Refers to the concluding rituals of recitation.

darśan. "Sight, vision."

Deśika. See Vedánta Deśika.

dīkṣa. Initiation that gives a person the right to be a priest in a temple.

divya deśa. "A sacred place." Refers to any one of 108 sacred temples sung about by the *āḻvārs.*

Divya Prabandham. *The Sacred Collect of Four Thousand Verses,* composed in Tamil by twelve poet-saints called *āḻvārs.*

Emperumāṉār. "Our Great One." Honorific title given to Rāmānuja.

gadya. "Prose compositions," not metrical yet framed with regard to harmony.

guru. Religious teacher, spiritual preceptor.

guruparamparā. A lineage of teachers.

Guruparamparā prabhāvam. "The Splendor of the Succession of Teachers." Thirteenth-century hagiography, including stories of the *āḻvārs* and the early *ācāryas.*

Harijan. "People of God Hari/Viṣṇu." Name given to "outcaste" communities by Mahatma Gandhi.

kaiṁkarya. "Loving service." See also *nitya kaiṁkarya.*

kali, kali yuga. The last and worst of the four "eons" in puranic concepts of time.

kīrtana. "Praise, glorification," especially by singing. See also *nāmasaṁkīrtana.*

Kōyil Tiruvāymoḻi. "Temple Tiruvāymoḻi," or 143 verses within the poem which are to be recited regularly, when there is no time for the recitation of the entire Tiruvāymoḻi.

Krishna. The ninth incarnation of Viṣṇu.

Kurattāḻvāṉ. A close associate and scribe of Rāmānuja. Father of Parāśara Bhaṭṭar.

Kurukeśa. A name of Tirukkurukaippirāṉ Piḷḷāṉ.

Lakṣmī. "Fortune, prosperity." Name of Śrī, the consort of Viṣṇu.

Mahābhārata. An epic of about 100,000 verses, attributed to the sage Vyāsa but probably composed over several centuries.

Maṇavāḷa Māmuṉi. Fourteenth-century Śrīvaiṣṇava theologian; one of the most important teachers for the Teṅkalai Śrīvaiṣṇavas.

maṇipravāḷa. "Gems and corals." A hybrid language composed of Sanskrit and Tamil, used by the Śrīvaiṣṇava community.

mantra. Sacred words or formula on which one meditates; when uttered the words may have power to cause events.

Mīmāmsa. A school of Hindu philosophy which believes in the eternal nature of the Vedas.

mokṣa. "Freedom, liberation" from the cycle of life and death.

muni. "A silent one." A holy man.

mūrti. "Form, image, likeness" of the deity.

Nalayirativyap pirapantam. The anthology of the sacred four thousand verses in Tamil composed by the twelve *āḻvārs*. See Divya Prabandham.

namasaṁkirtāna. See *kīrtana,* singing the names.

Nammāḻvār. The most important *āḻvār*. Author of four poems, including the Tiruvāymoḻi.

Nārāyaṇa. One of the most frequently used names of Viṣṇu.

Nāthamuni. The first Śrīvaiṣṇava *ācārya* and grandfather of Yāmuna. He is credited with collecting the four thousand verses of the *āḻvārs* into an anthology and instituting their recitation in temple and home liturgies.

nitya kaiṁkarya. Loving service that is rendered continuously and forever by a devotee.

nityānusandhānam. Daily meditations and recitation. A selection of hymns from the Divya Prabandham.

ōtuvār (Tamil, usually a Śaiva term). "One who recites."

pāñcarátra. "Five nights." A tantric tradition dedicated to Viṣṇu-Nārāyaṇa. Its texts are considered authoritative by the Śrīvaiṣṇavas, and the ritual books were extremely influential in shaping the liturgy of Śrīvaiṣṇava temples.

pañca saṁskára. "Five sacraments." Refers to the initiation of a person into the Śrīvaiṣṇava community and forms the ritual aspect of *prapatti.*

Piḷḷai Lōkācārya. Thirteenth-century Śrīvaiṣṇava theologian, considered to be one of the principal *ācāryas* of the Teṅkalai sect.

Piḷḷān, Tirukkurukaippirāṉ. Cousin of Rāmānuja and author of the first commentary on Nammāḻvār's Tiruvāymoḻi.

prasādam. "Favor, clarity." Refers to the symbols of favor distributed by a priest or religious teacher.

puṛam. "Outer." Refers to poems of war, heroism, and chivalry. One of two genres of classical Tamil poetry, the other being *akam.*

Purāṇa. "Ancient, old." Title given to well-known works that recount events that are believed to have taken place in "ancient" times.

puruṣakāra. "Mediator" between human beings and God. In Śrīvaiṣṇava theology the term usually refers to Śrī and *ācāryas* but occasionally to other gods as well.

Rāma. Seventh incarnation of Viṣṇu.

Rāmānuja. Eleventh-century theologian, considered to be the most important teacher of the Śrīvaiṣṇava community. Author of commentaries on the *Brahma Sūtra,* the Bhagavad Gītā, three hymns, and several other works.

Rāmāyaṇa. Tale of Rāma, the seventh incarnation of Viṣṇu. An epic attributed to Vālmiki.

Raṅganātha. "Lord of the stage." Name of the manifestation of Viṣṇu in Srirangam.

ṛṣī. "Seer." Traditional word used for those who are said to have seen the Vedas and communicated them.

Sacred Four Thousand, The. See *Nālāyirativyap pirapantam.*

sampradāya. Tradition; traditional knowledge and practice that is handed down through the generations.

Śaṅkara. A ninth-century theologian who taught the philosophy of *advaita* (nondualism). He is said to have established monastic orders in various parts of India.

Śaṭhāri. Name of Nammāḻvār. In Śrīvaiṣṇava parlance it refers to a silver crown kept in temples. This crown bears the feet of the Lord and is laid on a devotee's head after worship.

Śeṣa. Name of the serpent on whom Viṣṇu reclines in the ocean of milk; the paradigmatic servant.

Sevā Kālam. "Time of service." Refers to the time of Divya Prabandham recitation.

Splendor, The. See *Guruparampara prabhāvam.*

Śrī. "Radiance, splendor, auspiciousness." The inseparable consort of Viṣṇu.

Srirangam. Name of a sacred town near modern Tirucchirapalli. Its temple is the most celebrated in Śrīvaiṣṇava history. Almost all *āḻvārs* sang in praise of Viṣṇu (Raṅganātha) enshrined in this temple, and several *ācāryas* lived here.

Śrīvaiṣṇava. A community that worships Viṣṇu and his consort Śrī. It accepts the Tamil songs of the *āḻvārs* as equivalent to the Vedas and reveres Rāmānuja as its most important *ācārya.*

śruti. "That which is heard." Revealed literature, frequently used for the Vedas.

stava. A hymn, a panegyric.

stotra. A hymn of praise.

Stotra Ratna. "Jewel among hymns," a work composed by the teacher Yāmuna.

Teṅkalai. One of the two Śrīvaiṣṇava sects. The principal teachers it venerates are Piḷḷai Lōkācārya and Maṇavāḷa Māmuṉi.

Tiruvāymoḻi. "Sacred word of mouth, sacred Veda." A poem of Nammāḻvār considered as revealed literature by the Śrīvaiṣṇavas.

ubhaya vedānta. "Dual vedānta." Refers to the acceptance of the twofold heritage (Tamil poems of the *āḻvārs* and Sanskrit scripture) by the Śrīvaiṣṇava community.

Upanayana. A ceremony in which a boy is invested with a sacred thread and initiated to the study of sacred texts.

Upaniṣad. The last (and frequently considered to be the most important) part of the Vedas.

vacanas. "Sayings."

vaikuṇṭha. The abode of Viṣṇu. The residence for the soul that has attained liberation.

vaiṣṇava. "Relating to Viṣṇu." A devotee of Viṣṇu.

Vaṭakalai. One of the two branches of the Śrīvaiṣṇava community. It venerates Vedānta Deśika (13th c.) as an important teacher.

Vaṭivaḻakiya Nampi Tācar. Fifteenth-century (?) writer who wrote poetic biographies on all the *āḻvārs* and Rāmānuja.

Vedānta. "End of the Vedas." School of theological interpretation principally based on the Upanisads, the Bhagavad Gītā, and the *Brahma Sūtra.*

Vedānta Deśika. Thirteenth-century theologian who differed from Piḷḷai Lōkācārya on the understanding of *bhakti yoga* and *prapatti.* He is considered to be extremely important by the Vaṭakalai Śrīvaiṣṇavas.

Vēṅkaṭam. Name of a sacred hill in the state of Andhra Pradesh. It is sung about by the *āḻvārs* and is an important pilgrimage center for Hindus today.

Viśiṣṭādvaita. "Qualified nondualism." The philosophical name given to the form of Vedānta articulated by Rāmānuja.

Viṣṇu. "All-pervasive." The most important deity for the Śrīvaiṣṇava community.

Viṣṇu Sahasranāma. "The thousand names of Viṣṇu." A section from the epic Mahābhārata in which Viṣṇu is adored. An important work in the piety and ritual life of the Śrīvaiṣṇava community.

Yāmuna. One of the most important *ācāryas* in the Śrīvaiṣṇava tradition. Teacher of Rāmānuja's teachers.

BIBLIOGRAPHY

Tamil names like Tirukkurukai Pirāṉ Piḷḷāṉ and Aḻakiya Maṇavāḷa Nāyaṉār are treated as a single unit. The Tamil names cited do not contain a first name and a last name. Thus, the reference for Tirukkurukai Pirāṉ Piḷḷāṉ would be listed alphabetically under "Tirukkurukai" rather than under "Piḷḷāṉ."

GENERAL WORKS

Aḻakiya Maṇavāḷa Nāyaṉār. See B. R. Purushothama Naidu.

Acārya Hṛdayam. See B. R. Purushothama Naidu.

Aṇṇaṅgarācāriyar, P. B., *Nālāyira tivviyap pirapantam.* Kāñci: V. N. Tēvanātaṉ, 1971.

———, ed. *Tiruvāymoli.* 10 vols. Kāñci, 1949–63.

———, ed. *Rāmānujagranthamālā.* Kāñci, 1974.

———, ed. *Pakavat Viṣayam.* 4 vols. (with Nañjīyar's *Nine Thousand-paṭi,* Periyavāccāṉ Piḷḷai's *Twenty-four Thousand-paṭi,* and Vatakku Tiruvīti Piḷḷai's "*Īṭu*" *Thirty-six Thousand-paṭi* commentaries). Kāñci, 1975–76.

———, ed. *Stotramāla.* Kāñci: P. B. Aṇṇaṅgarācariyar, 1974.

Appadurai, Arjun. *Worship and Conflict under Colonial Rule.* New Delhi: Orient Longman, 1983.

Apte, Vaman Shivram. *The Student's Sanskrit-English Dictionary.* New Delhi: Motilal Banarsidass, 1982.

Arunachalam, Mu. *Nammāḻvār, varalārum nūlāraycciyum.* Srirangam: Śrīraṅgam Śrīnivāsa Tātācāriyar Svāmi Tirust Veḷiyīṭu, 1984.

as-Said, Labib. *The Recited Koran: A History of the First Recorded Version.* Adapted and translated by Bernard Weiss, M. A. Rauf, and Morroe Berger. Princeton, N.J.: Darwin Press, 1975.

Ayyangar, Satyamurti. *Tiruvaymoli-English Glossary.* Bombay: Ananthacharya Indological Research Institute, 1981.

Balasundara Nayakar, K. *Īṭṭurai Ārāychi and Commentary on Tiruvāymoḻi* (for Agapporul stanzas only), pts. 1 and 2. Tirupati: Tirumala-Tirupati Devasthanam Press, 1956–58.

Ballantyne, "Dr." "The Eternity of Sound: A Dogma of the Mi'ma'nsa'." *The Pandit* (Banaras) 1 (1866): 68–71, 86–88.

Beck, Brenda E. F. *The Three Twins: The Telling of a South Indian Epic.* Bloomington: Indiana University Press, 1982.

Blackburn, Stuart. "Oral Performance: Narrative and Ritual in a Tamil Tradition." *Journal of American Folklore* 94, no. 372 (1981).

Blackburn, Stuart, and A. K. Ramanujan. *Another Harmony: New Essays on the Folklore of India.* Berkeley: University of California Press, 1986.

Bonazzoli, Giorgio. "Composition, Transmission and Recitation of the Purāṇa-s (A Few Remarks)." *Purana* (July 1983): 254–80.

Bibliography

Brown, C. Mackenzie. "Purāṇa as Scripture: From Sound to Image of the Holy Word in the Hindu Tradition." *History of Religions* 26, no. 1 (1986): 68–86.

Cakticaraṇan̲. *Araṅkan̲ Kavitai Amutam*. Madras: Amuta Nilayam, 1986.

Caramōpāya Nirṇayam. See Nayan̲āraccān̲ Piḷḷai.

Carman, John B. *The Theology of Rāmānuja: An Essay in Interreligious Understanding*. New Haven, Conn., and London: Yale University Press, 1974.

———. "Ramanuja's Contemporaneity." *Sri Ramanuja Vani* 1 (1978): 37–45.

Carman, John B., and Vasudha Narayanan. *The Tamil Veda: Piḷḷān̲'s Interpretation of the Tiruvāymoḻi*. Chicago: University of Chicago Press, 1989.

Carpenter, David. "Language as Dharma: Vedic Revelation in the Post-Vedic Age." Paper presented at the national meeting of the American Academy of Religion, Chicago, November 1989.

Cilappatikāram. Madras: Murray and Co., 1957.

Clooney, Francis X. "Unity in Enjoyment: An Exploration into Nammāḻvār's Tamil Veda and Its Commentators." *Sri Ramanuja Vani* 6, no. 4 (1983): 34–61.

———. "Divine Word, Human Word: The Śrīvaiṣṇava Exposition of the Character of Nammāḻvār's Experience as Revelation." In *In Spirit and Truth* (festschrift for Ignatius Hrudayam). Madras: Aikya Alayam, 1985.

———. "Why the Veda Has No Author: Language as Ritual in Early Mīmāṁsā and Post-Modern Theology." *Journal of the American Academy of Religion* 55, no. 4 (1987): 659–86.

———. *Thinking Ritually: Rediscovering the Pūrva Mīmāṁsā of Jaimini*. De Nobili Research Series, vol. 17. Vienna: De Nobili Research Library, Institute for Indology at the University of Vienna, 1990.

Coburn, Thomas B. "Scripture in India: Towards a Typology of the Word in Hindu Life." *Journal of the American Academy of Religion* 52, no. 3 (1984): 435–59.

Coward, Harold, and David Goa. *Mantra: Hearing the Divine in India*. Chambersburg, Penn.: Anima Publications, 1991.

Coward, Harold, and Krishna Sivaraman. *Revelation in Indian Thought*. Emeryville, Calif.: Dharma Publishing, 1977.

Cutler, Norman. "The Devotee's Experience of the Sacred Tamil Hymns." *History of Religions* 24, no. 2 (1984): 91–112.

———. *Songs of Experience*. Bloomington: Indiana University Press, 1987.

Cutler, Norman, and A. K. Ramanujan. "From Classicism to Bhakti." In *Essays on Gupta Culture*, edited by Bardwell Smith. New Delhi: Motilal Banarsidass, 1983.

Damodaran, G. *The Literary Value of the Tiruvāymoḻi*. Tirupati: Sri Venkateswara University, 1978.

Dāsyai. See Tiruk kōnēri Dāsyai.

Dehejia, Vidya. *Slaves of the Lord: The Path of the Tamil Saints*. New Delhi: Munshiram Manoharlal, 1988.

Denny, Frederick. "The *Adab* of Quran Recitation: Text and Context." In *International Congress for the Study of the Quran, Proceedings*. Canberra: Australian National University Press, 1980.

———. "Exegesis and Recitation: Their Development as Classical Forms of Quranic

Piety." In *Transitions and Transformations in the History of Religions: Essays in Honor of Joseph Kitagawa,* edited by Frank Reynolds and Theodore M. Ludwig. Leiden: E. J. Brill, 1980.

———. "Quran Recitation: A Tradition of Oral Performance and Transmission." *Oral Traditions* 4, nos. 1–2 (1989): 5–26.

Denny, Frederick M., and Rodney L. Taylor, eds. *The Holy Book in Comparative Perspective.* Columbia, S.C.: University of South Carolina Press, 1985.

Divyasūri Caritam. See Garuḍa Vāhana Paṇḍita.

Dulles, Avery. *Models of Revelation.* New York: Doubleday, 1983.

Eck, Diana L. *Darśan: Seeing the Divine Image in India.* Chambersburg, Penn.: Anima Books, 1981.

Fitzgerald, James. "India's Fifth Veda: The Mahābhārata's Presentation of Itself." *Journal of South Asian Literature* 20 (1980): 125–40.

Garuḍa Vāhana Paṇḍita. *Divya suri Caritam* (The Story of the Divine Sages). Edited by T. A. Sampath Kumārācharya and K. K. A. Venkaṭācharya, translated into Hindi by Panḍita Mādhavāchārya. Bombay: Ananthacharya Research Institute, 1978.

Gill, Sam D. "Nonliterate Traditions and Holy Books: Toward a New Model." In *The Holy Book in Comparative Perspective,* edited by Frederick M. Denny and Rodney L. Taylor. Columbia: University of South Carolina Press, 1985.

Glory of the Āḻvārs, The. See Vaṭivaḻakiya Nampi Tācar.

Gnanambal, K. "Srivaishnavas and Their Religious Institutions." *Bulletin of the Anthropological Survey of India* 20, no. 3 (1971): 97–187.

Gonda, Jan. *The Vision of the Vedic Poets.* The Hague: Mouton, 1963.

Goody, Jack. *The Logic of Writing and the Organization of Society.* Cambridge: Cambridge University Press, 1986.

———, ed. *Literacy in Traditional Societies.* Cambridge: Cambridge University Press, 1968.

Gopalakrishna Naidu. *Lord Venkateswara and Alwars.* Tirupati: Tirupati Devasthanam, n.d.

Gopalan, L. V. *Sri Vaishnava Divya Desams (108 Tirupatis).* Madras: Visishtadvaita Pracharini Sabha, 1972.

Gough, Kathleen. "Implications of Literacy in Traditional China and India." In Goody, *Literacy in Traditional Societies.*

Govindacharya, Alkondavilli. *The Divine Wisdom of the Dravida Saints.* Madras: C. N. Press, 1902.

———. *Holy Lives of the Azhwars.* Mysore: G. E. Press, 1902.

———. *The Life of Ramanujacharya.* Madras: S. Murthy, 1906.

Graham, William A. *Beyond the Written Word: Oral Aspects of Scripture in the History of Religion.* Cambridge: Cambridge University Press, 1987.

Haberman, David. *Acting as a Way of Salvation.* New York: Oxford University Press, 1988.

Hardy, Friedhelm. "Mādhavendra Pūri: A Link between Bengal Vaiṣṇavism and South Indian Bhakti." *Journal of the Royal Asiatic Society* 1 (1974): 23–41.

———. "Ideology and Cultural Contexts of the Śrīvaiṣṇava Temple." *Indian Economic and Social History Review* 14, no. 1 (1977): 119–51.

———. "The Tamil Veda of a Śūdra Saint" (The Śrīvaiṣṇava Interpretation of Nammāḻvār). In *Contribution to South Asian Studies,* edited by Gopal Krishna, vol. 1. Delhi: Oxford University Press, 1979.

———. *Viraha Bhakti.* Delhi: Oxford University Press, 1983.

Hari Rao, V. N., ed. and trans. *Koil Olugu: The Chronicle of the Srirangam Temple with Historical Notes.* Madras: Rochouse and Sons, 1961. See also *Koyiloluku.*

———. *The Srirangam Temple: Art and Architecture.* Tirupati: Sri Venkateswara University, 1967.

Harman, William. *The Marriage of a Hindu Goddess.* Bloomington: Indiana University Press, 1989.

Hawley, John Stratton, in association with Srivatsa Goswami. *At Play with Krishna.* Princeton, N.J.: Princeton University Press, 1981.

———. "The Music in Faith and Morality." *Journal of the American Academy of Religion* 52, no. 2 (1984): 243–62.

Heart of the Teacher, The. See Aḻakiya Maṇavāḷa Nāyaṉār.

Hein, Norvin. *The Miracle Plays of Mathura.* New Haven, Conn.: Yale University Press, 1972.

———. "Caitanya's Ecstasies and the Theology of the Name." In *Hinduism: New Essays in the History of Religions,* edited by Bardwell Smith. Leiden: E. J. Brill, 1982.

Hiltebeitel, Alf. *The Cult of Draupadi: Mythologies from Gingee to Kuruksetra.* Chicago: University of Chicago Press, 1988.

Hooper, J. S. M. *Hymns of the Alvars.* Calcutta: Association Press, 1929.

Howard, Wayne. *Veda Recitation in Varanasi.* Delhi: Motilal Banarsidass, 1986.

Hudson, Dennis. "Bathing in Krishna." *Harvard Theological Review* 78, nos. 1–2 (1980): 539–66.

———. "The Vaiṣṇava Temple with Three Floors for Icons." MS.

Jagadeesan, Nainar. *History of Sri Vaishnavism in the Tamil Country: Post-Ramanuja.* Madurai: Koodal Publishers, 1977.

Juergensmeyer, Mark. *Religion as a Social Vision.* Berkeley: University of California Press, 1982.

Juergensmeyer, Mark, and N. Gerald Barrier. *Sikh Studies: Comparative Perspectives on a Changing Tradition.* Berkeley: Graduate Theological Union, 1979.

Kalyaṇāpuram Amutaṉ. *Tivyaprapanta Icai Mālai.* Srirangam: Sundaram Charities Trust, 1980.

Kapur, Anuradha. "Actors, Pilgrims, Kings and Gods: The Rāmlila at Ramnagar." *Contributions to Indian Sociology* 19, no. 1 (1985): 57–74.

Kaylor, R. David. "The Concept of Grace in the Hymns of Nammāḻvār." *Journal of the American Academy of Religion* 44, no. 4 (1976): 649–60.

Kaylor, R. David, and K. K. A. Venkatachari. *God Far, God Near: An Interpretation of the Thought of Nammāḻvār.* Bombay: Ananthacharya Indological Research Institute Series, no. 5 (supp.), 1981.

Kelber, Werner H. *The Oral and Written Gospel: The Hermeneutics of Speaking and Writing in the Synoptic Tradition, Mark, Paul and Q.* Philadelphia: Fortress Press, 1983.

Kōyil Kantāṭainayaṉ. *Periya Tirumuṭi Aṭaivu.* In *Āṛāyirappaṭi Guruparamparāprabhāvam,* edited by S. Krishnasvāmi Ayyaṅkār. Tirucci: Puttur Agraharam, 1975.

Kōyiloḻuku. Ed. Kiruṣṇasvāmi Ayyaṅkār Svāmi. Tirucci: Sri Vaisnava Grantha Prakācana Samiti, 1976.

Krishnasvami Ayyangar, S. ed. *Bhagavad Viṣayam,* 10 vols. (with Tirukkurukai Pirāṉ Piḷḷāṉ's *Six Thousand-paṭi,* Nañjīyar's *Twelve Thousand-paṭi,* Periyavāccāṉ Piḷḷai's *Twenty-four Thousand-paṭi,* and Vaṭakku Tiruvīti Piḷḷai's "*Īṭu*" *Thirty-six Thousand-paṭi* commentaries). Madras: Nobel Press, 1924–30.

Krishnaswami Iyengar, S. *Early History of Vaisnavism in South India*. Oxford: Clarendon Press, 1920.

———. *History of Tirupati,* 2 vols. Tirupati: Tirumalai Tirupati Devasthanam, 1940–41.

Krishnavarma, Shyamaji. "The Use of Writing in Ancient India." *Actes du sixieme Congres International des Orientalistes tenu en 1883 a Leide,* pt. 3, sec. 2: "Aryenne." Leiden: E. J. Brill, 1885.

Kurattalvar Aiyengar, N. *A Free Translation of Tiruvaimoli of Sathakopa,* 10 pts. Sri Penukonda Alvar Sannadhi Series no. 4. Trichinopoly: Vakulabharanam Press, 1929.

Leclercq, Jean. *The Love of Learning and the Desire for God: A Study of Monastic Culture*. Translated by Catharine Misrahi. New York: Fordham University Press, 1960.

Lester, Robert. "Rāmānuja and Śrī-Vaiṣṇavism (in the Light of the *Āṛayirappaḍi* to Nammāḻvār's *Tiruvāymoḻi*)." Paper presented in the Fifth International Conference-Seminar of Tamil Studies, Madurai, South India, 4–10 January 1981.

———. "Hinduism: Veda and Sacred Texts." In *The Holy Book in Comparative Perspective,* edited by Frederick Denny and Rodney Taylor. Columbia: University of South Carolina Press, 1985.

Levering, Miriam. *Rethinking Scripture: Essays from a Comparative Perspective*. Albany: SUNY Press, 1989.

Lullaby, The. See S. Muthuratna Mudaliyar.

Lutgendorf, Philip. *The Life of a Text: Performing the Ramcaritmanas of Tulsidas*. University of California Press, 1991.

Madras District Gazeteers. 7 vols. Madras: Government Press, 1957–83.

Maṇavāḷa Māmuni. "Upatecarattinamālai" (Upadeśaratnamālai). In Aṇṇaṅgarācāriyar, *Nālayira tivviyap pirapantam*.

Mangala Murugesan. *Sangam Age*. Madras: Thendral Pathipakam, 1982.

Martin, Richard. "Tilawah." In *Encyclopedia of Religion,* 14:526–30.

———. "Understanding the Quran in Text and Context." *History of Religions* 21 (1982): 361–84.

Moffatt, Michael. *An Untouchable Community in South India*. Princeton, N.J.: Princeton University Press, 1979.

Monier-Williams, Monier. *A Sanskrit-English Dictionary*. Oxford: Clarendon Press, 1974.

Mumme, Patricia Yvonne. *The Śrīvaiṣṇava Theological Dispute*. Madras: New Era Publications, 1989.

Muthuratna Mudaliyar, S., ed. *Nammāḻvār Tiruttālāṭṭu*. Tanjore: Tañcāvūr Carasvati Mahāl Publications, no. 43, 1951.

Naidu, Gopalakrishna. *Lord Venkateswara and Alwars.* Tirupati: Tirupati Devasthanam, n.d.

Nālāyira tivviyap pirapantam. Edited by K. Venkataswami Reddiyar. Madras: Tiruvenkatatan Tirumanram, 1981.

———. Edited by P. B. Aṇṇaṅgarācariyar. Kanci, 1971. See also *Śrī Tivyap pirapantam.*

Nammāḻvār. *Nammāḻvār aruḷiceyta Tiruvāymoḻi mutal pattu. Āṟayirappaṭi, irupattunālāyirappaṭi, captārttam, tramiṭōpaniṣad tātparya ratnāvaḷi ākiyavaṟṟutaṉ Śrī Vētānta Rāmānuja Mahātēcikaṉ aruḷiya pakavat viṣaya sāram.* Srirangam: Srirangam Śrīmatāṇṭavaṉ Ācramam, 1986.

———. *Nammāḻvār aruḷiceyta Tiruvāymoḻi iraṇṭu-mūṉṟu-nāṅkām pattukaḷ. Āṟāyirappaṭi, irupattunālāyirappaṭi, captārttam, tramiṭōpaniṣad tātparya ratnāvaḷi ākiyavaṟṟuṭaṉ Śrī Vētānta Rāmānuja Mahātēcikaṉ aruḷiya pakavat viṣaya sāram.* Srirangam: Srirangam Śrīmatāṇṭavaṉ Ācramam, 1987.

Narasimmayyankar, Uttamanampi S. *Vaikuṇṭa Ēkātaci Utsava Vaipavam.* Srirangam: Kōmatam Caṭakōpācāri, n.d.

Narayanan, Vasudha. "Arcāvatāra: On Earth, as He Is in Heaven." In *Gods of Flesh, Gods of Stone,* edited by Joanne P. Waghorne and Norman Cutler, in association with Vasudha Narayanan. Chambersburg, PA: Anima Publications, 1985.

———. "Hindu Devotional Literature: The Tamil Connection." *Religious Studies Review* 12 (1985): 12–20.

———. *The Way and the Goal.* Washington, D.C.: Institute for Vaishnava Studies (American University) and Cambridge: Center for the Study of World Religions (Harvard University), 1987.

———. "Renunciation in Saffron and White Robes." In *Monastic Life in the Christian and Hindu Traditions,* edited by Austin B. Creel and Vasudha Narayanan. Lewiston, N.Y.: Edwin Mellen, 1990.

See also Rajagopalan, Vasudha.

Nāyaṉāraccaṉ Piḷḷai. *Caramōpāya Nirṇayam.* In *Āṟayirappaṭi Guruparamparāprabhāvam,* edited by S. Krishnasvāmi Ayyaṅkār. Tirucci: Puttur Agraharam, 1975.

Nelson, Kristina. *The Art of Reciting the Qur'an.* Austin: University of Texas Press, 1985.

Ong, Walter J. *Orality and Literacy: The Technologizing of the Word.* London and New York: Methuen, 1982.

———. "Text as Interpretation: Mark and After." In *Orality, Aurality, and Biblical Narrative,* edited by Lou H. Silberman. *Semeia* 39 (1987): 7–26.

Palmer, David E. *Hermeneutics: Interpretation Theory in Schleiermacher, Dilthey, Heidegger, and Gadamer.* Evanston, Ill.: Northwestern University Press, 1969.

Parāśara Bhaṭṭar. "Śrī Raṅgarāja Stava." In *Stotramālā,* edited by P. B. Aṇṇaṅgarācāriyar. Kāñci, 1979.

Parthasarathy Vanamala. "Evolution of Rituals in Viṣṇu Temple Utsavas, with special reference to Srirangam, Tirumalai and Kāñci." Ph.D. diss., University of Bombay, 1983.

Periyavaccan Pillai. *Tiruppāvai Mūvāyirappaṭi vyākyānam,* edited by P. B. Aṇṇaṅgarācāriyar. Kāñci, 1974.

Peterson, Indira Viswanathan. "Singing of a Place: Pilgrimage and Poetry in Tamil Śaivaite Hagiography." *Journal of the American Oriental Society* 102, no. 1 (1982): 69–90.

———. *Hymns to Śiva.* Princeton, N.J.: Princeton University Press, 1989.

Pinpaḻakiya Perumāḷ. Jīyar. *Āṛāyirappaṭi Guruparamparāprabhā vam,* edited by S. Krishnasvāmi Ayyaṅkār. Tirucci: Puttur Agraharam, 1975.

Pope, G. U., comm. and trans. *The Tiruvacagam or "Sacred Utterances" of the Tamil Poet, Saint and Sage Manikka-vacagar.* Oxford: Clarendon Press, 1900.

Puliyur Kēcikan, ed. *Tolkāppiyam.* Madras: Pārinilayam, 1986.

Purushothama Naidu, B. R. *Acharya Hridayam with the Tamiḻākkam of the Commentary of Maṇavāḷa Māmunigaḷ.* 2 vols. Madras: Madras University, 1965.

Raghavachar, S. S. Introduction to the *Vedarthasangraha of Sri Ramanujacharya.* Mangalore: Mangalore Trading Association, 1973.

Raghavan, V. "Vedic Chanting; Music, Dance and Drama." In *International Seminar on Traditional Cultures in South-East Asia.* Bombay: Orient Longmans, 1960.

Rajagopalachariar, T. *The Vaishnavaite Reformers of India,* 3d ed. Delhi: A. D. Publications, 1982.

Rajagopalan, Vasudha [Narayanan]. "The Śrīvaiṣṇava Understanding of *Bhakti* and *Prapatti:* The Āḻvārs to Vedānta Deśika." Ph.D. diss., University of Bombay, 1978.

Raman, K. V. *Sri Varadarajaswami Temple—Kanchi: A Study of Its History, Art and Architecture.* New Delhi: Abhinav Publications, 1975.

———. "Divyaprabandha Recital in Vaishnava Temples." In *Professor T. K. Venkataraman's 81st Birthday Commemoration Volume,* edited by S. Nagarajan. Madurai: Madurai Tamilology Publishers, 1981.

Ramanathan S. *Tivviyap pirapanta paṇ icai.* Madras: Kalaimakaḷ *Icaik Kallūri,* 1969.

Rāmānuja. *Rāmānuja's Vedārtha Saṁgraha,* edited and translated by J. A. B. van Buitenen. Poona: Deccan College, 1956.

———. *Vedartha Sangraha of Ramanuja,* translated by M. R. Rajagopala Ayyangar. Chromepet (Madras): by the author, 1956.

———. *Vedartha-Sangraha,* translated by S. S. Raghavachar. Mysore: Sri Ramakrishna Ashrama, 1968.

———. *The Gitabhashya of Ramanuja,* edited and translated by M. R. Sampatkumaran. Madras: M. Rangacarya Memorial Trust, 1969.

———. *Śrībhāṣya, Vedārthaṣaṁgraha, Gītābhāṣya, Gadya traya.* In *Ramanujagranthamālā,* edited by P. B. Aṇṇaṅgarācāriyar. Kāñci, 1974.

Rāmānujācāriyar, P. S., and A. A. Mātavācāryan, eds. *Nammāḻvār aruḻiceyta Tiruvāymoḻi* (for the first four hundred verses, with Piḷḷaṉ's *Six Thousand,* Śrīsākṣātsvami's *Twenty-four Thousand,* and *Captārtam,* Vedānta Deśika's *Dramidopaniṣad Tātparya Ratnāvaḷi,* and Śrī Vētānta Rāmānuja Mahātēcikaṉ's *Pakavat-Viṣaya Sāram*), 2 vols. Srirangam: Srirangam Srimatāṇṭavaṉ Ācramam, 1986–87.

Ramanujachari, S. K. "A Note on Divinity of Archavatara and Greatness of Ramanuja at Srirangam." *Sri Ramanuja Vani* 10, no. 3 (1987): 37–39.

Ramanujam, V. V. "Pranaya Kalaham." *Sri Ramanuja Vani* 12, no. 1 (Oct. 1988): 7–8, 60–64.

Ramanujan, A. K. *The Interior Landscape: Love Poems from a Classical Tamil Anthology.* Bloomington: Indiana University Press, 1967.

———. *Hymns for the Drowning: Poems for Viṣṇu by Nammāḻvār*. Princeton, N.J.: Princeton University Press, 1981.

Ramanujan, A. K., and Norman Cutler. "From Classicism to Bhakti." In *Essays in Gupta Culture*, edited by Bardwell Smith. Delhi: Motilal Banarsidass, 1983.

Ramesan, N. *The Tirupati Temple*. Tirupati: Sri Tirupati Devasthanam, 1981.

Randhawa, Mohan Singh. *Farmers of India*. 3 vols. New Delhi: Indian Council of Agricultural Research, 1959–64.

Rangachari, K. *The Sri Vaishnava Brahmans*. Madras: Bulletin of the Madras Government Museum, 1931.

Rangachari, R., trans. *Dramidopanisad Tatparya Ratnavali and Sara*. Madras: Vedanta Desika Research Society, 1974.

Rangacharya, V. "Historical Evolution of Sri Vaishnavism." In *The Cultural Heritage of India*, vol. 2. Calcutta: Sri Ramakrishna Centenary Committee, n.d.

Ranganatha Mutaliyar, ed. *Sri Vaisnavam*. Madras: n.p., 1937.

Reddiyar, Venkataswami. See *Nālāyira tivviyap pirapantam*.

Renou, Louis. *The Destiny of the Veda in India*. New Delhi: Motilal Banarsidass, 1965.

Satyamurti Ayyangar. *Tiruvaymoli-English Glossary*, 2 vols. Bombay: Ananthacharya Indological Research Institute, 1981.

Sax, William S. "Ritual and Performance in the Pāṇḍavalīlā of Uttarakhand." In *Essays on the Mahabharata*, edited by Arvind Sharma. Washington, D.C.: University Press of America, forthcoming.

Schechner, Richard. *Between Theater and Anthropology*. Philadelphia: University of Pennsylvania Press, 1985.

Schechner, Richard, and Linda Hess. "The Ramlila of Ramnagar." *The Drama Review* 21, no. 3 (1977) 51–82.

Shekhar, Indu. *Sanskrit Drama: Its Origin and Decline*. Leiden: E. J. Brill, 1960.

Singer, Milton, ed. *Krishna: Myths, Rites, and Attitudes*. Honolulu: East-West Center Press, 1966.

Sivaraman, Krishna. "The Word as a Category of Revelation." In *Revelation in Indian Thought*, edited by Harold Coward and Krishna Sivaraman. Emeryville, Calif.: Dharma Publishing, 1979.

Six Thousand, The. See Tirukkurukai Pirāṉ Piḷḷāṉ.

Sjoman, N. E., and H. V. Dattatreya. *An Introduction to South Indian Music*. Sarasvati Project Karnataka series 1. Amsterdam: Sarasvati Project, 1986.

Smith, Brian K. "Exorcising the Transcendent: Strategies for Defining Hinduism and Religion." *History of Religions* 27 (1987): 32–55.

Smith, John D. "Worlds Apart: Orality, Literacy, and the Rajasthani Folk-*Mahābhārata*." *Oral Traditions* 5, no. 1 (1990): 3–19.

Somasundaram, J. M. *The Island Shrine of Sri Ranganatha*. Tiruchirapalli: St. Joseph's Industrial School Press, 1965.

Splendor, The. See Pinpaḻakiya Perumāḷ Jīyar.

Srimāṉ Aṣṭakōtram Nallāṉ Cakravartti Na Ca Parthasārati Aiyaṅkār Maṇi viḻā-Pārāṭṭu viḻā. Madras: Liberty Press, 1988.

Srinivasa Raghavan, *Sri Vishnu Sahasranama with the Bhashya of Sri Parasara Bhattar*. Madras: Sri Visishtadvaita Pracharini Sabha, 1984.

Śrīnivāsarākavaṉ, A. *Śrīmāṉ Nikamānta Mahatēcikaṉ Aruḷiceyta Śrī Vaiṣṇava Dinacari.* Madras: Sri Visistadvaita Pracharini Sabha, 1984.

Srirama Bharati. *Devagana: An Outline of South Indian Temple Music.* Melkote: Tyaga Bharati Music Education Mission, 1985.

Srirama Bharati, and Sowbhagya Lakshmi. *The Tiruvaymoli of Nammalvar Rendered in English.* Melkote: Tyaga Bharati Music Education Mission, 1987.

Sri Tivyap pirapantam. Edited by Tamil scholars, 4 vols., Madras: Murray, 1956. See also *Nālāyira tivviyap pirapantam.*

Staal, J. Frits. *Nambudiri Veda Recitation.* The Hague: Mouton, 1961.

———. "The Concept of Scripture in the Indian Tradition." In *Sikh Studies: Comparative Perspectives on a Changing Tradition,* edited by Mark Juergensmeyer and N. Gerald Barrier. Berkeley: Graduate Theological Union, 1979.

Subbu Reddiar, N. *Philosophy of the Nalayiram with Special Reference to Nammalvar.* Tirupati: Sri Venkateswara University, 1977.

Tacar. See Vaṭivaḻakiya Nampi Tācar.

Tamil Icai Caṅkam Viḻā Malar. 1988–89, 1989–90, and 1990–91.

Tamil Lexicon, 6 vols. Madras: Madras University Press, 1982–83.

Tamil scholars. *Pāṭṭum Tokaiyum.* Madras: Murray, 1958.

———. *Sri Tivyap pirapantam.* 4 vols. Madras: Murray, 1956.

Tiruk kōneri Dāsyai. *Tiruvāymoḻi Vācakamālai.* Tanjore: Sarasvati Mahal Library, 1950.

Tirukkurukai Pirāṉ Piḷḷāṉ. "Āṟāyirappaṭi Vyākkyānam." In *Bhagavad Viṣayam,* edited by Sri S. Krishnasvami Ayyangar, 10 vols. Madras: Nobel Press, 1924–30. See also Nammāḻvār.

Tiruvallikkēṇi Śrī Pārthasārathi svāmi tēvastāna vēta atyāpaka kōṣṭi cirappu malar (Sri Parthasarathi Temple Veda-Reciters' Felicitation vol.) Madras, 1985.

Tivyap pirapanta ilakkiya viḻā viḷakkam. Cuddalore: T. K. Narayanacami Nayutu, 1973.

Turner, Victor. *The Anthropology of Performance.* New York: PAJ Publications, 1986.

Uttamur Viraraghavacariyar, ed. *Nammāḻvār aruḷiceyta Tiruvāymoḻi, prabandha rakṣai,* 4 vols. Madras: Visishtadvaita Pracharini Sabha, 1970–78.

Varadachari, K. C. *Alvars of South India.* Bombay: Bharatiya Vidya Bhavan, 1970.

Vaṭivaḻakiya Nampi Tācar. *Āḻvārkaḷ Vaipavam* (The Glory of the Āḻvārs). Edited by R. Kannan Cuvāmi. Madras: R. Kannan Svāmt, 1987.

Vatsyayan, Kapila. *Classical Indian Dance in Literature and the Arts.* New Delhi: Sangeet Natak Akademi, 1968.

Vedānta Deśika. *Dramiḍopaniṣad Tātparya Ratnāvaḻi and Sāra,* translated by R. Rangachari. Madras: Vedanta Desika Research Society, 1974.

———. *Śrī Vaiṣṇava Tinacari.* Edited by Putukkottai A. Srinivasarakavan. Madras: Sri Visistadvaita Pracharini Sabha, 1984.

Venkatachari, K. K. A. *The Manipravala Literature of the Śrī Vaiṣṇava Ācāryas.* Bombay: Ananthacarya Research Institute, 1978.

Venkataraman, S. *Araiyar Cēvai.* Madras: Tamilputtakālāyam, 1985.

Wadley, Susan S. "Texts in Contexts: Oral Traditions and the Study of Religion in Karimpur." In *American Studies in the Anthropology of India,* edited by Sylvia Vatuk. New Delhi: Manohar, 1978.

Winternitz, Moriz. *A History of Indian Literature*. New York: Russell and Russell, 1971.
Wulff, Donna Marie. "On Practicing Religiously: Music as Sacred in India." In *Sacred Sound*, edited by Joyce Irwin. JAAR Thematic Studies 50, no. 1: 149–72. Chico, Calif.: Scholars Press, 1983.
Yocum, Glenn. "Shrines, Shamanism, and Love Poetry: Elements in the Emergence of Popular Tamil Bhakti." *Journal of the American Academy of Religion* 41, no. 1 (1973): 3–17.
———. "A Non-*Brahman* Tamil Śaiva Mutt: A Field Study of the Thiruvavaduthurai Adheenam." In Creel and Narayanan, *Monasticism in the Hindu and Christian Traditions*. Lewiston, N.Y.: Edwin Mellen, 1990.
Young, Katherine. "Beloved Places (Ukantaruḷiṉanilṅkaḷ): The Correlation of Topography and Theology in the Śrīvaiṣṇava Tradition of South India." Ph.D. diss., Mcgill University, 1978.
Younger, Paul. "Singing the Tamil Hymnbook in the Tradition of Rāmānuja: The Adhyayanotsava Festival in Śrīraṅkam." *History of Religions* (1982): 272–93.
———. "Ten Days of Wandering and Romance with Lord Raṅkanātaṉ: The Paṅkuṉi Festival in Śrīraṅkam Temple, South India." *Modern Asian Studies* 16, no. 4 (1982): 623–56.
Zelliot, Eleanor. "The Medieval Bhakti Movement in History: An Essay on the Literature in English." In *Hinduism: New Essays in the History of Religions*, edited by Bardwell L. Smith. Leiden: E. J. Brill, 1982.

BOOKS ON SACRED PLACES (STHALA PURĀṆAS)

Many of the books in this list have no authors; some are pamphlets without the name of a publisher, while others list the temple board as publisher. To facilitate the use of this bibliography I have listed them under the names of the sacred place they describe, because the authors are unknown in most cases. A few of these books are substantial historical works and are also listed among general works. Some of the temples have two or more names, but I have given the complete listing under the name used by the *āḻvārs*. The popular names are also given, with a cross-reference to those used by the poets. The sthala purāṇas of the "Divya deśas" (108 sacred places sung by the *āḻvārs*) are given first and are followed by the sthala purāṇas for other "esteemed" Śrīvaiṣṇava places (*abhimāna sthala*).

Books on 108 Sacred Places

Aṣṭōttara catati tivyatēca vivarṇam. Tirucci: Śrī Vaiṣṇava Grantha Prakācana Samiti, 1976.
Gopalan, L. V. *Sri Vaishnava Divya Desams (108 Tirupatis)*. Madras: Visishtadvaita Pracharini Sabha, 1972.
"108 Tirupati Antāti" (*Nūṟṟeṭṭut* tiruppati antāti). In *Aṣṭap pirapantam*. Madras: S. Rajam, 1957.
Svayam Vyakta Kshetra. Srirangam: Sriranganathaswamy Temple, n.d. (English).

Bibliography

Divya Desas

Ahobilam

Śrī Ahobilakshetramum Śrī Ahobila Maṭhamum. Triuvallur: n.p., 1955.

Pidatala Sitapati, *Sri Ahobila Narasimha Swamy Temple* (Temple Monograph). Hyderabad: Archaeology and Museums, Government of Andhra Pradesh, Archaeological Series no. 56, 1982 (English).

Aḻakar Kōyil. See Tirumāliruñcōlai.

Attigiri (Kanchipuram)

Chari, T. V. R. *The Glorious Temples of Kanchi*. Kancheepuram: Sri Kanchi Kamakshi Ambal Devasthanam Sarada Navarathri Kalai Nigazhchigal Trust, 1987.

Moorthy, C. K. *The Shrines of Kanchee*. Kancheepuram: Jayaram Publications, 1974.

Raman, K. V. *Sri Varadarajaswami Temple—Kanchi: A Study of Its History, Art and Architecture*. New Delhi: Abhinav Publications, 1975.

Ayodhya

Sri Rama Janma Bhoomi. Pamphlet. N.p.p., n.d. (printed c. 1970).

Kumbakonam. See Tirukkuṭantai.

Nacciyār Kōyil. See Tirunaraiyūr.

Oppiliyappan Kōyil. See Tiruviṇṇakar.

Srirangam. See Tiruvaraṅkam.

Srivilliputtur

Kaliyanam, G. *Guide and History of Sri Andal Temple, Srivilliputtur*. Srivilliputtur: Sri Nachiar Devasthanam, 1971.

Sanmukanatan, P. K. *Srivilliputtur Stala Makātmiyam*. 4th ed. Srivilliputtur: Sri Nācciyār Tirukkōyil, 1972.

Tiruccērai

Śrī Cāranātapperumāḷ Tirukkōvil: Tiruccērai (Kumpakōṇam-vattam). Tiruccērai: by the temple, 1985 (English and Tamil).

Tirukkovalur

Sri Tiruvēnkatarāmānujāccāriyar. *Tirukkōvalur Stala Purāṇam.* Tirukkovalur, 1978.

Tirukkuṭantai (Kumbakonam)

Tātācāriyar, N. S. *Aruḷmiku cāraṅkapāṇicuvāmi tirukkōyil tala varalāru.* Kumbakonam: Aru̱lmiku Cārankapāṇi Cuvāmi Tirukkoyil, 1984.

Tirumāliruñcōlai (Aḻakar Kōyil)

Aruḷmiku kaḷḷaḻakar tirukkōyil aḻakarkōvil varalāru. 2d ed. Madurai: Caṅkar Printing Press, n.d.

Tirunaraiyūr (Nācciyār Kōyil)

Śrī śrīnivāsapperumāḷ kōyil nācciyārkōyil kumpakōṇam tāluka tamiḷ arccanaiyum talap perumaiyum. Kumbakonam: Kīta Press, 1971.

Tātācāryar Cuvāmi, N. S. *Nācciyārkōyil aruḷmiku Śrīvañjuḷavalli cameta Cīnivācapperumāḷ tirukkōyil talavaralāru.* Kumbakonam: Kumar Press, n.d.

Tirupati. See Tiruvenkatam.

Tiruvallikkēṇi (Triplicane)

Triplicane Sri Parthasarathy Temple Sthalapurāṇam (Sri Brindaranya Kshetra Mahatmyam). Madras: Sri Parthasarathyswamy Devasthanam, 1953 (English and Tamil).

Tiruvallikkēṇi Śrī pārthasārathi suprapātam (poḻippuraiyuṭaṉ). Madras: Śrīmat Pakavatkīta, Śrīkītacārya Suprapāta Pracāra Nīti Kaiṁkarya Sapai, 1974.

Vaittiyanātaṉ, H. *Tiruvallikkēṇi Makātmiyam.* Madras: Bharati Book Center, 1978.

Tiruvallikkēṇi Śrī Pārthasārathi svāmi tēvastāna vēta atyāpaka kōṣṭi cirappu malar (Sri Parthasarathi Temple Veda-Reciters' Felicitation Volume) Madras, 1985.

Tiruvanantapuram (Trivandrum)

The Temple of Sree Padmanabha—Trivandrum. Trivandrum: Sree Padmanabha Swami Temple, 1977.

Tiruvaraṅkam (Srirangam)

Ikṣvāku kulatanam ennum śrīraṅka mahātmyam. Madras: Little Flower, 1986.

Cantiranāt, *Śrīraṅka makimai (tiruvaraṅka makimai).* Madras: Sri Intu, 1987.

Āḻvārkaḷ anupavitta araṅkattup perumāṉ. Srirangam: Sri Rankanatasvami Tevastanam, 1987.

Srirangam Rajagopuram Maha Samprokshanam 25-3-1987 Commemoration Souvenir. Srirangam: Sriranganathaswamy Etc. Devasthanams, 1987.

Tiruvayintirapuram

Tiruvayintīrapura stala purāṇam. Madras: Little Flower, 1963.

Tiruvenkatam (Tirupati)

Gopala Rao, T. *Sree Venkateswara Mahathyam*. Rajahmundry: Sree Sitharama Book Depot, 1971.
Raman, T. V. S., trans. *Tirumalai-tirupati Pilgrim Guide and Sthala Puranam*. Tirumalai Hills: Sri Venkateswara Book Depot, 1960.
Ramesan, N. *The Tirumala Temple*. Tirupati: Tirumala Tirupati Devasthanams, 1981.
Ravindranath, Sushila, and Javed Gaya. "Temple Trusts: Whose Business?" *Business India*, no. 170 (1984): 86–99.
Sharma, S. N., ed. *Tirupati Tourist Guide*. Rajahmundry: Gollapudi Veeraswamy Son, Sree Sita Rama Book Depot, 1971.
Viraraghavacharya, T. K. T. *History of Tirupati*. 3 vols. Tirupati: Tirumala-Tirupati Devasthanams, 1977.

Tiruviṇṇakar (Oppiliyappan Kōyil, near Kumbakonam)

Śrīrāmatēcikācārya svāmikaḷ, V. N. *Oppiliyappaṉ kōyil talapurāṇam*. Kumbakonam: Arulmiku Venkaṭacarlapati Cuvami Tirukkoyil, 1988.

Triplicane. See Tiruvallikkēṇi.

"Esteemed" Places (Abhimāna Sthalam)

Maturantakam

Citamparam, M. *Śrī Ērikātta Irāmaṉ talavaralāru*. Madurantakam: Śrī Kōtaṇṭarāmacuvāmi Tēvastāna Veḷiyīṭu, n.d.

Maṉṉārkuṭi

Ārumukam, I. *Irājamaṉṉārkuṭit tala varalāru*. Mannargudi: Devasthana Publishers, 1965.

Srimushnam

Srinivasaraghavachariar, R. *Srimushna Mahatmyam*. Virudhachalam: n.d. (English).
Srinivasaraghavachariar, R. *Srimushna Mahatmyam*. Virudhachalam: by author, 1973 (Tamil).
Aruḷmiku Pūvarākacuvāmi tirukkōyil Tirumuttam Tala Varalāru. Srimushnam, 1975.

Sriperumbudur

Srimat Pūtapuri Mahātmyam (Śrīperumputūr stala varalāru). Madras: Āḻvārkal Amuta Nilayam, 1985.

Vaṭuvūr (Vaduvur, Tanjore district)

Śrī Kōtaṇṭarāmasvāmi Tēvastānam, Vaṭuvur, Stala Purāṇam. Vaduvur: Sri Kothandaramaswami Devasthanam, 1987.

DAILY PRAYER MANUALS (*NITYĀNUSANDHĀNAM* BOOKS)

Tiruvāymoḻi. Madras: Śrī Ātinātar Āḻvār Kaiṁkarya Capā, 1988.

Vaṭakalai Nityānusantānam. Edited by Navanītam Śrīrāmatēcikācārya svami. Madras: Little Flower, 1978.

Nityānucantānam: Pūrvācāryarkaḷ anucantitta muṟai. Edited by S. Kiruṣṇasvāmi Ayyaṅkār. Tirucci, 1981 (Teṅkalai).

Nityānucantānam: Pūrvācāryarkaḷ anucantitta muṟai. Edited by R. Etiraja Ramanuja Tacar. Madras: Srivaisnava Nurpatippuk Kalakam, 1984 (Teṅkalai).

Mayarvara matinalamaruḷappeṟṟa āḻvārkaḷ aruḷicceyta Nityānusantānam. Tirupati: Tirumala Tirupati Devasthanam, 1982 (Vaṭakalai).

Nityānusantānam āḻvār pāṭalkaḷuṭaṉ. Edited by Kantāṭai Kiruṣna-mācāriya svāmikaḷ. Madras: Pālaji, 1983.

BRIEF LIST OF POPULAR DIVYA PRABANDHAM CASSETTES

Singing

Bombay Sisters. *Divyaprabandham. Periyazhvar Thirumozhi.* Sangeetha Live Cassettes. 4 MSC 4109. Stereo.

———. *Thiruppavai* (Tamil devotional). Sangeetha Live Cassettes. 9 MSC 1027.

Cirkali G. Civacitamparam. *Om Namo Narayana.* Indu Musik. IMR 1445. Stereo.

G. Damodaran. *Alwargal Amudha Ganam* (Tamil devotional). Geethanjali. GRC 1180. Stereo.

———. *Ramanuja Nurrantati 108.* Geethanjali. GRC 1188.

Mani Krishnaswamy. *Dhivya Prabandham.* AVM Cassette. MEI-SR 1011. Stereo.

Rajkumar Bharathi. *Thiruvengada Padhigangal (Periya Thiru Mozhi).* Sangeetha Live Cassettes. P6ECDB 10022. Stereo. 60 mins.

N. C. Soundaravalli. *Sri Parthasarathy Suprabatham. Divya Prabandham. Sri Andal's Varanamayiram.* HMV. STHVS 37052. Stereo.

Srirama Bharati. *Tiruvaymoli.* 4 vols. Amsterdam: Sarasvati Project.

R. Vedavalli. *Thiruvengada Padhigangal (Aara Amudham).* Sangeetha Live Cassettes. P6ECDB 10021. Stereo. 60 mins.

———. *Thiruvēngada Padhigangal (Aara Amudham).* Sri Venkateswara College of Music and Dance. TTD 4002.

———. *Āḻvār Pācuraṅkaḷ. Nammāḻvār Pācuraṅkaḷ*. Audio Fine. ARC 1026. Stereo.
Vimala Parthasarathy. *Thirumangai Kanda Thiruvengadam (Divya Prabandham)*. Keerthana. 6 CA 543. Stereo.

Recitation

Sevilimedu Srinivasachariar and Party. *Divya Prabandham*. 2 cassettes. Vani Cassettes. 4 SEI 131 132.
———. *Aazhvargal Pasuram*. Vani Cassettes. 4 SEI 142.
———. *Nammāḻvār Pācuraṅkaḷ, Tiruvaymoli*. 10 cassettes. Vols. 1–5. Vani Cassettes. 2 SEI 903, 904, 905, 906, and 907.
Sevilimedu Srinivasachari, Tirukannapuram Sadagopachari, and Party. *Tamil Devotional-Paasurangall*. Echo. 4 ECD 111.
Sevilimedu Srinivaschariar Raghavan and Party. *Āḻvār Pācuraṅkaḷ*. Geethanjali. GRC 1176.
Tuppul Srinivasaraghavachariar and S. K. Sridhar. *Thiruppavai* (traditional). RAJ audio. RA 006. Stereo.
T. A. Varadhachariar Swamigal. *Dhivya Prabandam (Perumal Thirumozhi)*. AVM audio. 45B 291.
———. *Dhivya Prabandam (Siriya Thirumadai-Thirunedunthandagam)*. AVM audio. 45B 290.
———. *Divya Prabandham Tiruppavai*. AVM audio. 60B 459.
———. *Divya Prabandham (Kōyil Tiruvāymoḻi, Cēvai Cāṟṟumurai)* AVM audio 60B 460.
———. *Divya Prabandham Rāmānuja Nūṟṟantāti*. AVM audio. 45B 274.

PRIVATE RECORDINGS FROM ADYAPAKAS AND TEMPLE PERFORMERS

Recitation

Ashtagothram N. C. Parthasarathy Iyengar. *Divya Prabandham, Ramanuja Nurrantati* and *Upadesratnamalai*. 18 × 90-min. cassettes. 1988.
T. Saranathan. *Tiruvaymoli and Nammalvar's life*. 5 × 90-min. cassettes. 1988.
Manavala Iyengar. *Nityanusandhanam and Koyil Tiruvaymoli*. 60 mins. 1979.

Songs

Veenai Rangarajan. *Nammalvar's Songs*. 30 mins. 1990.
———. *Songs from the Divya Prabandham*. 45 mins. 1991.
———. *Ekantam Songs at the Srirangam Temple*. 60 mins. 1991.
Venkata Varadhan. *Divya Prabandham Concert at Tamil Isai Sangam*. 90 mins. 1989.
Goda Mandali. *Divya Prabandham Concert at Tamil Isai Sangam*. 60 mins. 1990.
———. *Songs from the Divya Prabandham*. 1991 and 1992.
Sri Ranganatha Paduka Mandali. *Songs from the Divya Prabandham*. 1992.

INDEX

Index

Audience
for Festival of Recitation, 115, 126–27, 132
for secular performances, 142–43
Viṣṇu as the primary for rituals, 89, 115, 132, 142, 206 n. 13
Auspicious attributes, of Viṣṇu, 111, 210 n. 31, 216 n. 22
Authority (*Adhikāra*), 105–6, 208 n. 16, 219
Authorship of the Vedas, 16–17, 28–31
the Tiruvāymoḻi, 15–16, 20, 36–37, 136–37
Vedas as authorless, 20, 36–37, 38, 136–37
Avatāra, 220. *See also* Incarnation(s), of Viṣṇu
Ayaru aṛum, meanings of, 210 n. 27
Āyirakkāl maṇṭapam. *See* Hall of a Thousand Pillars
Ayyangar, Satyamurti, translation of the *Kōyil* Tiruvāymoḻi, 193 n. 8

Bangalore, Karnataka, India
Nammāḻvār Shrine. *See* Nammāḻvār Cannati
Pāṇ Perumāḷ Cannati, 67
Bhagavad Gītā, 49, 104, 208 n. 16, 215 n. 22, 225
Bhagavad viṣayam. *See* Commentaries
"Bhāgavata Mahātmya," 7
Bhāgavata Purāṇa (Sanskrit text), 2
Bhāgavatas. *See* Nonbrahmins
Bhajana maṇḍalis (song circles), 142–43
Bhakta, 220
Bhaktanjali (singers), 94–95
Bhakti (Devotion), 18, 220
electronic, 10, 95–98
Bhakti yoga, 111
Bharata Nātyam style of dance, 10, 79, 88, 214–15 n. 14
Bhāskara, viewpoint of, 21, 23
Bhaṭṭars. *See* Priests
Bhedābhedins, interpretation of the Vedas, 26
Bhoga upakarṇa (instrument of enjoyment), heaven described as, 131, 135
Bhūloka vaikuṇṭha. *See* Heaven, on earth
Bībī nācciyār (Muslim consort) for Viṣṇu, shrines, 83
Biographical literature on the *āḻvārs*, 21, 80, 195 n. 23
on Nammāḻvār, 31–36, 37–38, 39, 197 n. 48
see also Āḻvārkaḷ Vaipavam; Hagiographic literature
Birthdays, 60–63, 64, 93, 204 n. 13
domestic rituals connected with, 4, 58, 199 n. 15
Nammāḻvār's, 64, 70–72, 77
Birth stars, 60–63, 62, 69
Blackburn, Stuart, 8
Bliss, 22, 76
Boar, incarnation of Viṣṇu as, 23, 195 n. 26
Body-soul relationship. *See* Soul-body relationship
Bonazzoli, Giorgio, 211 n. 39
Book(s) (*Nūl*), Vedas perceived as, 20, 33–34, 38
"Bow song" tradition, 8
Brahmā (creator god), 20, 31, 32, 34, 137, 220
Brahman (Supreme Reality), 5, 8, 73, 195 n. 27
Brahma Sūtras (*Vedānta Sūtras*), 225
Rāmānuja's commentaries on, 16, 104, 203 n. 5, 208 n. 16, 215 n. 22
Brahma vidyā, 73–74
Brahmins, 26, 48, 51, 72, 102, 123
Carnatic music dominated by, 90, 91–92
investiture with the sacred thread, 72, 140, 205 n. 15
recitation by, 46, 54, 58, 141
smarta community, 85–86
at the Triplicane Temple, 52, 55–56
Veḷḷāḷas considered as *śūdras* by, 212 n. 7

Index

Converts to Śrīvaiṣṇavism, 27, 205 n. 16
made by Rāmānuja, 67, 202 n. 1, 203 n. 6
Costumes, for the festival image, 117, 120, 212 n. 3
Courtesans (Temple dancers), 80, 83–84, 91
Coward, Harold, 5
Creation, Viṣṇu's relationship to, 22
Cricket, 53, 55
Cymbals, 35, 43, 81, 84, 122, 145

Dalit, as term for scheduled caste, 202 n. 1. *See also* Scheduled caste
Dance, 4, 35, 41–42, 70, 109, 214 n. 13
Bharata Nātyam style, 10, 79, 88, 214–15 n. 14
choreography of the Divya Prabandham, 7–8, 42–46, 79, 80, 88
during the Festival of Recitation, 115, 124–25, 130, 132, 144
by women, 80, 83–84, 91, 214–15 n. 14
Darsán. *See* Vision
Dāsar (Disciples) of Nammāḻvār, Nammāḻvār Sabhā as, 74–75
"Daya Sathakam" (Vedānta Deśika), 196 n. 40
Death rituals, 58–59, 69
Denny, Frederick M., 6, 7
Detachment, 59, 72
Devadāsi tradition, 214 n. 14. *See also* Courtesans
Devagana Pathasala (Tyaga Bharati Mission), 93–95
Dīkṣa (Initiation) for priests, 48, 199 n. 15, 220
Disciples (*Dāsar*) of Nammāḻvār, Nammāḻvār Sabhā as, 74–75
Discus (Śrīvaiṣṇava emblem), 68, 85
Divinity or humanity of Nammāḻvār, 14, 30, 31–36, 37, 68, 137
Divya deśa, 220. *See also* Sacred places; Temples; *individual temples by name*
Divya Prabandham (The Sacred Collect of Four Thousand Verses), 2, 19–20, 53, 142, 220, 222
acceptance by Vaṭakalais and Teṅkalais, 56
daily cycle of prayers from, 40
dramatic performances of, 8–10
musical settings, 80–81, 90–95, 142, 199 n. 14, 206 n. 14
current popularity, 83, 96, 97
sung during the *ekānta sevā*, 87–88
sung in secular concerts, 88–90
See also Singing
pillars in Srirangam Temple as, 121
power of the words, 43–45
printed editions, 8–9, 60, 70, 98
quoted by Vipranarayana, 75
recitation of. *See* Recitation
revelation of to Nāthamuni, 36, 96, 137–38, 201 n. 9, 222
study and teaching of, 45–53, 55, 94–95
See also individual works by name
Divya Sūri Caritam (*The Story of the Divine Sages*) (Garuḍa Vāhana Paṇḍita), 21, 197 n. 48
Domestic rituals/worship, 46, 48, 68, 143, 199 n. 15
for pregnancy, 58, 69, 93, 199 n. 15
recitation of the Divya Prabandham, 4, 11–12, 32, 42, 55, 58–59, 116
instituted by Nāthamuni, 36, 100–101
Dosai, distribution of, 71
Dramatic performances. *See* Dance; Enactments; Performing arts
Dramiḍopaniṣad Tātparya Ratnāvaḷi (*The Gem Necklace of Reality in the Tamil Upaniṣad*) (Vedānta Deśika), 28, 101
Droṇa, Ekalavya as disciple of, 103
Dṛṣṭi kāvyam (Visual poem), 125. *See also Araiyar cēvai*
Dualism, denied by the Advaitins, 23, 195 n. 27

Index

at the Nammālvār Cannati, 70–72
See also Festival of Recitation
Fingers, use in counting verses, 49–50
Flag, hoisting of, at the Tillai Citrakūṭam Visnu temple, 45
Food
given as *prasādam*, 52, 55
offered to the festival image, 127–28
Formulaic phrases
use by the *araiyars* during the Festival of Recitation, 122
use in commentaries, 110–11, 139, 210 nn. 27, 31
Funerals, 4, 58, 199 n. 15

Gadya, 220
Ganda Gopala, 55
Gandhi, Mohandas (Mahatma Gandhi), 202 n. 1, 221
Ganeśa, Viśvaksena in place of in households, 202 n. 10
Garbha gṛha (inner chamber/shrine), 82, 87–88, 131, 199 n. 15, 217 n. 35, 219
Garuḍa Vāhana Paṇḍita, 21, 33, 35, 197 n. 48
Gates of Heaven (*Vaikuṇṭha vācal; Paramapada vācal*), opening of, 115–16, 118–19, 120–21, 135
Gaudiya Vaiṣṇavas, plays of, 8
Gāyatri mantra, 199 n. 17
Gem Necklace of Reality in the Tamil Upaniṣad, The (*Dramiḍopaniṣad Tātparya Ratnāvaḷi*) (Vedānta Deśika), 28, 101
Gestures, use of, 124, 216 n. 26
Gill, Sam D., 6
Glory of the Ālvārs, The (Vaṭivalakiya Nampi Tācar). *See Ālvārkaḷ Vaipavam*
Gnanambal, K., 203 n. 6, 203–4 n. 7, 204 nn. 9, 12
Goa, David, 5
Goal in itself, recitation of the Tiruvāymoli seen as a, 76–77, 141
God. *See* Viṣṇu
Goda. *See* Āṇṭāḷ
Goda Mandali (class conducted by Venkata Varadhan), 91–93, 95, 206 n. 14
Gonda, Jan, 5
Good fortune, role of lineage in, 75–76
Gopalakrishna Ekangi Swami, 66
Govindacharya, Alkondavilli, 203 n. 6
Govinda Ramanuja Dasar, 66, 72–74, 203 n. 5
Gowthamapuram, Bangalore, India, scheduled caste community, 12, 66–79
Grace, divine, 76, 102, 130, 133
Nammālvār as recipient of, 59, 74, 127
Graham, William A., 5
Guru, 220
Guruparamparā, 220
Guruparamparā prabhāvam (Pinpalakiya Perumāḷ Jīyar). *See Splendor, The*
Gypsy fortune-teller, role of assumed by the *araiyars*, 130, 212 n. 4

Haberman, David, 8
Hagiographic literature, 9, 58–59, 61, 72, 115
on Nammālvār, 32–36, 129
Haidar Ali, 84
Hall of a Thousand Pillars, in Srirangam Temple, 145, 214 n. 13
Viṣṇu enshrined in, 116, 119–24, 127, 212–14 n. 8
Hanumān temples, 92
Harijan, 202 n. 1, 221. *See also* Scheduled caste
Hari Rao, V. N. *See Koyil Oḷuku*
Hawley, John S., 7, 8
Hearing, 11, 12, 21, 26, 35, 93
the Divya Prabandham on cassette or radio, 98
during the Festival of Recitation, 116, 133

Index

Mūrti, 7, 222. *See also* Image
Music, 2, 7, 48, 125, 134, 142–43
 araiyar tradition, 80–85, 214 n. 13
 Divya Prabandham set to. *See* Divya Prabandham
 the Tiruvāymoḻi interpreted through, 5, 35, 41–42, 46, 100
 See also Singing
Music Academy, in Madras, India, 93
Musical instruments, 56, 70, 92, 97
 vīṇās, 85, 86, 87
Muslim consort (*Bībī nācciyār*) for Viṣṇu, shrines, 83
Muslims. *See* Islam
Mutaliyāṇṭāṉ, 62, 201 n. 7
Mutal Tiruvantāti (poem), 62
Mysore (presently Karnataka), state, India, 27, 67. *See also* Nammāḻvār Cannati
Mythology, 15, 33, 81, 202 n. 10

Nācciyār Tirumoḻi (poem, Āṇṭāḷ), 62, 95
Nāda. *See* Sound
Nādaswaram (musical instrument), 56, 70
Nadhamuni Araiyar, 84, 85, 90, 121, 122, 215 n. 21
 on *adhyapaka* style, 43–45, 198 n. 12
 on the *araiyar cēvai*, 124, 212 n. 2
Naina Pillai, 91
Nakkīrar, 207 n. 9
Nālāyira Divya Prabandham (*Nālāyirativyap pirapantam*). *See* Divya Prabandham
Nallan Chakravarti Ramanujachari, 52
Namasaṁkirtāna, 221, 222
Naming of a child, domestic rituals connected with, 199 n. 15
Nammāḻvār, 2, 3, 27, 31–36, 102, 222
 ascent to heaven, 36, 115–16, 128–29, 212–14 n. 8
 biographical information. *See* Biographical literature
 birthday celebrations, 12, 62, 64, 71–72, 77
 depiction in traditional paintings, 39
 divinity or humanity. *See* Humanity
 in image form during the Festival of Recitation, 71, 118, 119, 121–22
 as medium of revelation and as redeemer, 74–79
 as a messenger of the gods, 114
 name given by the Lord at Srirangam, 193 n. 1
 names used in referring to self, 16, 32
 as primary focus of worship at the Nammāḻvār Cannati, 68–69, 74
 quest for union with the Lord, 3–4, 28–29, 31, 116, 122, 133, 137
 as recipient of divine grace, 59, 74, 127
 revelation to Nāthamuni, 36, 37–38, 39, 96, 137–38
 said to be born of the lowest caste, 25, 196 n. 31
 salvation, 132
  enactment of, 59, 116, 127–29, 212 n. 4
 Saranatha Bhattar's oral discourse on, 48, 111, 210 n. 34
 stories of heard by children, 12
 temple shrine location, 68
 travels seen as mental journeys, 25, 196 n. 33
 Viṣṇu's words uttered through, 124, 215 n. 18
 See also Tiruvāymoḻi
Nammāḻvār Cannati/Shrine, in Bangalore, 12, 66–68, 141, 203–4 n. 7
 recitation and rituals, 66–79, 141
 Sabhā (congregation), 12, 66, 78–79
Nammāḻvār Tiruttāllāṭṭu, 21, 197 n. 47, 207 n. 8
Naṁpiḷḷai (Nampūr Varadarājān), 105–7, 113, 208 n. 15, 209 nn. 22, 24
 Nine Thousand-pati rewritten by, 207 n. 7
Nampi Tācar. *See* Vativalakiya Nampi Tācar

Index

Index